BEER IN THE BILGES

BEER IN THE BILGES

Sailing Adventures in the South Pacific

JOHN KNAPPETT,
ENJOY THE ADVENTURES!
Alan Boreham.
January 2013

ALAN BOREHAM,
PETER JINKS,
AND BOB ROSSITER

iUniverse, Inc.
Bloomington

Beer in the Bilges
Sailing Adventures in the South Pacific

iUniverse books may be ordered through booksellers or by contacting:

iUniverse
1663 Liberty Drive
Bloomington, IN 47403
www.iuniverse.com
1-800-Authors (1-800-288-4677)

ISBN: 978-1-4759-2879-2 (sc)
ISBN: 978-1-4759-2880-8 (hc)
ISBN: 978-1-4759-2881-5 (e)

Library of Congress Control Number: 2012909680

Printed in the United States of America

iUniverse rev. date: 07/26/2012

For Dixie Carter

If you spend any time in the remoter places in the world, you will meet some people who don't seem to fit into normal society. These are not always evil people or even peculiar people. These are just people who seem to thrive in an environment with fewer rules and much less scrutiny than most of us are accustomed to. Even in paradise you're likely to find people like this, as we did. Some of these people are still there.

The Professionals: Alan Boreham, Peter Jinks, and "Hollywood" Bob Rossiter

"An old sailor without his beer is like corned beef without cabbage."

John Wray, *South Sea Vagabonds*

Contents

Preface xiii

Part One A Kiwi from the East

Chapter 1   *Hollywood Bob* 3
Chapter 2   *Three Old Men in the Clouds* 9
Chapter 3   *Anchoring in the Ha'apai Group.* 18
Chapter 4   *A Wing and a Prayer* 24
Chapter 5   *Dancing Across the Pacific* 31
Chapter 6   *Tongan Delights* 41
Chapter 7   *Shoot-Out.* 48

Part Two An Aussie from Down Under

Chapter 8   *The Adventure Continues.* 61
Chapter 9   *Sydney to Suva* 68
Chapter 10   *One for the Road.* 83
Chapter 11   *Chiefly Traditions* 91
Chapter 12   *And You Said It Was Only Superstition"* 100
Chapter 13   *"Wood, Yes, But Will She Float?"* 106
Chapter 14   *A Little Bit of Paradise.* 111
Chapter 15   *Kidnapped* 121

Part Three A Canadian from the North

Chapter 16   *There's a Moose in My Way.* 127
Chapter 17   *The Way South* 132
Chapter 18   *Let There Be Light.* 140
Chapter 19   *The Love Boat.* 147
Chapter 20   *Taking a Second Chance* 161
Chapter 21   *Has Anyone Seen an Island?* 168

Part Four The Professionals

Chapter 22   All Roads Lead to the Waikiki Yacht Club 193
Chapter 23   The Grave 203
Chapter 24   Do You Smoke? 208
Chapter 25   Flight to Samoa 219
Chapter 26   Rosie 230
Chapter 27   Heartbeat 237
Chapter 28   And He Didn't Even Get His Feet Wet. 245
Chapter 29   The Haulout 249
Chapter 30   Sharkbite Charlie and the Bowling Alley 261
Chapter 31   The Haulout Continues 265
Chapter 32   A Suspicious Sinking 276
Chapter 33   A Mission of Mercy 283
Chapter 34   Flying the Flag. 287
Chapter 35   Diving on the Tuna Seiners 293
Chapter 36   Rust Bucket Rodeo 304
Chapter 37   Final Preparations 309
Chapter 38   The Aborted Trip 321
Chapter 39   Tiki 334

About the Authors 341
Glossary 345

List of Illustrations

1. Chart of the Pacific Ocean showing origins and destinations of the authors. xviii

2. "Hollywood" Bob Rossiter on his motorcycle in Hawaii 5

3. Maupihaa Island, French Polynesia, renamed "Spook" Island 13

4. Rising storm off Suwarrow, Cook Islands. 14

5. Hal Holbrook drawing a cool beer from the bilges of *Yankee Tar*. . 21

6. *Yankee Tar* at anchor off the Paradise International Hotel, Neiafu, Vava'u Islands, Kingdom of Tonga 28

7. Hal Holbrook, Dixie Carter, and Bob Rossiter at the Paradise International Hotel, Vava'u Islands, Kingdom of Tonga 38

8. Tongan girls in formal dress 39

9. Bob inspecting the diesel fuel in Neiafu, Vava'u Islands, Kingdom of Tonga. 45

10. Hal Holbrook and Bob Rossiter at gunnery practice 55

11. Preparing for a day on Sydney Harbour aboard *Ron of Argyll* with owner Andrew Clubb. 67

12. *Ron of Argyll* leaving Sydney Harbour. 72

13. *Ron of Argyll* beating to windward 74

14. Drying sails after a storm 76

15. Peter's catch 77

16. The main saloon of *Ron of Argyll* 78

17. Andrew Clubb receiving award from the governor general of Fiji. . 81

18. Crew of *Ron of Argyll* (left to right) Don Graham, Terry Carrol, Peter, Chantal, and Andrew at the awards ceremony for the 1982 Sydney-to-Suva race 82

19. Peter Jinks (right) and visitors aboard *Ron of Argyll* in Suva, Fiji. . . 84

20. *Ron of Argyll* (center) tied stern-to at the Tradewinds Hotel in Suva, Fiji. 85

21. Children row out to meet the yacht at Totoya Island, Lau Group, Fiji 95

22. Andrew Clubb going to see the chief, bearing gifts. 96

23. *Ron of Argyll* at anchor in Totoya Island lagoon 97

24. Totoya Island women dancing at the farewell feast. 101

25. Andrew Clubb enjoying a deck shower. 104

26. Peter and friendly villagers of Oneata Island, Lau Group, Fiji. . . . 107

27. *Ron of Argyll* at anchor in Neiafu Harbour, Vava'u Islands, Kingdom of Tonga. 113

28. Carter Johnson at work. 114

29. Little girl near Neiafu, Vava'u Islands, Kingdom of Tonga 118

30. The shoreline near Neiafu with visiting yachts at anchor 123

31. Alan (center) and crew wishing final farewells as *Second Chance* prepares for departure from Vancouver. 133

32. *Second Chance* leaving Vancouver 134

33. Alan on watch off the coast of British Columbia 144

34. A fishing boat off the coast of California 153

35. *Pacific Princess* leaving San Francisco Harbor 157

36. *Second Chance* approaching the Golden Gate Bridge 158

37. *Second Chance* at the St. Francis Yacht Club in San Francisco . . . 159

38. Scott at the helm, with Gary on watch, as *Second Chance* leaves San Francisco 163

39. *Second Chance* in the North Pacific en route to Hawaii 164

40. Andy at the wheel as *Second Chance* emerges from the storm 169

41. Alan having a wash during a calm mid-Pacific 170

42. Some of the crew going for a swim during the calm 171

43. *Second Chance* under full sail in the trade winds. 176

44. Anybody want flying fish for breakfast? 177

45. Jury-rigged storm jib after upper hanks tore out in the gale 183

46. John enjoying champagne to celebrate the discovery of Oahu . . . 187

47. *Second Chance* on arrival in Ala Wai Harbor 188

48. Andy indicating the hole in the hull of *Second Chance* 189

49. Graveyard near Neiafu, Vava'u Islands, Kingdom of Tonga 205

50. American Samoa International Airport 224

51. The Rainmaker Hotel at the entrance to Pago Pago Harbor, American Samoa 225

52. *Ron of Argyll* anchored near derelict fishing vessels in Pago Pago Harbor, American Samoa. 226

53. Aerial view of yachts tied up to rock mole in Pago Pago Harbor . 227

54. *Aiga* buses at the market in Pago Pago, American Samoa. 228

55. Gary Green aboard his yacht *Heartbeat* in Pago Pago Harbor . . . 239

56. Asian long-liner awaiting repair at the marine railway 252

57. Alan, Bob, and Don place fenders as the *Ron* is secured on the marine railway 253

58. Alan places a fender as some of the boatyard crew swim below . . 254

59. Boatyard worker nicknamed Slim takes a rest 255

60. Long-liner pulls in to the marine railway behind the *Ron*. 256

61. Foreman checks that the *Ron* is secure 257

62. The "Black Ship" passing the Rainmaker Hotel to dump offal at sea. 267

63. Don Coleman caulking the hull of the *Ron* 269

64. Caulking finished and ready for bottom paint 270

65. View of Pago Pago Harbor entrance and reefs from the cable car atop Rainmaker Mountain. 278

66. A still and humid day in Pago Pago Harbor 279

67. Sunken long-liner *Kwang Myong 65* 281

68. American tuna seiner *Montana* in Pago Pago Harbor. 296

69. *Ron of Argyll* leaving Pago Pago Harbor en route to Honolulu . . . 322

Preface

————◆◆✦◆◆————

There was a point in time when there was a real possibility that this book would never be written. It was November 1982, and we were five days out of Pago Pago, en route to Honolulu, sailing a classic, fifty-five-foot gaff-rigged ketch named *Ron of Argyll*. She was built in Scotland in 1928 for one Colonel McKay, who was a frequent guest of King George V aboard the *Royal Yacht Britannia*. The colonel had reputedly hired the marine architect who produced that lovely yacht to design one for him. Her traditional hull, built of one-and-a-quarter-inch-thick teak planks copper-fastened to oak frames, had over the years furrowed the waters of the Atlantic, West Indies, and Pacific, hosting, it is said, such celebrities as Marilyn Monroe, and it had been sold to an Australian owner in the 1970s.

For we three sailors—"Hollywood" Bob Rossiter is a New Zealander who was then forty-one, Peter Jinks is from Australia and was thirty-two, and Alan Boreham is from Canada and was twenty-seven—this was a delivery job, a contract with the current Australian owner to bring the yacht to Hawaii and then on to Los Angeles for sale. We were all young at heart and living the dream of sailing a beautiful yacht through some of the most amazing cruising destinations in the world. It was an adventure, but one that was suddenly testing our resolve.

The winds had risen to gale force, and as the old girl punched into the growing seas, water was gushing in somewhere—we couldn't tell where—and filling the bilges. With 1,800 miles to go, we took to the manual bilge pumps to try to dry her out so that we could find the source of the leaks. The search proved futile, and we worked just to stay afloat. With each of us following an exhausting, nonstop routine of an hour on the tiller, an hour on the pump, and an hour of sleep, after two days we were stumbling around like zombies. Bob swore that he had seen an empty beer bottle full of cockroaches washing around in the bilge, with the butt of the biggest one stuffed into the opening like a cork, making a cockroach lifeboat. That may have been the incentive we needed to turn around and try to make it the five hundred miles back to Samoa. Otherwise it was just three miles to land—straight down. As we were to find out later, it was a wise decision, as we unwittingly avoided an approaching hurricane that surely would have spelled the end of that lovely yacht—and us along with it.

———————

In the ensuing years, we relived these and other experiences in the South Pacific in conversations between pairs of us, usually over a beer or two, but we didn't all get together again until 1999, when we met at the Harbor Pub and Pizza overlooking the Ala Wai Harbor in Waikiki. Over the course of that rather long session, we talked about how lucky we had been to sail through the South Pacific islands and experience them while they were still relatively unspoiled. We also marveled at the variety of amazing characters we had encountered along the way, such as Sharkbite Charlie, Rosie the three-hundred-pound dancer, and Gunter, the mysterious chef from South America. These were people so unusual that you couldn't hope to invent them. We decided then and there that we wanted to share these sailing experiences and these characters with people who would never have the opportunity to venture out there themselves.

We chose to organize the book into four parts. The first three follow each of us as we venture forth into the Pacific. Part One highlights Bob's adventures sailing from California across the Pacific to New Zealand with actor Hal Holbrook and actress Dixie Carter, who joined them along the way, Part Two follows Peter in the Sydney-to-Suva yacht race and then on into the Polynesian islands, and Part Three describes Alan's first offshore voyage from Vancouver to Honolulu. Part Four focuses on our yacht delivery from Pago Pago to Hawaii.

The events that we describe in these memoirs took place between 1981 and 1983, but we didn't begin writing until after our gathering in 1999. Even then it took about eight years to complete the original manuscript. All three of us had busy lives and lived in different countries. Bob had a prospering yacht services business in Hawaii, Peter was married and growing his retail shoe business in Sydney, and Alan was managing a new fisheries program for Aboriginal people across Canada. It made the most sense to us to set aside a week or two every twelve to eighteen months to get away together to concentrate on writing.

To help us in writing these memoirs, we went back to Marina del Rey in California, to Hawaii, Fiji, and Samoa, to Rarotonga in the Cook Islands, and to Australia and New Zealand. It helped enormously to go back to the "scene of the crime" to sail the waters, talk with people, and generally soak in the atmosphere of these places again. Besides the clarity and focus that those trips provided, they were all part of another adventure. After all, that is what life is all about.

We made tremendous progress on each trip, approaching this project like a job and working about eight hours a day, allowing adequate time afterward for mental stimulation and recreation. In between these sessions, we filled in some of the missing details by contacting people who had been involved in the events we describe or by making reference to publications like navigation charts. All of the photographs we have included reflect the era, while some, like those of the ocean and the islands, are timeless.

The telling of stories from one's past is usually done from the writer's own perspective, in the first person, and less often from the perspective of an independent observer, in the third person. In writing these memoirs, we had to decide how best to describe our individual paths that led us to join forces in American Samoa as well as our shared experiences, while at the same time portraying the remarkable people and events that we encountered along the way. Our choice of using the third person narrator gave us the liberty of collaborating on the description of these episodes in our lives so that we could write in a consistent voice, hopefully making the flow of the chapters easier for the reader to follow.

What emerged from this collaboration is a series of short stories describing voyages, people, and events. Although some consecutive chapters take us through a single voyage or event, such as Alan's crossing from Canada to Hawaii in Part Three, other chapters are focused solely on an interesting event or encounter in the Pacific. Collectively, these vignettes capture the cruising experience, Pacific life and culture, and the unexpected elements that are to be found in these remote places.

Sailors reading this book will be familiar with the sailing jargon that runs through it. For those who are not familiar with sailing and for any reader who is unfamiliar with the Polynesian words that we have occasionally included, don't worry. We have included a glossary of terms at the end, choosing to put it there rather than adding explanations in the text itself so we wouldn't disturb the narrative flow.

We would like to acknowledge those who have helped and supported us in the writing of these memoirs. We appreciate the encouragement and advice provided by Krista Hill during the review and editing process, and the insight and expertise of Cheri Madison and the other editors to improve the final manuscript. We would also like to thank Tania Jinks and Pat Rossiter, the long-suffering wives of Peter and Bob, who have been supportive throughout this process and who must have wondered more than once whether this book would ever be finished.

Anyone who traveled to the Pacific islands in the early 1980s will already be aware of the cultural and religious traditions that existed then and still exist to a large extent today. For the three of us (although less so for

Bob), these traditions were unfamiliar, and when combined with the uncertainties of blue water sailing, our travels were truly adventures into the unknown. We approached the situations described here with a naïveté and the sometimes foolhardy bravado of any adventurer, and somehow we lived to tell about them. We all learned to have great respect for the people of these different cultures, who welcomed us to their islands and into their homes and who shared with us their traditions and wisdom. We hope that we also contributed something to their lives.

Much more is known and can be learned about the world now than when we were setting out. We would encourage anyone planning to follow in our wake to familiarize themselves with the local cultures before visiting these faraway places and to respect the traditions of these wonderful people. For those adventurers—and especially for those who will never have the opportunity to experience the Pacific islands—read on.

Chart of the Pacific Ocean showing origins and destinations of the authors.

Part One

———◆▸◀◆▸◀◆———

A Kiwi from the East

Chapter 1

―――――◆≻≺◆―――――

Hollywood Bob

The Harley-Davidson thundered down Wilshire Boulevard, the sound of the motorcycle's engine reverberating off the plate glass windows of the exclusive boutiques and startling the shoppers as the rider rumbled past. Traffic was light, and he slowed only enough to turn onto the road that would lead into Beverly Hills. He leaned into a curve and accelerated, a big smile spreading across his face and his white hair streaming back from the force of the wind. Black shades protected his eyes, and the bright sunshine glinted off a small gold earring that he wore in his right ear.

Too soon Bob had to leave the main roads and pull his Harley into a long, tree-lined boulevard. He slowed almost to a crawl, scanning both sides of the street to find the number of the house he was after. He found it on a mailbox that was almost obscured by the tall, dense hedge that secluded the house. There were several black limousines, a couple of BMWs, a Ferrari, and two Lincolns clogging its narrow, twisting driveway. He came to a stop on the street and looked over the scene, then revved the bike and slowly eased past the limos, stopping opposite the entrance. It was a very impressive house, although modest by Hollywood standards. Bob switched off the engine, swung the side stand out with a deft kick, and stepped off the motorcycle. The limousine drivers ignored him and continued

3

polishing the headlights and buffing the chrome, strains of Kenny Rogers singing his new hit song "Lady" wafting from one of the car radios.

He strode over to the entrance, unbuckling his black leather jacket. A large, well-dressed security guard looked the tall, confident guest up and down respectfully.

"Excuse me, sir. Do you have your invitation?" he asked.

"No, I don't. Hal invited me. The name's Rossiter."

The security officer glanced down at his list. He looked up and with a smile said, "Welcome, Mr. Rossiter. Please go right in."

———————

Bob pulled off his shades and stuffed them into the pocket of his T-shirt. As his eyes became accustomed to the light, he looked around, taking in the impressive entry, the sweeping staircase, and the large room beyond. He dug one hand into his Levi's and pulled out a crumpled pack of cigarettes, and then he took a few steps into the hall before stopping to take one out. He held it vertically by the filter, inspecting its deformed profile as he rotated it. He carefully smoothed it out between the thumb and forefinger of his other hand before inserting it into his mouth. As he reached into his back pocket for a match, one of the catering staff appeared and held up a flickering lighter. The little man tried not to stare at the mangled cigarette.

"May I offer you a light, sir?" he asked.

Bob hesitated for a second before leaning down, lighting the end of the cigarette, and inhaling deeply. "Thanks," he said.

"A cocktail, sir?" the little man asked.

Bob looked at the array of delicate glasses on the silver tray and swung his stare back to the little man. "Where's the joker with the beer?" he said plainly.

Stunned by the unfamiliar accent and puzzled by the language, the waiter managed a weak smile and inquired, "Would you like a beer, sir?"

"Yes, mate. Make it nice and cold." Bob surveyed the crowd in the inner room and added quickly, "You'd better make that two."

"Hollywood" Bob Rossiter on his motorcycle in Hawaii

"Very good, sir," replied the waiter, who disappeared through a side door.

No sooner had Bob taken the five or six steps to the entry of the main lounge than the waiter appeared at his elbow with two bottles of beer and two crystal glasses on a tray.

"Here we are, sir," he offered and picked up one of the bottles to pour it into a glass.

Bob swiftly intercepted the upturned bottle, put it to his mouth, drained the contents in a series of gulps, and replaced it on the tray. "Thanks, mate," he said with a wink. "We'll save the bloke in the galley a little work." He took the other bottle from the tray and walked into the room, leaving the stunned waiter behind.

———

Bob recognized several movie actors and stars of television, as well as a number of influential people in the Hollywood game. From their dress, some of the people obviously had heavy-duty money. Some, he knew, also had yachts at Marina del Rey, and a few of those were clients of his. For the last several years, Bob had developed a reputation as a no-nonsense shipwright in the area, specializing in doing custom work on the yachts of the Hollywood crowd. As a young man at home in Auckland, New Zealand, he had begun studying mechanical engineering, math, and draftsmanship, but had slipped into the marine world. This training had put him in good stead, and he had worked his way across the Pacific from New Zealand to Tonga and Fiji and finally to California over the last fifteen years as a shipwright. He was also a licensed ship's captain, game fishing charter boat operator, and delivery skipper. With a green card, he could make a future here, but Los Angeles was beginning to wear on him, and it felt like it could be time to move on again.

Today he was here to see the host of this shindig, Hal Holbrook, the well-known actor. Hal was probably best known for his one-man stage performance *Mark Twain Tonight*, but also for a dozen movies and his roles on television. An accomplished sailor himself, Hal had approached Bob about helping him realize a dream of sailing across the Pacific.

Bob had met Hal a couple of years before, when Hal was planning his first trip across to Hawaii. A mutual friend named Peggy Slater, a boat broker in Marina del Rey, had suggested that Hal talk to Bob about going with him. Peggy knew boats and what it took to sail them. She herself had sailed her own yacht single-handed to Hawaii. In writing his foreword to Peggy's book *An Affair with the Sea*, Hal described how she told him that she knew just the guy if he would go. Hal wrote that he "vaguely knew of Rossiter, a tall handsome man around forty with a shock of pure white hair, tanned and tough, a New Zealander." Hal located Bob, and they had discovered an instant liking and respect for one another.

Bob was particular about whom he sailed with and had quickly learned that Hal possessed the heart of a sailor. Hal had proved to be very down to earth and a good shipmate. The trip to Hawaii had cemented their friendship, so when Hal had come to him with the idea of sailing in the single-handed Transpac race from San Francisco to Kauai and then having Bob join him to carry on to New Zealand, Bob was ready to give it serious consideration. The thought of visiting the South Pacific again and returning home to New Zealand after all these years sounded pretty good.

Bob was looking around the crowded room when his eyes fell on a stunning blonde in a wispy summer dress coming down the staircase. She may have been an actress—Bob didn't know—but at any rate, he immediately recognized that she had long since lost her amateur status. As she reached the bottom and moved toward him, his gaze was fixed on her. It wasn't until she was almost within reach that he realized that Hal was with her. Hal called to him. "Bob! Great you could make it!"

Bob took the few steps to close the gap between them and reached out to Hal's outstretched hand. Hal was as tall as Bob and looked healthy and fit. He had a full head of hair, graying slightly and cut fairly long, as was the style of the day. In his early fifties, he was dressed in well-tailored gray trousers and an open-necked shirt.

Hal said, "Let me introduce you to a friend of mine. Bob, this is Monica. Monica, meet Bob Rossiter. He's the guy I was telling you about. I've asked Bob to sail with me on *Yankee Tar* to New Zealand."

"Ooh, that sounds exciting!" cooed Monica as she sidled up to Bob.

Hal looked Bob square in the eye and said, "Well, Bob, have you made up your mind?"

"Yep," Bob said decisively. "Let's go. When do we leave?" he asked, flashing a big smile.

"That's great!" said Hal. "As soon as I get to Hawaii, we'll be on our way. Let's celebrate!"

Bob slipped his arm around Monica's waist. "Yeah," he agreed. "Let's celebrate!"

Chapter 2

———◆◆◆———

Three Old Men in the Clouds

Bora Bora, July 1981

It was early morning when *Yankee Tar* slipped out of the harbor of Bora Bora in French Polynesia, leaving the eight other yachts anchored quietly in the deep basin. To an observer on shore, the low, steady throbbing of the engine would have been almost inaudible amid the chatter of the water as the bow broke the surface in its gentle push forward to the open sea. The sun appeared over the jagged green ridge of the volcanic island as they passed through the break in the reef, the bow now rising and falling in the gentle Pacific swells. Hal sat at the wheel of the Gulf 40, a center-cockpit, cutter-rigged sloop of William Garden design built in fiberglass by Cheoy Lee shipyards in Hong Kong. He sipped a cup of coffee, enjoying the easy motion of the seas. Once they were well clear of the reef, he turned off the engine and trimmed the sails. Then he set the wind vane that controlled the self-steering gear and went below.

Hal and Bob laid out the course to Maupihaa Island, one of the leeward islands, some one hundred miles to the southwest. If the weather cooperated, they planned to stop at this small group of islands on the way to Suwarrow, five hundred miles farther on. The morning weather forecast looked favorable, and in these typical trade wind conditions, Hal planned to have the islands in sight by daylight. They both double-checked the plot before resetting the wind vane to this new course.

Hour after hour the water burbled past the stern of the yacht as it sailed gently along in the low seas, the wind vane barely moving in the steady breeze. Bob and Hal took turns on watch, relaxing in the cockpit, the motion of the boat almost hypnotizing. Their only toil was their religious dedication to navigation. Hal took a noon sun sight with the sextant to determine their position in the same way that sailors had done since the development of a reliable seagoing chronometer over two hundred years before. Between sextant shots, they kept an hourly deck log, recording their speed from the yacht's knot meter and the course from the compass along with the wind and sea conditions. They transferred this information to the navigation chart to advance their position hour by hour, a method called dead reckoning. With no means of electronic navigation, sailors corrected their dead reckoning position with subsequent sextant shots, often taken at noon on ocean passages. Dead reckoning could be extremely accurate if done with precision. Any difference between the two methods usually indicated an error in the dead reckoning caused by variations in course or speed between hourly log entries or sometimes unknown influences such as magnetic anomalies or ocean currents.

All day Bob had been looking at the amorphous shapes of the bulbous white clouds. The shapes changed as they moved along, and from time to time, the faces of three old men would appear. The serious countenance of the faces was striking. Unlike most imaginary objects we see in cloud formations, this image persisted for several minutes before disappearing. Without explanation, the image reappeared to Bob numerous times over the course of four or five hours. They seemed to keep projecting to him a warning, their persistence emphasizing the urgency of the message.

That night the wind was light and the seas fairly flat, so Bob was bunking on a sail bag on deck to avoid the stifling heat in the cabin; he couldn't sleep for the images of the old men in the clouds. Finally he went below to check their progress on the chart, concerned that they would approach the islands during the night. Up until now, he hadn't said anything to Hal about the images, thinking that Hal would question his sanity. Now Bob returned to the cockpit, his senses tuned to maximum pitch, but he couldn't see anything up ahead of them. He eventually settled against the stainless steel rails of the pulpit at the bow, the seas illuminated only by the mass of stars.

Hal left the cockpit and went forward to join him on deck. "What's bothering you, Bob?" he asked, obviously concerned by Bob's mood.

"I have a feeling that we're closer to the island than we think."

"Well, our dead reckoning shows that we're fourteen miles off yet."

"I can't explain it, but I think that's wrong. I can't sleep, and it's just about time for my watch anyway. Why don't you take a break and I'll stay up here to keep an eye out."

"Suits me."

Hal went below to get some sleep, but not long after, Bob called down. "Hal! Hal, come up and listen to this!"

Hal carefully made his way up to the bow, dozy from being awakened from a sound sleep. He crouched beside Bob, holding onto the stout lifelines. "What is it?"

"Listen. Do you hear that?"

"I don't hear anything. What can you hear?"

"Shhh. Just listen, for Christ's sake!"

Bob could see that Hal was listening intently to hear anything from the direction Bob was indicating. "I don't think there's anything there, Bob."

"Well, I heard something."

Unconvinced, Hal walked back a few paces across the flush deck and sat with his back to the mast, wedged between two deck boxes, and shut his eyes. Bob continued to peer into the darkness. After only a few minutes, he thought he could discern a thin white line dead ahead.

"Reef! Dead ahead!" he bellowed. "Hard to port!"

Shocked awake, Hal hesitated only for a moment, and then jumped up and dashed back to the cockpit. He disengaged the wind vane and spun the wheel to port.

"Hard over! Hard over!"

"I've got the damned thing hard over!" Hal called back. He reached to harden the sheets just as the breakers on the reef came into view off the starboard bow. They sailed along on this course until they were certain to be clear of danger and then eased the main and jib sheets to slow the boat. They sat opposite one another in the cockpit for a few minutes in contemplation.

"That was weird," said Hal finally.

"I can't explain it, but those three old men were right."

"Who?" asked Hal with surprise. Bob explained the images that he had seen. "You and your damned spooks!" Hal declared. "Tell me about them next time. I can't explain it either, but from now on, we're both going to triple-check our navigation and then consult with your paranormal friends."

"Yeah, who knows," said Bob. "We might have found one of those unrecorded currents that seem to live around some of these places that only they know about."

They hung off until daylight to see if they could find the entrance to the reef, but the ordeal had left them both with an uneasy feeling.

"Let's forget this place and move on," said Hal.

"Too right," replied Bob. "We'll rename this place 'Spook' Island!"

Hauling the sheets, they sailed well clear of the island before bearing away to a broad reach and setting off in the direction of Suwarrow in the northern Cook Islands. After four uneventful days of sailing, they sighted the low coral island made famous by the hermit Tom Neale in his book *An Island to Oneself.* Neale had lived alone on this tiny remote atoll for five years, visited by passing boats only every twelve months or so. As beautiful as this little paradise was, its extremely low profile and shallow lagoon made anchored yachts easy targets to passing storms. As *Yankee Tar* approached, the sky became lightly overcast, and the wind and sea picked up slightly. They had been having trouble with the engine overheating, so

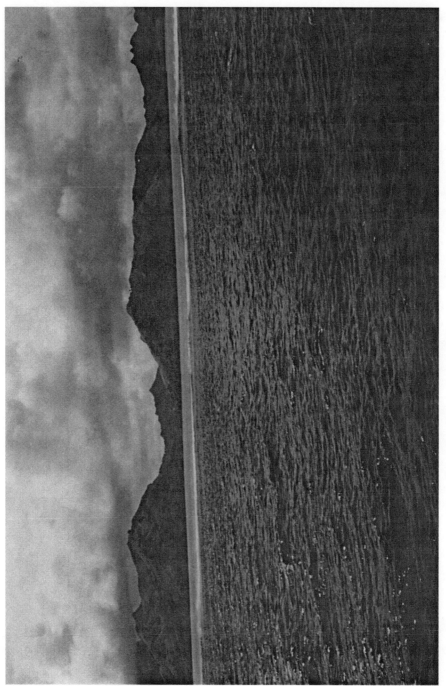

Maupihaa Island, French Polynesia, renamed "Spook" Island

Rising storm off Suwarrow, Cook Islands

as there wasn't much light left, they turned about to get plenty of sea room for the night, planning to make landfall the next morning.

While preparing to heave to, they were hit by a sudden squall. The sea made up rough and the wind increased dramatically. Bob had hanked on a storm jib and was on the deck trying to tie a second reef into the mainsail, but the rapidly deteriorating conditions made the work much harder. Frustrated by the change, he called on his imaginary wind god, Fred, to help him out. According to Bob's interpretation of the world, seeing that God was so busy, he had delegated the control of the weather to his assistant, Fred. Hal, Bob, and Fred had developed a good relationship during the trip, and Hal and Bob talked to Fred quite often. The conversation was always one-sided, but sometimes Fred wasn't too busy to accommodate their requests.

"Hey, Fred! Knock it off for a minute!" Bob called out.

Against all odds, the wind abated long enough for Bob to finish taking the second slab out of the main. He made his way back to the cockpit, and the wind picked up again to its full strength.

Hal surveyed the situation and said, "We should have put three reefs in the main and tidied up a bit. Do you think Fred would give us another break?"

"We can give it another shot." Bob cupped his hand to his mouth and shouted, "Hey, Fred! We didn't get our shit together that time! Could we try it again?"

As they awaited a response, the seas gradually calmed and the wind dropped. Hal put on the spreader lights to augment the fading daylight, and they both went forward to tie in the third reef.

"Do you believe this?" Hal remarked as they finished the work on deck and just stood there, incredulous. "Look at the ocean now."

"Unbelievable," said Bob. "It's as flat as a plate of piss!"

Their tiny, visible world was now created solely by the loom of the spreader lights, but just beyond, they could hear the cries of hundreds of seabirds circling the boat. Suddenly a deep, bell-like sound rang out and a huge bird fell to their feet, its eyes going around in circles as it tottered unsteadily on the deck.

"It's run into the top of the mast!" Hal declared. "Pick him up and put him back in the water."

Bob looked at it warily. "You pick him up! Look at the size of that fucking beak!"

As if to emphasize the point, the bird clacked its beak menacingly. Discretion being better than getting their fingers chopped off, they left it alone to recover. After a few minutes, the bird more or less regained its faculties, fell over the side, and swam drunkenly away into the dark. Hal switched off the lights, and they were once again in darkness.

"I bet he'll have a story to tell his mates!" laughed Bob.

"He'll have his own spooks to tell them about!" agreed Hal.

The next morning, the sky was overcast and the wind had swung more to the east, creating an uncomfortable sea. Intuition told them to keep clear, so they reluctantly set a course for American Samoa, about three hundred miles to the southwest. Within thirty minutes, any sign of the low-lying atoll had disappeared in an ever-increasing gloom.

Hal said, "I think we've made the right decision. That's not one of those places you would want to be trapped in."

The winds increased steadily over the next two days to storm force of fifty knots from the east, with seas building to steep, twenty-foot peaks with long troughs between them—menacing, but not necessarily dangerous for this sturdy, oceangoing yacht. By now they had reduced sail to only the smallest of three storm jibs, a hanky-sized sail made as tough as boilerplate and sheeted in tight fore and aft. That turned out to be prudent because in another twenty-four hours, the conditions got even worse, with the wind increasing to gusts of seventy knots at times and the seas to thirty feet. With the wind almost dead astern, *Yankee Tar* was making over eight knots, but the handling of the boat was becoming very difficult. Although the waves were exceedingly large, they were not breaking, so they made the decision to heave to, gauging their speed and the timing of the waves to head up and tack before lashing the wheel hard over to leeward. The yacht settled into a comfortable position and Bob sat in the cockpit on watch, while Hal took advantage of the easier motion to prepare some hot food. After a good feed, they rinsed off the salt and took the opportunity to get some sleep.

In the morning, the wind had dropped to a more moderate gale of thirty-five knots, leaving a confused mass of waves. They put on some more sail to increase speed and give them better control of the boat, at the expense of increasing the strain on the sails and rigging. Bob was at the wheel and Hal was sitting on the cockpit coaming when the boat suddenly lurched and the boom came in a couple of feet, causing the mainsheet to slacken momentarily. As it did, it formed a perfect circle and dropped neatly over Hal's head, snugging around his neck as the boom momentarily rocked unsteadily. Even if he had had the time, there was enough weight to the sail that Hal couldn't release himself; if the boom swung back to its original position, the noose would certainly snap his neck. Faced with this predicament—and with only a split second to make a decision—two or three options flashed through Bob's mind. He made the choice to momentarily make the boat "stagger" by luffing the mainsail to slacken the mainsheet so Hal could pull off the noose. The problem was that if he swung the boat too far, the boom would swing across the boat and the mainsheet would tighten and still break Hal's neck. There was no time to explain anything. Their eyes met, and Hal gave the slightest nod. Bob swung the wheel hard to weather and almost immediately swung it back again. In that instant when the mainsheet went slack, Hal was able to free himself just before the boom crashed back across to its original position.

Hal sat like a stunned mullet, speechless for a few minutes, and Bob knew that Hal realized just how close he had been to death. His capture had been a one-in-a-million chance. Hal said simply, "I'm going down to pour a stiff rum. Want one?"

"Just bring up the bottle," Bob replied.

On arrival in Pago Pago, they learned that five of the seven yachts anchored in the lagoon at Suwarrow had ended up on the reef during the storm.

Chapter 3

Anchoring in the Ha'apai Group

The *Pacific Islands Pilot, Volume II,* describes the center or Ha'apai Group of islands in the Kingdom of Tonga this way:

> *The Ha'apai Group is composed of numerous coral islands ... most of the islands present similar features; from a distance they appear low and flat-topped, and on nearer approach a white sandy beach is seen encircling a densely-wooded island entirely surrounded by a reef. The principal anchorage in the Ha'apai Group is off the township of Pangai on the west side of Lifuka Island. Elsewhere anchorages are few in number, especially in the north part of the group.*

Yankee Tar motored very slowly toward a low-lying island. It was almost indistinguishable from many of the other islands in the group, with coconut trees reaching about eighty feet into the perfect blue sky and no sign of life. The wind and sea were calm here among the islands, and as they approached, they could see the low ocean swell spilling over the fringing reef with a tumble of foam, forming a visible line that marked its location. It had been a three-day sail in good weather from the commercial harbor of American Samoa but over four thousand nautical miles from the smog and chaos of Los Angeles to this tiny speck in the middle of the Pacific Ocean.

Hal stood at the wheel and looked up the mast to where Bob was sitting on the lower spreaders, about twenty-five feet above the deck. Hal shielded his eyes from the midday sun with his hand and squinted. "I can't see an opening in the reef. Are you sure this is the place?" Without waiting for an answer, he peered ahead again. "All these little islands look the same," he said with a frown, and then called up to Bob again. "What do you see from up there?"

"It's okay," Bob called down. "We're right on track. Back off the throttle a bit." Hal eased the throttle and the engine slowed to just above an idle. With the reef twenty yards away, Bob called down again. "Okay, now get ready to make a very slight turn to port." With that, a narrow opening that was formed by the overlap of the two reefs became visible. Hal looked relieved and Bob called again. "Right down the middle." Bob slid down the mast and walked forward to take a position on the foredeck.

Hal called to him over the thrumming of the engine. "I can't see where to go! It looks like a dead end!"

"Watch the color of the water!" Bob called back. "We're almost in!"

The seemingly bottomless clear, green water that they had entered when they reached this group of islands continued until the ocean floor rose up steeply to the edge of the reef, the color gradually bleeding out of the water as it shallowed until it became utterly transparent, exposing the irregular shapes of the coral beneath. The sun overhead illuminated the darker tops of the coral that they needed to avoid so Hal could steer safely along the narrow channel and into a small bay.

Bob stooped and picked up one of the two anchors that they had prepared on the deck. He looked back over his shoulder. "Ready with the anchor!" Their momentum carried them another twenty yards. "Stop us right here!" Hal shifted into reverse, and as the boat came to a stop, Bob lowered the anchor over the bow roller until it hit the sandy bottom. *Yankee Tar* slowly started to back away from the anchor.

Hal looked over the side. "It doesn't look very deep here, Bob. What is it, eight feet?"

"It looks like it, but it's at least twenty."

"Shit, it's clear!"

Hal steered the boat back as Bob paid out the anchor chain that they had carefully laid out on the deck to the set length and secured to a cleat, and then revved the engine to half throttle to set the anchor firmly in the sand.

"Ready on the second one?" Hal called.

"Yeah, nudge her forward a bit."

Yankee Tar moved ahead to the appointed position, and they set the second anchor. After a few minutes, the boat settled itself to lie comfortably on the two anchors, which spread out in front of them at an angle of sixty to seventy degrees, the bow facing to the east and the island forming a perfect windbreak.

Hal shut off the engine and looked around to survey their tranquil location. He could see the reef barely fifteen yards off the stern and saw that it extended in a horseshoe-shaped shelf just below the surface all around their anchorage. Fifty yards ahead into the shallows lay the coral sand beach of the island.

"How did you ever find this place?" Hal asked in disbelief. "This isn't a lagoon; it's like sitting in a hand basin!"

"Let me bring up a couple of beers from the bilge and I'll tell you."

They sat back in the cockpit and Bob took a drink before saying, "I sailed a yacht through here in the sixties. The first time I came in here, I brought along an old Tongan sea captain. I felt like you did when the reef got close. Once we were in, the old man told me to lay out two anchors to stop the boat from swinging. The anchors had to be set at a certain angle. We dropped one all right, but the old captain wasn't happy about the second one. He told me that he would set it for me and would wave his hand above his head to indicate that I should pay out more chain. I thought that he would signal from the foredeck, but the old guy surprised the shit out of me when he jumped over the side and swam down about twenty feet to

Hal Holbrook drawing a cool beer from the bilges of *Yankee Tar*

the anchor. He pulled it up with one hand and walked along the bottom with it, motioning to me with his other hand to pay out more chain. He put it where he thought it should be, swam to the surface, and climbed aboard as if it was an everyday occurrence. I thought to myself, *if I can do that when I'm your age, I'll be doing all right!"*

Hal shook his head in disbelief. "I'm with you on that!"

"There's no light on the end of this reef," Bob continued. "You should try coming in here at night!"

"Why the hell would you want to do that?"

"Six months after the old Tongan guy showed me this place, I was heading back up to Vava'u. I wanted to break the trip, so I thought I'd stop in here. By the time I got close, the sun was going down, and I knew I wasn't going to make it before dark. The weather was quiet so I edged the yacht close to the reef looking for the entrance, but I couldn't see jack shit. Just as I was turning the boat seaward to wait it out until morning, I spotted a light, which surprised the shit out of me. Tongan charts are notorious for showing lights that aren't there because the locals haven't been out to fill up the gas bottles for years. Or sometimes a big sea has come over the reef and, even though the gas bottle was full, all you'd find was a pile of rusty angle iron. Light maintenance wasn't a high priority, I can tell you. They would have done better hiring some little dude to take out a canoe full of firewood every night.

"Anyway, I altered course and approached with extreme caution. As I neared the light, I was astounded to see a young boy with a hurricane lamp at the top of an eight-foot-long marker stick that had been jammed into the coral at the end of the reef. As I passed through the entrance, I could see his small outrigger canoe tied to the stick. He had been sent out by the chief of the village to guide me into the lagoon.

"I looked over at him as I passed and said, 'How ya doin'?' The boy just grinned, slid down the pole, jumped into his canoe, and paddled off. When I had anchored and rowed ashore, the chief was on the beach waiting for me. The young boy stood by his side, still with a huge grin on his face.

"The chief said to me, 'Hey, Captain Bob. This afternoon we see you coming. We know you not be here before nighttime, so we try to make it easy for you.' He put his hand around the boy's shoulders and said, 'You know my son.'

"I tousled his head and said, 'Too right! He's the lighthouse keeper.'"

Hal shook his head again, chuckled, and just said, "Amaaazing."

Chapter 4

———◆◆◆◆◆———

A Wing and a Prayer

Yankee Tar swung at its anchor in Neiafu Harbour in Vava'u, just off the Paradise International Hotel. Hal and Bob had cleaned up the yacht so that it was shipshape before their arrival in Vava'u and ready for the customs, immigration, and health inspections. Once at anchor, they had cleaned and ordered all of the gear on deck. They organized the charts and equipment down below and stowed it away. Hal exceeded even Bob's high standards of orderliness for a seagoing yacht, a trait that gave Bob a source of material for good-natured teasing. Hal found lots to kid Bob about as well, but while they both enjoyed the ease of their friendship, they also knew from the discipline they had each learned during their early sailing days—Hal's off the east coast of the United States and Bob's from Auckland Harbour to the coastline of New Zealand—that the comfort and safety of a yacht at sea depended on good habits.

Hal was packing his bag in his cabin, getting ready to fly back to Hollywood for a movie contract. His plane was scheduled to leave in the morning. He had cleaned and stowed his gear from the last leg of their voyage so that it would be ready to go when he got back. Now he would need to begin to make the transition back to his work life and the separate discipline that it required. For one thing, he would have to get used to wearing more than the shorts and light cotton shirts that he had become accustomed to—and shoes. Both he and Bob had learned that bare feet were safer on board because flip-flops or shoes could catch on deck fittings or rigging and cause an accident.

Hal called up to Bob in the cockpit, "Bob, have you seen that cruising permit?"

"You mean the shopping list?"

"Yeah," Hal said with a chuckle. "I'm going to take that back and get it framed."

"It's down on the chart table. I'll go get it for you." Bob stepped down into the main cabin and pulled a wine-stained, five-by-six-inch piece of paper from under a stack of nautical charts. On the top half of one side of the paper was written a list of supplies. Scribbled on the bottom half was a rough rendering of the islands that Bob and Hal had planned to visit. The names of the islands were written in such a way that they were roughly interspersed with the list of coconuts, rice, bananas, bread, and beer. He took the paper, climbed back into the cockpit, and passed it down to Hal in the aft cabin.

"Thanks, Bob." Hal chuckled again and shook his head. "That was the funniest thing I've seen in a long time!"

When Bob and Hal went to the police office to request a cruising permit for the outer islands, the officer asked where they wanted to go.

"We want to go to five islands," Bob replied and laid the shopping list down on the table.

The officer asked, "Are those the places?"

"Yeah," Bob said.

The police officer had many duties in Tonga, among them acting as customs and immigration officer, but he appeared to be unsure how to deal with this situation. He took the paper and had a cursory look, and then took his rubber stamp, pounded it onto the stamp pad, and proceeded to try to apply a big square stamp over each of the five islands and their names that were arrayed across the grocery list.

"There you are," he said, very officially, and thrust the paper back to Bob.

Hal and Bob looked at each other and without a word put the paper into their bag and left, barely able to contain themselves. Once outside, they burst out laughing.

"I guess we're approved to buy our groceries," Bob said.

"And to visit the island of rice!" Hal added.

<hr />

As Hal was finishing his packing, Bob stepped into the aft cabin. "Here's something to ensure that you make it back after the movie," he said, and handed Hal a small package.

"Why thanks, Bob," said Hal. He unwrapped the paper and revealed a leaping dolphin, about an inch and a half long, finely carved by an island artist from a boar's tusk and inset with black coral for the eyes. It had a small loop so that it could be worn as a necklace. "I've admired these. Leonati does great work."

"Well, this is a magic one. As long as you wear this, you'll come back."

Hal nodded and caressed the satin smooth surface, staring silently for a few moments. He looked up and smiled. "I'm about done here. Let's go up for dinner."

<hr />

Bob and Hal climbed down into the dinghy wearing clean shorts and shirts and carrying their flip-flops for the walk up the steep, stony steps to the hotel. Bob kneeled in the stern. He wound the rope around the top of the two-horsepower Seagull outboard motor and gave it a sharp pull. The motor burped to life and bubbled away happily.

"How do you *do* that?" asked Hal. "I pull the snot out of that thing and it still won't go!"

"You've got to talk to it," Bob confided as they motored across the still harbor to the hotel wharf. Bob had developed a special understanding of Seagulls after using them for many years. He reckoned that the British

Seagull motor was so old that it had probably originally been assigned to
Noah and that it required almost divine intervention to keep them going.
Somehow the Tongan government had received a large number of them
under a foreign aid program—more than they could possibly use—but
cruising yachts had to order spare parts from Britain at great expense. In
the past, Bob had bought several of the Tongan motors for spares and to
sell to some boaters in New Zealand, at a tidy profit.

When Bob and Hal scaled the hill to the hotel, they found the dining
room to be surprisingly full of people. Along one side of the room was
placed a long table, where a group of high officials from Samoa and their
staff were just beginning their dinner. The headman recognized Hal and
called, "Mr. Holbrook! Please come and join us."

Two chairs were quickly found, and Bob and Hal sat down. Before
the restaurant staff had an opportunity to set the places, the dignitary on
Hal's left looked to his subordinate next to him, who was poised with knife
and fork about to dig in to his dinner. With the speed of a gunfighter, he
whisked the plate away from him and slid it in front of Hal. His minion
was barely able to pull up on his fork before it dug into the tabletop. Still
poised with his irons, he shot a surprised look at his boss, who returned
a withering stare and then turned an obsequious smile to Hal. Hal and
Bob exchanged questioning glances, both delivering star performances to
maintain their composure. Bob's meal, however, took somewhat longer
to arrive.

The next morning, Hal was exchanging pleasantries with the hotel staff
while Bob stood outside nervously watching for the transport that was
supposed to take them to the airport. He was becoming worried that the
car was late. Every few minutes, he would step into the road to look for the
car, and then step back and pace nervously. After a few more minutes, a car
came into view, driven by Heinz, the agent for the local airline. He was a
pudgy, arrogant German man in his late thirties, balding prematurely and
always rumpled and unkempt. He pulled up in a cloud of dust. Bob hurried

27

Yankee Tar at anchor off the Paradise International Hotel, Neiafu, Vava'u Islands, Kingdom of Tonga

into the lobby and hustled Hal out to the road. As they approached, Heinz reached out of the window and held up his hand in a signal to stop.

"Zee plane vill not come. It haz ze major oil leak. Ze mekanik is verking on it now. It vill be three days. Have a vunderful time in paradise!" he concluded with an insincere laugh. With that he put the car in gear and pulled away, leaving them in a fresh eruption of dust.

"Knowing them, they've probably got the engine in the kitchen sink," said Bob.

"I've got to be back in L.A. by tomorrow night!" said Hal with agitation. "I've got a contract to keep!"

"Well, let's get a taxi and get out to the airport. There's another small airplane that flies to Nuku'alofa. Maybe we can get you on that."

"But that flight was full. Let's call them."

"Never mind. Let's just get out there and see what we can do."

When they arrived, Hal looked around at the crowd and his shoulders sagged. "I'll never get on the flight," he said dejectedly.

In the distance, they could hear a plane approaching. They watched it descend, and when it landed, it took the whole length of the dirt runway to stop, one engine sounding very rough. As it taxied up to the airport building, the suspect engine spluttered to a stop. The pilot got out and threw his hat back into the cockpit in disgust.

Bob walked out to the pilot and asked, "What's the problem?"

"The flaps are shot. I'll never be able to get off the ground if I put her down in Ha'apai. I'll just have to go straight on to Nuku'alofa."

"What about the Ha'apai passengers?"

"They'll just have to stay here."

Bob rushed back to Hal. "There are some empty seats!" he said excitedly. "Get yourself on board!"

"But what about changing my ticket?"

"I'll take care of that. Just get yourself on board."

The pilot stood by the steps of the plane, surrounded by the confused passengers, trying to explain the change of plans.

Bob hustled Hal through this chaos and up to the pilot. "He's going to Nuku'alofa."

The pilot nodded and gestured to the cockpit. Hal climbed inside and into the right-hand seat.

The hubbub died down as the departing passengers boarded the plane and those remaining returned to the airport building. The pilot fired up the good engine without difficulty, but the other one started only reluctantly. He taxied to the runway, set the brakes, and ran up the good engine to an even roar. He throttled the engine back. The errant engine sputtered, blew out a cloud of blue smoke, and died. Bob winced. This did not look good. Two or three times, the pilot tried to start it. Each time, the engine turned over with a putaputaputaputa sound and then stopped. Finally one cylinder fired, followed by others in an erratic rhythm. The pilot must have thought that this was as good as it was going to get because he gunned the stubborn engine, then revved the good one and took off with the best speed he could make.

As Bob watched, the plane passed over the reef and climbed slowly into the distance, the stuttering sound of its engine disappearing with it and taking Hal on to his next adventure.

Chapter 5

Dancing Across the Pacific

Hal took care to fly back to Vava'u via a different route. After a month back in the real world, he had finished his part and was glad to be back in the South Pacific. He and Bob spent time catching up on the local events and pursuing the needed provisions for their trip to New Zealand. It was the end of August and they planned to leave in two to three weeks to avoid the cyclone season, which runs from about November to March, the summer months in the southern hemisphere.

Hal was particularly intent on cleaning the boat again from stem to stern. The original Mr. Clean, he exceeded even his own unbelievably high standards in these preparations. The reason for his fastidiousness was the anticipation of his southern belle, the actress Dixie Carter, joining them for the voyage. Hal had met Dixie during the filming of *The Killing of Randy Webster*. Dixie herself had a busy career and was already well known for her roles in Broadway theater and in several television series. She would go on to star in the hit television show *Designing Women* as the much-loved Julia Sugarbaker.

Hal and Dixie had grown close in the time they had known each other, and things had progressed gradually from there. Bob had met Dixie in Marina del Rey before he and Hal had left for the voyage to New Zealand

and had quickly recognized the special feelings that Hal had for her. It was Bob who had suggested that Dixie join them for the trip to New Zealand, not knowing that Hal had secretly wanted to ask her but didn't want to without Bob's approval. This would be an opportunity for Dixie to share in Hal's passion for sailing.

A week later, Bob and Hal again made the twenty-minute trip to the local airport. They steadied themselves in the back of an old Toyota pickup truck as it bumped over the rough road, lifting their battered backsides off the rattly, wooden-planked floor over the roughest parts.

"Shit!" Bob exclaimed at a particularly brutal section. "This place is like a dumping ground for potholes!" The incessant rattling that accompanied this "Toyota tango" resulted from the total absence of maintenance, the front suspension probably not having seen grease since it left Japan. "Unbelievable!" commented Bob at the racket. "This contraption sounds like two skeletons making out in a tin bathtub!"

"I know!" Hal called to Bob over the noise, and then in a worried tone said, "We can't bring Dixie back to the boat in this!"

"Don't worry about it," Bob called back, wincing at an unexpected series of large holes. "We'll just have to bullshit ourselves into something else."

They arrived in a cloud of coral dust at the Tongan *fale* that served as the international terminal for South Pacific Island Airways, known locally as South Pacific Island "Scareways." They tumbled out of the truck, brushed themselves down to a modicum of respectability, and wandered out past the waiting Tongans onto the runway apron. After only a few minutes, Hal began pacing back and forth in the hot sun, his path on the dull red dirt traced by little clouds of dust that rose from each of his footfalls. He stared anxiously for a speck in the distance. "I don't see it yet, Bob!" Hal called back.

Bob sat quietly in the shade of the thatched roof. "Well, you'll probably hear it before you actually see it coming."

"But it's late!"

"They're always late. I don't think we have to worry."

Hal was not comforted. A few minutes later, the sound of an uncertain engine could be heard, the signature popping sound and misfire announcing the arrival of the flight. Hal was, if anything, more nervous as the plane approached the dirt airstrip. The big balloon tires of the aircraft hit the ground with a resounding wallop; it bounced several times and rolled on to the end. With a characteristic sputter, the plane turned and taxied up to the *fale* before coming to a stop, each of the engines finally expiring with a gasp like an asthmatic elephant. The oil dripping from one of the cowlings was an all-too-familiar sight.

The ground crew dragged the boarding steps across the ground and set them against the airplane. From inside, the door was unlatched and swung open. Hal bobbed his head from side to side amid the crowd, searching.

Dixie appeared at the door and descended the five steps with the flair of the accomplished stage and Hollywood actress that she was. She had an elegant beauty. She was slender, with long black, wavy hair and a delicious smile, looking like a character from *Gone with the Wind* in a spaghetti-strap summer dress, sandals, and a broad-brimmed hat to shade her cream complexion from the tropical sun. Seeing Hal and Bob emerge to the forefront of the group, her smile widened and she waved gaily to them. Hal moved eagerly toward her, but before he could reach her, she announced in a honeyed, southern accent, "Boys! Have I got a surprise for you!"

Hal came to an abrupt halt, and Dixie turned to the pilot, who came down the steps behind her holding two bottles of chilled champagne and a large package of what turned out to be caviar.

"How did you keep those cold for the flight?" asked Hal, incredulous.

"Well," she cooed in her delicious Scarlett O'Hara accent, "I simply said to the captain, 'Please help me, sir,' and he was so very accommodatin'!"

Hal rushed the final few feet and threw his arms around her. "Welcome to the Kingdom of Tonga, my love!"

The three of them walked back toward the *fale*, Hal and Dixie talking excitedly. "And the Tongan people are so friendly!" Dixie exclaimed. "That large gentleman over there in the black skirt talked to me for almost the entire trip."

Bob looked over to the man who was approaching an official black car, a tired old Checker taxi, the ultimate in Tongan luxury. As one of the official's assistants was opening the rear door, Bob had a sudden inspiration and darted ahead, accosting the man just as he was getting into the backseat. "Excuse me, sir," he said to the official.

The big man halted and turned toward him.

"Would it be possible for you to give the lady a ride to the hotel?" Bob asked respectfully, gesturing to Dixie.

The official looked across at her, and Bob was unsure whether it was a smile or leer that spread over his face. "Of course," he obliged, and after a quick stream of commands, his two servants scurried away from the car and stood dejectedly aside.

Bob waved to Dixie and she approached, followed by Hal, who struggled with two large suitcases that he had extracted from the pile of sacks, baskets, and rolled-up grass mats that constituted the passengers' baggage.

An observant immigration officer intercepted Hal en route. "You must clear customs first!" he insisted, but with a sweep of his large hand, the official waved off the officer and turned to Dixie enthusiastically.

"Hello again!" he welcomed. "Please accompany me. I will be glad to give you a lift to your hotel."

While Dixie and the official chatted, Bob hurried to the trunk, helped Hal heave in the bags, and slammed the lid. Then, quickly opening the rear door on the opposite side of the car to the official, he hustled Hal into the center position and walked briskly around to the other side to talk to the official. "Excuse me, sir," he interrupted, and without waiting, took Dixie by the arm, guided her into the backseat beside Hal, and closed the door. Before the official could act, Bob gave him a polite nod, dashed back around to the open back door, and jumped in beside Hal, leaving the official with no option but to ride in the front with the driver. One of the displaced assistants jumped forward to open the door for the outsmarted official, who climbed unhappily into the front seat.

Driving back in the relative luxury of the official's car, the potholes appeared to be a little shallower, but the pervasive lack of grease was abundantly obvious. The discussion on the trip was noticeably subdued.

As they approached the hotel, Hal whispered to Bob, "What do we do now?"

"I think we just leave it to Dixie."

When the car rattled to a stop, Bob and Hal quickly unloaded the luggage. Dixie stepped out of the car, walked up to the open window of the passenger door, and expressed a gracious "thank you" to the official before turning and sweeping elegantly up the few steps of the hotel. The car pulled away quickly and was soon obscured by the swirling coral dust, the official left to plot an outlet for his frustration. Certainly everyone in his office was going to have a bad day. Bob made a mental note to steer clear of him.

The first Friday night of every month, the Paradise International Hotel presented a Polynesian dinner and floor show in their dining room. It was a large area with perhaps ten wooden tables, each seating groups of six. The room was open on the side that faced the terrace and the pool to allow for natural ventilation on the hot summer nights. At the back wall of the room, the dance floor was set against a backdrop of woven grass mats and a host of local flowers.

The crowd consisted mainly of Tongans, together with a few travelers and yachties. The last time this number of people had gathered together was a few weeks before at a reception held for the reopening of the Paradise International Hotel. The new hotel owner had mistaken Bob for a Hollywood actor because he was sailing on Hal's yacht. All of the yachties had thought it was a laugh, so they had started to call him "Hollywood" Bob; the name spread quickly among the small, closely-knit cruising community.

Hal, Dixie, and Bob sat at a table in front of the dance floor for the best view. Two young men sat on low stools, playing on a ukulele and a guitar, serenading the guests with slow, melodic tunes that helped to create an authentic Polynesian atmosphere. They wore the traditional tau lava around their waists, a wrap of colorfully patterned cloth that extended to their knees. One wore a necklace of shark's teeth.

Meanwhile, a chorus of staff set out what seemed an endless supply of food on a row of dining tables that lined one of the side walls. The guests were invited to select their dinner from this exquisite buffet. The first course included a whole variety of delicacies that had been prepared in an underground oven or *umu*. The umu takes all day to prepare. It is started by digging a pit and lining it with hot rocks that have been heated in a fire. Fresh green banana leaves are laid over the rocks before the meats and vegetables, which are wrapped in more leaves, are placed on top. More green leaves are layered on top, followed finally by a blanket of earth to contain the heat. The umu is tended all afternoon, the smaller, more delicate foods being taken out and moved to the outside while the larger pieces carry on cooking.

The centerpiece of the umu was roasted joints of local pig. It was presented on a wooden platter, the meat so tender that it fell off the bones. This was accompanied by a host of vegetables. There was taro, a purpley, potato-like root vegetable that had been wrapped in leaves and cooked in a rich, sweet coconut cream. There were yams and breadfruit—the heavy, yellow-fleshed vegetable the size of a melon with a thick, knobbly skin—as well as tender taro leaves and tapioca, all roasted to perfection. Chicken and delicate, whole reef fish rounded out the spread of hot food.

Farther along were displayed platters of fillets of raw fish—wahoo, tuna, and mahi mahi—marinated in lime juice, squeezed from fruit picked fresh from the trees just outside the hotel, and coconut cream, along with crayfish boiled in seawater and delicately spiced with lemongrass and butter. Next was a cascade of fruits, sliced and presented in a rainbow of colors: papayas, mangos, passion fruit, sweet finger bananas, guava, and spiny-skinned pineapples.

Dixie was amazed by the quantity and variety of the food and puzzled by some of the peculiar-looking dishes. She inquired politely, "Hal, I just don't know what to eat! It's all so strange!"

"Don't worry, my dear," he replied gallantly, rising to his feet. "I'll find something you'll like."

Bob followed Hal to the buffet. Hal carefully selected a small assortment of the meats and vegetables. Bob looked over his shoulder. "Give her some of that raw fish," he suggested.

"She won't eat raw fish!" Hal protested.

"She'll like it; it'll just melt in her mouth," Bob assured him. "She'll never know what it is if you don't tell her."

Hal and Bob returned to the table. "Here, try this, my love," said Hal as he placed the plate on the table in front of her.

Dixie started somewhat tentatively and then tried the fish. She turned to Hal and remarked, "It's delicious! What is it?"

"My lips are sealed. I cannot tell you," said Hal, with a sideways glance at Bob.

Dixie looked suspiciously at Bob, who responded with a look of angelic innocence. She continued gamely, relishing each of the samples Hal had brought, enjoying the ambiance created by the happy company and simple hospitality.

While they finished their meal, the musicians continued to play, joined now by two men playing wooden drums fashioned by cutting a long slit into a length of log. After a few more tunes, the lights were turned off and the drummers began a hypnotic pounding of the wooden slit drums in the darkness. From behind the crowd, eight dancers—four men and four women—jogged into the room and spread out across the dance floor, illuminated only by the fire burning at either end of the clubs that the men carried. The men wore dark tau lavas around their waists and their faces were streaked in black paint, so that they appeared almost as shadows. They swung and thrust the clubs dramatically, while the four women in front of them danced at a frantic pace, the upper half of their bodies staying almost stationary while each pelvis moved as if mounted on a large ball bearing. Amazingly, the low-slung grass skirt attached to it seemed to defy gravity by remaining affixed to the frenzied hips. The primitive performance transfixed the crowd.

Bob leaned over to Dixie and spoke over the din. "I hope those guys with the torches don't get too close to the grass skirts! I'd hate to have to go and put the fire out!"

Hal Holbrook, Dixie Carter, and Bob Rossiter at the Paradise International Hotel, Vava'u Islands, Kingdom of Tonga

Tongan girls in formal dress

Dixie gave him a quizzical look and raised her eyebrows.

They were interrupted by the rapid and resounding *boom! boom! boom!* as the drummers suddenly halted the beat and the men disappeared outside and into the darkness. The lights returned, and the musicians resumed a more peaceful rhythm. The dancers slowed, swaying with the accompanying music and describing with their languid, aquiline movements the storytelling of their art.

"The dancing is very sensuous," said Dixie, looking over at Hal.

Hal was clearly rapt by the happy and peaceful atmosphere and smiled at the dancers, apparently catching the eye of one of them who smiled back. It appeared that it was this tacit introduction that targeted Hal, and by association, Bob, as students of Polynesian dance. At the end of the tune, each of the dancers walked into the audience to select "volunteers," including the two male crew of *Yankee Tar,* who joined, not reluctantly, to dance with the provocative performers. The lesson started with a simple stomp of the feet to emulate the men and progressed quickly to a short series of steps, punctuated by a bold lunge and battle cry. The beautiful women danced close to them, swinging their hips in time and egging them on with laughs and smiles. The men clearly enjoyed the lessons, and before they had embarrassed themselves too badly were returned to their tables, sweating from the exertion and laughing.

Hal flopped into his seat and let out a big, "Whew!" and added, "I don't know what it is, but I sure love this dancing!" He laughed, and it appeared to Bob that an idea struck him. "You know, Bob," said Hal, holding up his open hand and counting off on his fingers, "we've performed in Moorea, Bora Bora, Samoa, and now Tonga. We've danced our way across the Pacific!"

Chapter 6

———◆◆◆———

Tongan Delights

The early morning sun angling across the pool and surrounding deck of the Paradise International Hotel cast the solitary shadows of Hal and Dixie as they sat at one of the round breakfast tables. They chatted and picked randomly at the assortment of fruits that adorned their table, the stillness of the day cloaking them in a quiet intimacy. Bob sat slightly apart from them, sipping a cup of coffee and reviewing his list of things to do. He had liked Dixie from the word go, seeing in her the smart, gutsy lady that had attracted Hal. Already there was a strong bond developing among the three of them, a good sign for a yacht's crew that has to depend on one another.

Hal squeezed half a fresh lime, dripping some of the juice onto two halves of a papaya. He followed this with a sprinkling of shredded coconut before setting one of the halves on a plate before Dixie. She tasted the succulent combination, savoring it. "That really is delightful!" she said. "And so fresh!"

"All right off the trees here," Hal replied, gesturing toward the tropical forest.

Dixie appeared to consider something for a minute, and then leaned engagingly across to Hal and placed a delicate hand on his arm. "Tell me,

Hal darling," she said, "would you be so kind as to acquire some fresh coconut milk for me?"

"But of course, my love," Hal replied without hesitating. He looked around for a waiter, but with none in sight, he strolled across to a small, elderly man who was bent over double, slowly and deliberately sweeping the pool deck with a peculiar broom that emitted a kind of rattling sound as he swept. It was a Tongan broom, manufactured with the fibers harvested from the center ribs of coconut palm fronds and dried to give them a springiness. These whiplike sticks were bunched together and bound at one end with a fiber twine to form a grip and then cut to about three to four feet long. The man operated the broom by holding it in one hand, bending over, and sweeping with the entire length of the broom. The old man straightened and smiled as Hal approached. "Is there someone who could get some fresh coconut milk for the lady here?" he asked politely.

A happy look came to the old man's face, as if relieved of his detention, and he padded deliberately over to a nearby coconut tree. Before Hal could say anything, the man grasped the trunk of the tree with both hands, set his bare feet against the coarse, platelike bark, and nimbly moved up the tree in a practiced walking motion as easily as if he were climbing a ladder. He scaled the twenty-odd feet to the top in a matter of seconds. Then, steadying himself with one hand, he gripped the bottom of a coconut as it hung and spun it three or four times until the stalk parted. He looked down to choose a spot, dropped the heavy husk into the soft, sandy soil, and then called to one of the girls in the dining room, who came out with a large, broad-bladed bush knife.

The old man descended the tree as easily as he had climbed it. When he had reached the bottom, he took the bush knife that the girl had brought him. He held the husk firmly, upright in his left hand, and then deftly lopped the top off it with three successive whacks. With a twist of his hand, he used the tip of the blade to carve an opening in the soft inner shell. He smiled again and handed the fresh beverage to Hal.

"Well, thank you!" said Hal, taking it in both hands. "Thank you very much. That was more than I had expected!" he said, turning to Bob with a broad smile on his face. Bob saw how impressed Hal was with what the man had just done, scaling the palm like that. That was one of the things Bob liked about Hal, the fact that everything seemed new to him and that he, like Bob himself, appreciated the rich culture of the Tongans as deeply as he appreciated the sea.

Without a word, the old man cast a happy glance across to Dixie and turned back to continue his sweeping.

Hal walked over to the table, shaking his head. "Well, my love, that's about as fresh as it gets!" he chuckled and offered the coconut to her.

Dixie looked quizzically at Hal. "What do I do, Hal?" she asked. "I was expecting it would come in a glass!"

"Just drink it out of the husk," Hal suggested.

Dixie took the nut and peered inside it. Where the light green outer skin had been sliced away, there was a dense, white fibrous husk about two inches thick. The inside of the actual nut was lined with a smooth, almost reflective surface, and filled to the top with a clear liquid. She looked up at Hal and then raised it to her lips to drink. A little of the milk ran down her chin from the imperfect rim, and she smiled as she drank. "It's wonderful!" she declared as she lowered the nut and dabbed at her chin with a napkin. "Chilled, with a delicate coconut taste. And it's fizzy!"

"Isn't nature wonderful?" said Hal.

"We really are in paradise!" Dixie concluded.

···············

There were some final preparations to make before they were ready to leave port. Hal had arranged to take Dixie to the market and to the few local stores that were clustered near the harbor, as much to show her the simple wares that the Tongans relied upon as to pick up a few souvenirs.

Bob called out to them as they left, "Don't overdo it on the bananas!"

"I just love bananas!" said Dixie.

"You have to be careful with Tongan bananas," warned Bob. "There's a banana conspiracy going on. You turn your head for a minute, and when you look back, they all go yellow at the same time. Try eating eighty pounds of them! You'll have them baked, fried, mashed, raw, boiled, and when you feel a little brown stalk coming out of the top of your head, throw the rest of them over the side!"

Bob had arranged a local adventure for himself: to top up the diesel fuel while they were gone. Like so many things in these remote parts of the world, this was no simple task. He was very familiar with the common problems of contaminated fuel. Bad fuel could clog the fuel filters and kill the engine—always at the worst possible time—and lead to disaster. He had run into that situation before in the South Pacific and so had taken the necessary precautions. He had tied the dinghy to the little jetty fore and aft with breast and spring lines to prevent it from any movement during the process. To look at this arrangement, more common to mooring a yacht, it appeared to be overkill, but Bob knew the delicate operation that lay ahead. He had lined up four five-gallon plastic jerricans along the dock within easy reach of the dinghy, and arrayed around him on the floor of the dinghy were a plastic funnel, seven boxes of paper coffee filters, six pairs of nylon stockings, and eight rolls of paper towels. He took stock of these supplies, nodded with satisfaction, and stepped ashore to begin the operation.

The barrels that the diesel came in were never cleaned and were battered up almost beyond recognition. Bob had inspected several of the barrels the day before. The store manager had told him, "All good, Captain Bob." But Bob had pulled the bungs out and stared in with a flashlight and found otherwise. The color of the contents varied from that of India ink to decidedly porridge looking. He had marked one of the less venomous looking barrels for their use.

Bob went looking for a handcart to transport his chosen barrel to the dinghy, but when he returned, he found that the kindhearted storekeeper had rolled the barrel down to where the dinghy was tied up, ensuring a homogenous soup of rust, water, diesel, and whatever curious additives it contained. It was difficult to fault this act of kindness, so he thanked the storekeeper and carried on with the work.

Having done this before, Bob had brought his own barrel valve to control the flow. With the help of the storekeeper, he stood the barrel

Bob inspecting the diesel fuel in Neiafu, Vava'u Islands, Kingdom of Tonga

upright and installed the valve, and then laid it back down, overhanging the side of the dock. In a delicate and bizarre operation, he passed the diesel fuel through a stocking that he tied around the valve as a strainer to take out the big lumps, through a coffee filter nestled inside the top of a funnel, and finally through the funnel and into one of the five-gallon jerricans. After filtering fifteen gallons in this way, he could see that this was going to be an all-day job. He continued, stopping every so often to discard the stockings and renew the coffee filters, roughly at a ratio of one pair of stockings for every ten coffee filters. As careful as he was, though, the dinghy was soon wet with the fuel, and the rubber dinghy became greasier than a pork sausage. When he had filled up the four jerricans, he drove the dinghy out to the boat to transfer the fuel to the tanks. This was a perilous journey, as he had to master the art of not slipping over the side of the greasy pontoons.

Filtering the second load was even more time consuming because now he was getting down to the sand, rust, dead cockroaches, and whatever else was in the bottom of the barrel. The mortality rate of the coffee filters was astronomical toward the end, but he finally finished, satisfied with the result. Once he had transferred the last of the fuel aboard, he turned his mind to cleaning up. He squirted two bottles of dishwashing liquid into the dinghy and flushed it out with buckets of water. Then he squeezed what was left of the dishwashing liquid over himself, lathered up, and jumped in the harbor to rinse off.

Shortly after he finished, Hal and Dixie returned. Hal triumphantly displayed their find, a cardboard box the size of a basketball that he held aloft like a waiter balancing a tray.

"What's that?" asked Bob, looking quizzically at their treasure.

"Wine!" explained Hal. "In a plastic bag! No bottles to break, no corks. It's a great idea!"

Bob looked it over skeptically. "Yeah, it is. Where's it from?"

"Australia. I've never seen it before."

"Neither have I. Is there a date on it?"

Hal turned it around and inspected every side. "Can't see one," he declared brightly, undeterred.

"Well, this will be a new adventure," said Bob. "Let me give you guys a hand to get you and your 'bag of wine' aboard. I'm looking forward to us trying this new Tongan delicacy."

Chapter 7

———◆►✕◄◆———

Shoot-Out

A few days later, *Yankee Tar* slipped out of Neiafu Harbour and out to sea. The conditions were perfect. It was a warm, clear day, with a light breeze from the southeast, as if Fred, the wind god, had turned his weather machine to "nice" to give Dixie a gentle introduction to sailing life. With the yacht prepared for sea, Hal was below organizing the charts for the final leg of the voyage to New Zealand. It was mid-September and they were approaching the cyclone season in the South Pacific. Hal and Bob had calculated that their trip would take up to ten days in reasonable conditions, arriving in Auckland soon enough to avoid the early-season cyclones.

Bob was in the cockpit with Dixie, instructing her on how to steer a course. While Dixie had no knowledge whatsoever of sailing, she was a willing student.

They started with the basic skills of steering a sailboat. Bob stood behind her as she took the helm. "Now, what you want to do is keep an eye on your course, but always be aware of how the sails are set. Right now, the sails are set for a course of 180 degrees," he said, pointing at the compass that sat atop the binnacle in front of the wheel. "Just try to maintain that course for now."

"Aye-aye!" she replied cheerfully, looking down at the compass. Seeing she was steering about 170 degrees, she turned the wheel and steered a little to port. The compass swung to 160. "I guess I have to go the other way," she deduced and turned the wheel back to starboard.

"Right," said Bob, "but not too fast." The boat came round and the compass indicated 200 degrees. "Slower," he coached. Dixie turned the wheel back to port, the compass following to 150, and the sails began to luff. "Hold it there. Look behind us at the wake."

Dixie looked and saw the S-shaped wake that the boat had left in the water. "What am I doing wrong?"

"The idea is to keep the wake straight," he said. "You're chasing around the compass. That's normal for beginners. Now look up." Dixie looked up at the flapping sails. "And what you want to do is keep the sails full. It's easy to do when you've had a little practice. Just steer a little to starboard and hold it there. You'll be right."

"Mr. Rossiter, you are exceedingly patient!" Dixie remarked.

"You'll catch on soon enough."

Some time later, Bob joined Hal below. "How's she doing?" asked Hal.

"Good! She learns fast."

"I'm really glad you approve of Dixie joining us. It means a lot to me having her along."

"No worries, mate!" Bob smiled. "She's no trouble."

"Well, she has a lot to learn, that's for sure!" Hal laughed. "And it's better to have you show her the ropes than me."

"I'll have her trained in no time. Just leave it to me! The way she's going, we'll soon be able to rate her 'bosun.'"

Bob set about teaching Dixie the essential shipboard duties for standing watch. She quickly learned how to move about safely on deck, trim the sails, and keep the ship's log. She demonstrated another valuable talent that helped to endear her to her male crewmates: making phenomenal meals from shipboard rations. But at the same time, there were some special considerations that Bob had not foreseen. It was soon apparent, for example, that Dixie's lovely long hair posed a potential problem. When she brushed it in the cabin or in the head down below, the strands that fell into the bilge presented the risk of clogging the bilge pump. The only practical solution was for her to brush her hair on the rear deck so that it blew downwind and over the side. Dixie accepted this small concession with grace.

A few days out, Bob came up on deck and sat down next to Hal in the cockpit. He pulled a pack of cigarettes out of his pocket, lit one, inhaled deeply, and slowly exhaled. He turned to Hal. "Hal, this is a bit delicate," he said, choosing his words carefully, "but you've got to explain to Dixie how to use the head."

"What's the matter?"

"That's the second time I've had to fix it. The next time she blocks it up, she'll have to unplug it herself."

Hal looked at Bob in horror. "She can't do that!" he exclaimed, trying to keep his voice low enough to stop Dixie from hearing.

"Well, someone will have to! Just tell her the usual palaver—that she can't stuff three yards of toilet paper down it and that nothing goes into it unless she's eaten it first. She'll understand."

"I guess you're right," Hal replied without enthusiasm. "I'll have a word with her."

That issue was quickly and delicately resolved, but water use was a problem. At sea, water is a very precious commodity and used primarily for drinking. This was before the common use of watermakers, and sailors learned to wash dishes and brush their teeth using saltwater and rinse both with fresh. Showers are a rare treat, replaced by washing with limited amounts of water. *Yankee Tar* carried 120 gallons of water in three separate water tanks, as well as four five-gallon jerricans on deck. These extra containers were placed strategically so that they could be grabbed easily if the crew had to abandon ship and, most importantly, were only filled to 80 percent capacity so that they would float if jettisoned over the side from the stricken vessel.

Without proper instructions, Dixie went through a tank of water in three days.

"At this rate, we'll all die of thirst in a week," Bob commented to Hal. "You're going to have to explain to her about conserving water."

Hal broached this subject with Dixie, and once again, she was very understanding of the constraints of shipboard life and eager to do her part.

"You can use rainwater to shower on deck if you like," teased Bob. "If I'm on watch, you can be guaranteed that my eyes will be averted."

"You really are a true gentleman, Mr. Rossiter, sir," she replied good-naturedly.

As the days progressed, Dixie became a capable member of the crew, and Bob and Dixie's relationship less one of teacher to student and more one of sailor to sailor.

They had plotted a course that would take them past the northern tip of New Zealand, roughly west by south, for as long as possible to keep the trade winds. They planned to sail slightly past the tip of the North Island, and then drop due south and parallel the east coast. This would give them the fastest passage. At the same time, they had to watch for a weather system that was spinning counterclockwise and moving from Australia toward New Zealand. This was a common occurrence at this time of year and would last three or four days. They hoped to be able to drop down the west side of it to take advantage of the favorable winds, saving time on their passage.

Hal and Bob had learned this information from their friend Bernard Moitessier, the famous round-the-world ocean sailor and author. One of the reasons Bernard was famous was because, when leading the single-handed British *Sunday Times* Golden Globe round-the-world race in 1969, he had decided not to finish the race and just kept on going around the world again via the Southern Ocean. This was the same race in which Englishman Donald Crowhurst, knowing that he couldn't win the race, devised a plan to report false positions while sailing in circles in the Atlantic Ocean. He planned to eventually rejoin the fleet in first position to emerge the winner and collect the £5000 prize to repay the money he had borrowed against his home to enable him to compete in the race. On July 11, a royal mail ship found his abandoned yacht six hundred miles west of the Azores. His log entries suggest that he had gradually gone mad. The last deranged entry in his logbook from July 1 read, "It is finished, it is finished. It is the mercy. It is the end of my game. The truth has been revealed." It is suspected that he stepped over the side and committed suicide. In a showing of grace and chivalry, the eventual winner, countryman Robert Knox-Johnston, contributed the purse for winning the race to Crowhurst's widow to save her house.

Bernard didn't talk about the race. He was a typical single-handed sailor, very solitary with solid beliefs. He appeared happy with himself and without the need to prove anything to anyone—a real seaman. Hal and Bob first encountered Bernard in California, where he was giving lectures on his sailing experiences. They spent many hours exchanging stories and told him of their upcoming trip. It was Bernard who had given them this advice about the fastest route from Tonga to New Zealand.

Bernard was a small, slightly-built Frenchman with an intense air about him. He had an amazing wealth of knowledge of weather that was useful even to a seasoned cruising sailor like Bob. When they met him again in Tahiti on board his yacht *Joshua,* he gave them the advice on approaching Suwarrow and New Zealand and gave Bob his hand-drawn charts of these areas.

Yankee Tar had fine sailing conditions, with consistent winds of fifteen to twenty knots out of the southeast. Under a full main, 100 percent jib, and staysail, they sped along at about seven knots, and each day their heading took them closer to their next port. After five days, the wind dropped away, barely filling the sails, so that the boat was hardly making any way. The ocean took on an oily appearance, its surface undisturbed. The crew lounged about the boat in the warmth, spending their waking hours on deck awaiting a change of weather.

Hal and Dixie were reading in the cockpit in the shade of the dodger. Hal put his book down and glanced around the horizon. Apart from the distant haze, the sky and sea were featureless. Bob went below, and a few minutes later Hal called down the companionway. "Hey, Bob! Where's all this rough New Zealand weather that you're always telling me about? It's as smooth as a parking lot!"

"Well, it might let us in, but it doesn't always like to let me out!" Bob called from below. "The last time I left, it was a real bastard!" He emerged from the companionway with a long, irregular bundle under his arm. "While we're waiting, I think it's a good time for some target practice!" he declared.

Dixie looked up with surprise. "Target practice?"

"Now there's a good idea!" Hal said, closing his book and getting up.

"What are we practicing for?" Dixie asked again, with a hint of concern.

"You never know when you're going to encounter pirates," Bob declared dramatically, and then added, "and besides, it's fun!"

He unzipped the bag and pulled out a Remington pump-action shotgun. It had a stainless steel barrel—the shortest available, like a riot gun—and a composite stock, making it impervious to the salt air.

Dixie looked around the vacant horizon. "But what will you shoot at?"

"Well, in the old days, they'd set out an old powder keg and let loose a broadside until it was smashed to bits," said Bob. "We'll improvise: beer cans!" he said, pulling a can out of his pocket. "Empty, of course." Bob loaded the shells into the magazine and checked the safety. "You go first," he suggested to Hal, handing him the gun. "I'll set out the targets."

While Hal was moving to the aft deck, Bob hurled a series of three beer cans as far as he could. Each landed with a smack and sat motionless on the surface, drifting almost imperceptibly astern. Hal jokingly tested the wind with a wetted finger and then shouldered the gun. He set his feet in a wide stance to steady himself on the deck and took careful aim. The eruption of the first shot was a startling contrast to the solitude of the still ocean. The roar was deafening but strangely instantaneous, with no echo, like sneezing in the middle of a desert. The pulverized beer can catapulted twenty feet back with the impact and sank quickly below the surface. A fine spray of water spattered silently onto the surface of the sea, creating a small rainbow that hung temporarily, like a mirage, before evaporating into thin air.

"Nice shootin', Sheriff!" Bob complimented him. "Let's see if ya can take care of those other two varmints!"

Hal grinned and pumped another shell into the chamber. He took aim and blasted the second one in similar fashion. The third shot hit just in front of the last target, so that it leaped twenty feet in the air, giving Hal time to chamber another shell and take another quick shot just as it hit the water, driving it out of sight and into Davey Jones's locker. He reset the safety and turned back to the cockpit while the acrid blue smoke floated lazily downwind.

"Let me go down below and bring up some more ammunition," said Bob enthusiastically. He disappeared below and returned with several boxes of shells, a rifle, and some more targets. Hal launched the beer cans while Bob deftly loaded the 30-shot clip of the semiautomatic Ruger Mini 14. Bob handed it to Hal and took up the shotgun himself. When they were both set, they merrily blazed away, making short work of the intruders.

They stopped to reload, and Dixie called to them from the cockpit. "I just haaave to get a picture of this," she said, holding her camera, "because you two look like Butch Cassidy and the Sundance Kid!" Hal and Bob posed on the aft deck with their weapons, trying to look the part.

When Dixie had finished, she put down the camera and Hal walked back to the cockpit. "Would you like to give it a try, my dear?" he offered.

"I don't know if I could," Dixie replied demurely.

"It's easy," Bob encouraged.

Hal held out the Ruger to her. Dixie looked at it with disdain and looked admiringly at the gleaming shotgun Bob was holding.

"Being as delicate as you are, that would be a better weight," Bob said reassuringly, "because this shotgun'll knock you on your ass!"

Hal Holbrook and Bob Rossiter at gunnery practice

"Mr. Rossiter, you rogue!" she said with mock indignation. "Well, I guess I could," she agreed, and climbed onto the aft deck. She took the gun from Hal and hefted it in both hands, judging the weight.

Bob gave her some essential instructions. "Now listen, as long as you're pulling the trigger, it's going to fire, and if you keep pulling the trigger, it will keep firing," he emphasized. "The first thing to remember is to always hold the gun with the barrel pointing away from the ship. Don't shoot out the self-steering gear or knock down the backstay! After that, all you have to do is make sure you stand solid, with your feet slightly apart, hold it firmly to your shoulder, point it, and squeeze the trigger."

He tossed a couple more beer cans a short distance, disengaged the safety for her, and then stood quietly behind her as she took aim. The first shot smashed one of the cans, sinking it without mercy and producing a plume of water that spread fifteen feet in diameter. Dixie cried out with delight and started to swing around to share her triumph with Hal, the barrel of the gun swinging dangerously with her. Bob had anticipated the possibility of this reaction and quickly grabbed her by the ears, arresting her turn, and gently turned her head slowly back out to sea, the muzzle of the gun following obediently behind.

"Oh," Dixie gasped, watching the smoking barrel. "Be still, my heart!"

"Remember," Bob said, still holding her by the ears, "always point the gun away from the ship!"

"I declare," Dixie said with surprise, "you certainly have an effective manner, Mr. Rossiter, sir!" Then she laughed and said, "I promise not to sink the boat! Now let's shoot us some varmints!"

Among the three of them, the crew disposed of several dozen "pirates," but one form of intruder survived unscathed. Every so often, one or two flying fish would launch themselves out of the water to elude a predator and glide thirty or forty feet across the surface of the water before collapsing their long, winglike fins and diving back in. Like a seagoing game of skeet, the defenders would try to hit the airborne invaders, always without success. After an hour of this sport, they had had enough and retired to more peaceful purposes.

It was just at sunset that a light breeze rippled the surface of the water and the sails began to pull. Dixie was asleep below, so Hal and Bob set the course and trimmed the sails, and then did a quick check of the deck and gear. Once they were satisfied that the boat was set and secure, they returned to the cockpit. "It's my watch, Bob," said Hal. "We're all set here. Why don't you turn in and get some rest. I'll call you if we need to change sail."

"Suits me!" Bob replied and disappeared below.

The sky in the east was brightening when Bob poked his head up through the companionway, accompanied by the aroma of fresh coffee. It was the end of Dixie's watch. Bob offered her a steaming cup. "Coffee?" he asked cheerfully.

"Oh, bless your heart! It sure smells good!" she responded, taking the cup from him. "How did you sleep?"

"Like a man with a clear conscience! Any problems?"

"Not a thing. It was a beautiful night! There are some interesting clouds today, though. And that dark line up ahead. What is that, Bob?"

"Where?"

She pointed just off the starboard bow. "It's got that low cloud over it."

Bob climbed the few steps into the cockpit and turned toward the bow to look.

"See?" said Dixie. "I couldn't see it until the sun came up."

Bob ducked his head slightly to see past the sail and squinted into the low light. "That's Aotearoa," he stated plainly. "It means 'Land of the Long White Cloud.' It's a Maori story." He paused, looking into the distance before adding quietly, "It's New Zealand. I'm almost home."

Yankee Tar made landfall at Cape Brett in the Bay of Islands where the lighthouse stands on the rocky promontory. Nearby they could see the passage in the rock headland that was large enough for a forty-foot yacht to pass through. They continued down the east side of the north island on a comfortable broad reach, sailing along past miles and miles of unspoiled coastline and the rugged countryside and subtropical rain forests that lay behind. It was a two-day trip from there, past Whangarei Heads, and through the Hauraki Gulf to Auckland. This was going to be the end of the voyage for some time, as both Hal and Dixie had to leave to fulfill their obligations in Hollywood. They spent a few days organizing the yacht and arranging for its safekeeping.

On the evening before their departure, the three of them were sitting in the bar at the Brickhouse Hotel overlooking Auckland Harbour. Hal took a long sip on his drink and gazed out at the lights of the marina. He turned to Bob and said, "You know, I've really taken to this place."

"It's pretty easy to like," agreed Bob.

"There's only one thing that worries me, though."

"What's that?" Bob asked with concern.

"All these jokers talk like you!"

Part Two

An Aussie from Down Under

Chapter 8

The Adventure Continues

Sydney, Australia, June 1981

Cab 883 wound its way from Vaucluse down through the curves of New South Head Road toward Rose Bay in the eastern suburbs of Sydney, Australia. The windshield wipers fought to clear the heavy winter rain, and the big droplets danced through the illumination of the headlights. Peter Jinks yawned. It was a quiet Wednesday night, and he was only halfway through his fifth twelve-hour shift in as many days. As he scanned the street in vain looking for a fare, his mind wandered, and he thought how he would rather be back in the sun and excitement of Rio. He'd left his home in England at age seventeen to immigrate to Australia, taking the overland route to India and then a freighter to Sydney. With this first taste of adventure, he realized that he wanted more, so over the next fifteen years he had worked just long enough to be able to take off to some distant and exotic destination. His travels had taken him to Iceland, Russia, South America, Africa, and Japan, as well as to other less-exotic places. When the money ran out, he'd started a window-cleaning business in Denmark, bought furs in Afghanistan to sell in Munich, worked as a crocodile hunter for a taxidermist in Costa Rica, and opened a marriage agency between the Philippines and Australia with a business partner. His thoughts were interrupted as the radio came to life.

"Car 454, come in."

Peter heard the response come back, "454, Base."

"What happened to the Dover Road job? I've got the customer on the line again."

"Base, I honked my horn and nobody came out."

"Well, next time, driver, get your lazy backside out of the seat and knock on the door. Where are you now?"

"Uh, Base, I'm in Bondi Junction with a passenger."

"Carry on, 454. I'll recall the job." The operator paused and then said, "First call, Rose Bay to Rushcutter's Bay."

Peter grabbed the mike and called in. "883. Dover and New South Head."

"We won't go any further, cars. 883, pick up 'Oddy' at 430 Dover Road, and I'll tell the gentleman thirty seconds."

"Roger, 883." Peter checked the rearview mirror, swiftly did a U-turn over the double yellow lines, made a right turn through the red light at Dover Road, and pulled up a hundred yards down the road in front of a stately stone home. He started to open his door, but then he glanced through the passenger window and saw the door of the house open and a huge shape silhouetted in the doorway.

Oddy Karlsen strode briskly down the path and pushed through the heavy wrought iron gate with apparent ease. As he stepped onto the sidewalk, the streetlight reflected off the polished brass buttons of his double-breasted navy blazer and illuminated the shock of silver hair that now glistened from the rain. He pulled open the front door of the cab, as is the Australian fashion, and positioned himself in the seat beside Peter.

"Where would you like to go, mate?" asked Peter, glancing across and seeing him looking straight ahead.

A deep voice commanded in a slightly accented tone, "The Cruising Yacht Club of Australia, young man, and don't spare the horses."

Peter swung back into New South Head Road and down along the harbor toward the yacht club. Turning to the big man, he asked, "You're not by any chance Swedish, are you, mate?"

Oddy swung his head around and fixed Peter with his cool blue eyes. "How dare you swear at me?" he replied with mock indignation, a grin pulling at the corners of his mouth. "I'm Norwegian!" he replied emphatically.

Oddy was indeed of proud Viking ancestry and looked the part with his six-foot-five-inch, muscular frame. He had been smuggled out of German-occupied Norway to England in 1942 at the age of fifteen to join the Royal Norwegian Navy and served aboard a Norwegian destroyer on runs to Murmansk and aboard a corvette as part of the North Atlantic convoys from Liverpool to St. John's and Halifax. One of his final naval duties was the distinction of being one of two young sailors to hoist the Norwegian flag at the German surrender ceremony at Bergen, probably, he later said, "because we were the youngest or perhaps the soberest."

Peter and Oddy exchanged stories about some of their adventures and soon discovered that they had a lot in common. "I've been to Norway a few times, you know," said Peter.

"Oh really?" said Oddy. "When was that?"

"The last time was in '77. I had a great time!"

Oddy observed Peter for a moment before responding in his regal manner, "From your curly blond mop and blue eyes, you look like you may be blessed with some Viking ancestry yourself."

"Not that I know of. Anglo Saxon by birth, but I love Scandinavia. Especially the beautiful women!" Peter saw Oddy smile at this remark.

"What were you doing over there besides chasing our Viking women around?" he asked.

"Just traveling around and having a good time. I went sailing up some of the fjords. They're pretty spectacular."

"So how do you come to be driving a cab in Sydney, young man?" Oddy asked with interest.

"I've just got back from a couple of years traveling in South America. I'm trying to get a few bucks together so I can take off again. And what are you doing in this neck of the woods?"

"I came here with the Vikings many years ago for a refresher course in pillaging and plundering, and I've been here ever since." He grinned. "Tonight's session was rather tiring, though."

As the cab passed Edgecliff Station, Peter put on the indicator and pulled into the outside lane. He turned into New Beach Road, drew up in front of the double doors of the yacht club, and switched off the meter. The rain had tapered off to a light sprinkle. "Five dollars forty, thanks," said Peter.

Oddy paid the fare and said simply in his forthright manner, "Now, come in. I'll buy you a drink."

"Nah, I'd better keep working."

"Ah, but I insist," he commanded, fixing him again with his gaze and emphasizing the point with a raised finger. Oddy got out of the cab and turned toward the front doors without waiting.

Peter hesitated momentarily. He knew that he had six hours to go, and the money he would make would put him closer to his next adventure. But he felt the excitement that surrounded this curious character and was intrigued to know him better. He went with his gut feeling and quickly locked the cab and followed.

Oddy hurriedly scaled the fifteen steps to the landing, burst through the double doors, and strode purposefully toward the bar, Peter hurrying to catch up. Oddy hailed the barman. "Sir, a jug of mutton bird repellent if you please, with a dash."

"A dash of what, sir?" asked the barman blankly.

"Speed. I'm rather thirsty," he announced. "I've just done ten rounds with the Polish countess."

There were chuckles from some of the nearby club members who knew Oddy's reputation. Oddy acknowledged his friends and commandeered two spots among them at the crowded bar, motioning Peter to the place on his right. He reached behind Peter and touched a distinguished elderly gentleman on the arm. "Seaweed, meet my very good friend Peter, the taxi driver. Peter, this is Captain Seaweed, who is married to the lovely Mrs. Seaweed, nee Kelp." Peter shook hands with him, thinking that this was an odd nickname and wondering what Seaweed had done to deserve it.

The jug appeared on the bar in front of them. Oddy picked it up, along with two glasses, and then stood and turned on his heel. "Come on, Peter, I'll introduce you to a few of the local scallywags."

Peter was to discover that Oddy was both well-liked and mischievous, and in his witty way had taken it upon himself to christen every regular in the club with a nickname. With a series of quick introductions, Peter soon met Doctor Death, Ming the Merciless, Boy Messenger, Dennis the Menace, Ace, and many more. Peter was left wondering how on earth Oddy had come up with all these names. He couldn't contain his curiosity. When they were out of earshot, he ventured quietly, "Why is that bloke called Doctor Death?"

"Simply because he has no living patients," Oddy replied, as if the answer were obvious.

"Ah, I see." With the jug nearly empty, they returned to the bar, where it was quickly refilled. Peter took a drink and commented, "This is good. What's in it?"

"*Overproof* Bundaberg rum," Oddy emphasized, "and bitter lemon. Just a splash only."

"So why is it called mutton bird repellent?"

Oddy illustrated by taking Peter by the elbow and steering him to the bank of windows overlooking the yacht harbor. Peter gazed with fascination at the hundreds of sailing yachts below him and the lights of the marina reflecting off the water. He had never seen anything like it. "Do you see any mutton birds?" Oddy queried with an expansive sweep of his hand.

"Uh, no, Oddy," Peter observed.

"Well, there you are then," he concluded decisively, satisfied that he had dispelled any doubt. Then, with a twinkle in his eye, he said, "But perhaps we'd better have one more jug," and he added conspiratorially, "just in case."

Sitting back at the bar, they took up their conversation about their travels and talked for some time about their experiences until the conversation inevitably turned to the sea. "Ever done any sailing?" Oddy asked Peter.

"Yeah, I spent four months on a seventy-two-foot ketch up on the Great Barrier Reef in '75." He told Oddy about sailing around the reef and how good the diving had been. "You sound like you might have done a lot of sailing yourself," Peter suggested.

"If Viking longboats and sailing square-riggers around the Horn qualify, then yes, I suppose you could say I have a wee bit of sailing experience." In fact, Oddy was well-respected among the yachting fraternity for his sailing skill as much as for his strength and stamina, as well as for his vast knowledge of boats, from square-riggers to modern racing yachts. Oddy's achievements included completing ten Sydney to Hobart races, widely recognized as one of the toughest ocean races in the world, earning line honors in 1973 aboard *Helsal 1*, a seventy-two-foot ferro-cement sloop nicknamed *The Flying Footpath*, breaking the previous record set by *Ondine* in 1962.

Oddy told Peter about some of the yachts at the club and their owners. "In fact, I'm going sailing on the harbor with Captain Clubbenheimer on Sunday," said Oddy. "Why don't you come along?"

"That'd be great!" said Peter enthusiastically. "What do I bring?"

"Bring yourself, some food, and of course, any adventurous young ladies that you may or may not be acquainted with!"

Preparing for a day on Sydney Harbour aboard *Ron of Argyll* with owner Andrew Clubb

Chapter 9

Sydney to Suva

Peter stood on the balcony of the third floor flat overlooking Bondi Beach, sipping the black coffee that he hoped would clear his head from the aftereffects of the alcohol and the torrid night with the young brunette that he had met at the farewell party the night before. He gazed at the wide expanse of the Pacific Ocean, feeling the excitement building in him about the upcoming Sydney-to-Suva yacht race. He had learned an enormous amount about sailing traditional yachts in the last twelve months from Oddy aboard the fifty-five-foot, gaff-rigged ketch *Ron of Argyll*. And he had found a real appreciation for the charm and simplicity of the old wooden yacht. Being built in 1928, before the invention of the technology found on modern yachts, it used block and tackle instead of winches, used wooden cleats or belaying pins to secure the sheets and halyards instead of their modern alloy counterparts, and was steered with a tiller instead of a wheel. Simplicity was paramount for this traditional gear, and these time-tested devices would rarely jam or break. Now his knowledge would be tested by an ocean voyage. The crew would have to rely on their skills and their senses, much like the sailors who had sailed this yacht from Scotland decades before.

He was brought back to the present by the honking of a car horn and looked down to the street to see the Legion cab at the entrance. Peter leaned over the rail and called to the cabby, "I'll be down in a minute, mate!" He gulped back the rest of the coffee and walked into the bedroom.

The young lady stirred, awakened by the noise. She lifted herself onto her elbow and said sleepily, "Are you leaving already?"

"Yes. Sorry, I'm running late. Thanks for a great night." He bent down and gave her a kiss and said, "I'll drop you a postcard from Fiji." He grabbed his Line 7 sailing bag with all his worldly belongings and raced down the stairs. Peter threw his bag into the back of the cab and jumped into the front seat. He smiled to himself as he said to the driver, "The Cruising Yacht Club of Australia, young man, and don't spare the horses."

———

Peter weaved his way through the crowds of people on the marina. He passed boats' crews pushing wheelbarrows full of provisions and sails toward their yachts as they made their last-minute preparations for the 1,763-nautical-mile yacht race to Fiji. Hoses stretched from the docks to the boats as some of the crews topped up the water tanks, while others were up the masts making final adjustments to the rigging and gear. The halyards played a now-familiar tune against the masts in the fresh northeaster amid the shouts and calls of the crews. Reporters, racing officials, and well-wishers added to the activity.

Ron of Argyll lay bow-to the marina, the elegant, six-foot wooden bowsprit marking its position. When Peter reached the yacht, he dropped his bag, leaned over, and took the bow line in both hands, squinting at the reflection of the immaculate white hull in the water under the brilliant autumn sun. Slowly he eased the twenty-eight-ton yacht to within reach and picked up his seabag again in one hand. With the other, he grabbed the wire forestay that ran from the top of the mast to the end of the bowsprit, stepped up onto the bowsprit, and swung aboard.

He took a few steps past the open hatch and dropped his bag on the teak deck before stopping to take in the activity on the classic yacht. Aside from the cases of KB beer stacked at his feet, the preparations seemed to be almost complete. Only yesterday morning, the decks had been overflowing with provisions and gear that had since been inventoried and stowed safely away. Now the mahogany cap rails that trimmed the deck, as well as the mahogany hatches, skylights, and coach house, could be clearly seen, together with the two Douglas-fir timber masts and booms that supported the main and mizzen sails. He recalled the hours and hours that he and others had spent sanding the wood and applying coat after coat of varnish to bring all of the brightwork to its final deep luster. He gazed upward to the maze of rigging that not long ago had seemed totally confusing and recognized that everything was in order.

A number of well-wishers were alongside the yacht as well as onboard saying their good-byes to the crews. Peter had just started toward them when from behind him he heard, "G'day, Pete, how are ya?" and turned to see Andrew Clubb, the owner and skipper of the yacht, lifting himself up through the hatch and getting to his feet. Andrew was fair-haired, in his midthirties, and stood just over six feet tall. He had a wicked sense of humor, a love of traditional wooden boats, and a taste for fine women and the odd drink.

"I'm as fit as a Brahma bull!" Peter replied.

"Stay that way until we get to Suva!" said Andrew with a grin. "Now, Pete, the sponsor dropped off these eight cases of beer for us teetotalers! Can you grab Don to give you a hand? Stow what you can in the bilges and put the rest of them under the starboard bunk in the aft cabin. Then come back up on deck and give me a hand to get anyone who's not part of the crew off the boat so we can prepare to cast off."

Two hours later, the *Ron* passed between the rock promontories of Sydney Heads under full sail. The yacht was a spectacular sight among the twenty-five other racers and the flotilla of spectator craft. She plunged through the swells with the bowsprit pointing the way, the water streaming past the bronze portholes that dotted her sides. The gleaming mahogany brightwork contrasted against the sun-bleached teak decks and the heavy timber masts that held aloft the cloud of sails, the vessel seemingly suspended in the cobalt blue of the Pacific Ocean. She headed into the stiff northeaster, the eight-man crew working together to set and trim the sails. Five miles out of the heads, the *Ron* headed up to tack.

"Ready about!" Andrew called out.

All the crew leaped to their positions on the sloping deck. On the leeward side, one of the crew took two turns of the jib sheet off the stout wooden cleat, ready to release it at the skipper's command. Two of the crew took up the slack in the lazy sheet and prepared to haul it in as the sail came across. The call came back from each of the crew, "Ready!"

"Helm's a-lee!" returned the skipper as he turned the boat to bring the bow through the eye of the wind. The crisp curve of the sails slackened as the pressure of the wind came off them, and then the sails luffed for a moment, the lighter headsails crackling with the rapid movement, followed by the din of the heavier main as it snapped in powerful undulations. The sheets lashed the deck and rattled the wooden blocks that guided them to the cleats. The bow struck a wave and a spray erupted, showering the foredeck crew, followed by a sluice of blue water along the decks. The staysail tackle rattled on the iron horse that secured it. As the wind began to backwind the jib, the skipper bellowed, "Let it go!"

The crew called out as they worked, coordinating their actions. The jib sheet was whipped off the cleat, and the slack was taken up on its counterpart on the other side and secured. The two crew amidships worked in unison to manage the running backstays, the heavy wire rigging that helped to support the mast. They released the leeward side backstay as the pressure came off, and then quickly secured the windward backstay before it was loaded by the filling of the mainsail. The deck came level for an instant as the bow passed the eye of the wind, and then the yacht heeled over to port as the wind filled the sails.

The yacht gained speed on its new course, and the skipper brought her close to the wind. "I'll luff her up so you can get that sheet in a little more!" he called.

The crew heaved in on the jib sheet, taking up the slack on the wooden cleat before Andrew bore away to fill the sails again to maintain her speed. They repeated this once more to bring the sail to its final trim. As the

Ron of Argyll leaving Sydney Harbour

crew tidied up the lines, Peter glanced up to see Australia begin to slip out of sight over the horizon and felt the excitement and anticipation of the voyage ahead.

The crew was assigned to two watches of four people each, working four hours on and four hours off. They were experienced and fit, but the next six days tested the endurance and character of every person aboard. The yacht was close-hauled to make their northing, and the weather steadily deteriorated, with a strong easterly gale producing a rough and confused sea. With a growing swell and waves washing over the deck, the motion of the boat made it very uncomfortable, increasing the challenge of sailing the *Ron*. To compound the challenge, the ship's batteries failed on the third day, making radio communication with the racing fleet impossible and causing the crew to have to pump the bilge by hand. To add to the discomfort, a constant rain chilled the crew and dampened the inside of the boat. Despite the conditions, the ship's cook, Chantal, a feisty French blonde woman, continued to prepare the tucker for the crew in spite of the need to make occasional trips up the companionway to throw up into a bucket to alleviate her seasickness.

These conditions persisted for six days as the *Ron* was lashed by the tail end of a cyclone. As they were to find out, half of the fleet abandoned the race and put in to New Caledonia due to gear failure or chronic seasickness. The *Ron's* crew labored on, with the stalwart skipper maintaining order on the ship, including leading "happy hour" between five and six o'clock in the afternoon, which consisted of two standard drinks per crewman. He designated himself as barman to ensure that each person received his or her ration or, in his case, a very healthy ration. The storm finally abated to a fairly regular ten to fifteen knots of wind as the lumpy seas died away. When they approached New Caledonia, Andrew extended his generosity to a passing Italian yacht that agreed to pass on their location to the race committee in Sydney to allay their concerns and those of family and friends back home as the *Ron* continued on its way. As the Italian passed

Ron of Argyll beating to windward

alongside, Andrew lobbed a bottle of Chivas Regal scotch whiskey across the fifteen-foot gap that separated them and landed it squarely in the hands of the smiling helmsman.

The fair winds were not to last. For the third day in a row, the *Ron* sat motionless on the calm ocean ten miles north of the Loyalty Islands, the calm having descended as quickly as the previous storm had arrived. The hatches were now all open to ventilate and dry out the boat, and the sails hung limply from the spars. Bags of sails had been brought up on deck to dry them as well, and billows of sail lined the lifelines. The crew relaxed on deck, waiting for the elusive southeast trade winds to materialize.

Peter's mind drifted to Sydney and the hustle and bustle that he and the others had left behind. Everyone was always rushing around to get here and there, meeting deadlines and never taking enough time to spend with friends and family. These schedules all seemed very artificial now. Even though the crew all had a rigid watch routine, he realized how much better he felt after only eight days at sea. Despite the disruptions in sleep for sail and course changes, he was fitter and healthier than he could remember for many years. The clear air and warmth of the open tropical ocean lifted his spirits after the cool, damp start to the trip.

He was perched on a sail bag on the foredeck, luxuriating in the heat of the sun and holding a spool of heavy fishing line that led over the side to a yellow plastic lure. As he slowly wound the line in to produce the action on the lure, he felt a fish strike. He jumped to his feet and frantically retrieved the line to try to cheat the circling sharks of a free meal. The heavy line removed any sportsmanship, and he was soon able to overcome the weight of the three-foot-long mahi-mahi and pull it toward the boat. With his catch only yards away, a thrash in the water, a violent jerk, and sudden slackening of the line ended the game. Sharks: three, humans: two.

Peter pulled up the rest of the line, finding only part of the head remaining. "Bastards!" he exclaimed. Giving up for the day, he slipped the hook from the remains and tossed it into the water. "I hope you choke on it, you greedy bastards!" Peter turned to his previous catch—two nice tuna—and took them to the heavy wooden cutting board he had brought on deck to gut, scale, and fillet the evening meal.

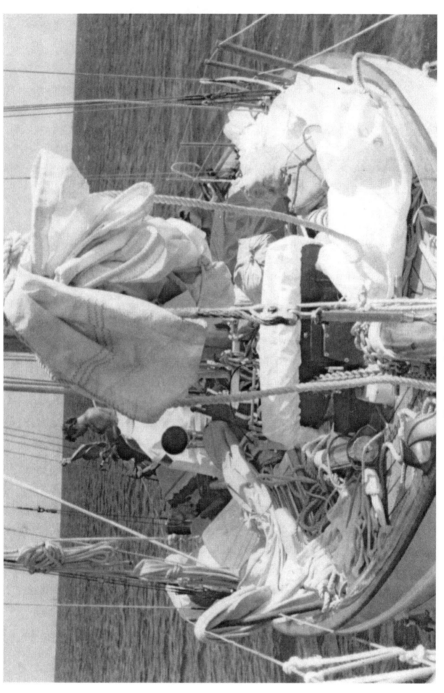

Drying sails after a storm

Peter's catch

The main saloon of *Ron of Argyll*

"Do you want to give me a hand, Peter?" the cook called up through the forward hatch.

"Yeah, in a minute. I'm just finishing up the fish. This is great. Probably the sweetest fish in the Pacific! There's enough here to go along with the bread you baked to feed the five thousand!" He finished up and passed the bucket full of fillets down through the hatch to her and then tossed the guts begrudgingly into the ocean.

Standing at the lifeline, Peter took the deck bucket by the handle and turned it upside down. Making sure the rope lanyard was tied securely to the stanchion, he dropped the bucket straight down and then quickly pulled on the lanyard, flipping it back upright and retrieving a full bucket of water. He sluiced down the deck to get rid of the fish scales and then tossed a bucketful over his head to cool off. This was the only shower on the boat as, apart from drinking water, the crew was restricted to one cup of water a day per person for personal use, such as brushing their teeth and washing.

Peter walked back to the cockpit and climbed down the companionway. The steps were about eighteen inches wide and raked at a steep angle so that the crew had to face the steps when climbing up or down and hold onto the railings that ran down either side. He descended the four steps to a little landing, down the next four steps, which took him to the cabin sole, and turned forward to go to the galley. On the starboard side was the chart table and communications equipment, which comprised a VHF radio and an ICOM720A single-sideband radio that Andrew had modified, as many people did, by cutting the blue wire at the back to make it into a fully functioning ham radio. There was also a Walker Sat Nav that they could use when the weather was too cloudy to take a sight with the marine sextant. The Sat Nav, or satellite navigation, was emerging and expensive technology that was not very reliable. It could take half an hour for the device to capture enough of the six available satellites to get a fix and do its complex computations (unlike the modern GPS, which uses eighteen of twenty-four available satellites) only to lose contact with one of the satellites, resulting in the dreaded and frustrating "no fix" result. It could take hours for it to recapture enough satellites to start again, depending on whether the ones you needed were available. The real danger with the Sat Nav in the South Pacific, though, was the outdated charts of some of the remote areas. A yachtsman could get a very accurate fix of his position and then plot it on a British Admiralty chart surveyed by the HMS *Beagle* in 1840, which might be a mile or two out of place.

To the port was the skipper's cabin, which closed with a sliding door. It contained a single bunk, with a washbasin that supplied water with a foot pump and drained into the bilge. He passed through the main saloon, a seating area that was paneled in a beautiful French-polished mahogany with brass hardware, looking like a piece of fine furniture. A similarly-finished gimbaled mahogany table in the middle was flanked to port and starboard by upholstered settees that doubled as bunks, with bookcases behind. Above the settees, two brass ports on either side of the hull helped to illuminate the saloon, while overhead the light streamed in through an ornate skylight. The sun-bleached jaws of a tiger shark, complete with a full complement of teeth, adorned the mahogany bulkhead, a reminder of the sometimes hostile environment in which they traveled.

Peter stepped from the main saloon into the galley, where the cook was preparing the fish on the top of the gimbaled stove. "How you planning to do them?" he asked.

"I thought I'd sauté them in olive oil with lots of garlic and black pepper," she suggested. "If you get one of the guys on deck to peel some potatoes, I'll cook them to go along with it."

"Sounds great!" replied Peter. "And I'll get Clubby to get a couple of bottles of his best wine from the top shelf. We may as well make the best of this weather!"

————

The warm southeast trade winds arrived the following day, and after five more days of glorious sailing, the *Ron* sailed slowly into the bay in front of the Royal Suva Yacht Club. Andrew cupped his hands to his mouth and hailed a passing dinghy. "How deep is the water here?"

"How much do you draw?" came the reply.

"Eight feet!" shouted Andrew.

"Then you are about to go aground!" returned the dinghy.

And with a gentle nudge, the *Ron* slowly oozed its way into the muddy bottom. After fifteen days at sea, they had arrived.

Andrew Clubb receiving award from the governor general of Fiji

Crew of *Ron of Argyll* (left to right) Don Graham, Terry Carrol, Peter, Chantal, and Andrew at the awards ceremony for the 1982 Sydney-to-Suva race

Chapter 10

―――◆◆✦◆◆―――

One for the Road

The *Ron* sat stern-to the boardwalk of the Tradewinds Hotel, its gangplank secured to its aft deck and leading conveniently to the hotel pool and bar. Just a few steps away, Peter sat sipping a Fiji Bitter beer at a table with Don, the only other crewman who had not had to return to work over the last three weeks, and with several other yachties of varying nationalities. One of these was Ted, a fair, redheaded sailor from New York. Ted had been sailing around the tropics for a while—at least long enough to contract dengue fever, a common tropical disease transmitted by mosquitoes that results in very severe flulike symptoms. Locally it was called "broken bone disease" due to the aching in the joints that it causes. The combination of the sickness and the oppressive humidity of the tropics resulted in him sweating profusely. To counteract this effect, he carried a hanky the size of a small bath towel that he used nonstop to wipe his brow. Since common flu medications could cause internal bleeding as a consequence of this illness, he self-medicated daily with generous quantities of rum. The medical result was questionable, but his humor was much improved.

In the heat of the afternoon, nothing much stirred in the bay, so the sound of an outboard drew everyone's attention. Peter put his beer down

Peter Jinks (right) and visitors aboard *Ron of Argyll* in Suva, Fiji

Ron of Argyll (center) tied stern-to at the Tradewinds Hotel in Suva, Fiji

and remarked, "That's the second Fijian sheila that I've seen that bloke take out to his boat in the last hour."

"That's the Dutch bloke, a single-hander who's obviously got tired of his own company," said Don. "Apparently he advertised for a wife in the *Fiji Times* and he's been as busy as a bee conducting 'interviews' ever since."

"Clever bastard! How come we didn't think of that?" said Peter.

There was a general murmur of agreement and laughter around the table. A short time later, they again heard the sound of an outboard motor starting out in the bay.

"That was quick!" chuckled Don.

They all turned in the direction of the sound. A few seconds later as the dinghy came into view, Ted said, "That's not the Dutchman; that's 'Hollywood' Bob."

Peter turned to Ted and asked, "Who's he, some sort of actor or something?"

"No," replied Ted, dabbing his brow, "although he certainly looks like one. He'd fit right into a spaghetti western."

"Then why's he called 'Hollywood'?" asked Peter.

"Because he looks after a sailboat for a Hollywood actor named Hal Holbrook. Bob's a Kiwi—a real character. I met him the other night over a few beers, and he told me about how he used to build and race dragsters back in New Zealand in the '60s. The bartender told me that one of his cars is in a museum in Wellington." A short distance away, Bob was bending down to tie up the dinghy. Ted called to him, "Hey, Bob!"

The solid, six-foot-three-inch New Zealander stood up, turned, and ambled the dozen or so steps along the boardwalk to stand opposite their table.

"Howdy, Bob. What're ya doin'?" said Ted.

Bob unwrapped an object from an oily, sodden rag and held it out for them to see. "I've been fucking around with this bilge pump all day. I've stripped it down twice and rebuilt it, and it still doesn't bloody work. I think the motor's rooted. All these jokers in Suva have got in stock is that cheap Taiwanese shit."

"Then you'd better sit down and have a beer with us! Sounds like you could use it," said Ted.

"I was going to go down the road to that new chandlery to see what they've got, but I suppose I've got time for a quick one."

A couple of hours and numerous pitchers of beer later, they were all still sitting in the bar. It was then that Andrew appeared on the deck of the *Ron* with a bottle of Gordon's gin, a bottle of tonic, and a small bucket of ice.

Peter turned to Bob and said, "It must be five o'clock. Happy hour! You were asking me all about the yacht. Why don't you come on board and have a drink and meet the owner. He knows more about it than I do."

Without the need for any further encouragement, Bob said, "Yeah, let's go," and the two of them crossed the pool deck and went up the gangplank to the cockpit of the *Ron*. Andrew, who had been an officer in the Australian merchant marine, was only too happy to show him around, and Bob soon realized the affection that Andrew had for the lovely old yacht. The two men of the sea chatted for hours, so it was long after midnight when the outboard motor of Bob's dinghy could be heard making its way back across the bay.

The Royal Suva Yacht Club represented the decaying of the colonial presence in the South Pacific. Dark and dank, the structure still bore the royal charter, while the acolytes clung to the image of the proper British culture. A pair of dartboards was located strategically by the bar, where two large, curly-haired Fijian men, dressed in uniforms of starched white shirts and knee-length black *sulus* tied around their waists, dispensed the gin and tonic, martinis, and pints of beer. Even the atmosphere inside suffered from this deterioration. In the oppressive humidity, the ceiling fans managed only to move the hot air from one place to another, ensuring a uniform discomfort. In spite of this fading glory, the club remained a center of activity for both the local and visiting yachties alike.

In the midst of the southern tropical winter, the assembled crews were following the daily schedule of midday refreshments at the bar.

The international crowd comprised Americans and other nationalities in about equal numbers. It was one of these Americans who mentioned in the course of conversation that it was the Fourth of July. "I thought I'd go into town to find some fireworks and have a celebration," he declared.

"Why would you do that?" Peter asked, baiting him.

"Why? Well, it's Independence Day!" he retorted.

"And from whom would that independence be, sir?" asked the Fijian barman in perfect Oxford English.

"From the British!" he declared without thinking, but then caught himself. "That was a long time ago, of course," he added in a less-enthusiastic tone.

"What kind of celebration did you have in mind?" asked Bob from down the bar.

"You know, fireworks, that kind of thing."

A few minutes went by while the men considered the possibilities.

"We could give you a hand," suggested Peter. "Make it into a party."

"I've got some noisemakers left over from New Year's Eve," offered Olaf from the Norwegian yacht.

"And I've got some shotgun shells to make a little more noise," suggested Ted.

"I don't know whether you Americans really know how to have a genuine celebration," chided Bob. "Maybe a few Kiwis and Aussies could give you a lesson!"

"And just how would you do that?" challenged the American.

"I've got a shitpot full of expired flares aboard that would give you a pretty impressive show!"

There was a general agreement among the crowd for this idea, and others offered their expired flares to benefit the celebration, the enthusiasm growing with each jug of Fiji Bitter. Eventually everyone at the international gathering had convinced themselves that they would help to create a celebration that would rival anything in America. This odd frenzy mystified the Americans. Nevertheless, plans were made, and a few hours later the crowd dispersed to prepare for the extravaganza.

Just after dusk, an armada of dinghies motored unsteadily out to the entrance of the bay, a couple of hundred yards away from the hotel, the crews clamoring to be heard above the noise of the outboards. The disorganized mob bumped into one another quite often in the gathering dark, untroubled by these encounters. In deference to the Americans, the fleet allowed the original perpetrator to stand unsteadily in his dinghy to make a slurred tribute to his country and countrymen. Before he had finished, the first multistar flare shot a hundred feet into the darkened sky. In the disorganized symphony that followed, the assembled crews displayed their handheld flares from their dinghies, while others jettisoned their smoke flares to float on the surface of the bay. For a finale, the rocket flares erupted a thousand feet into the air, the parachutes slowly descending to earth. Amid all of this racket was heard the roar of Ted's shotgun as he let go both barrels at the same time, followed by the spatter of the shot as it rained down into the bay.

Bob called over the din to Peter in the adjacent dinghy, "I hope Ted keeps that thing aimed up in the air!"

"I didn't think he was sober enough to manage it!" Peter called back with a laugh.

The noise and accumulating smoke gave the effect of the Battle of Trafalgar, and the collisions became more enthusiastic and intentional. Before long, the battle had begun, with a demolition derby of dinghies roaring around the bay. High over the skirmish, a parachute flare coasted slowly toward shore, finally alighting on the roof of the hotel. For a moment, the battle ceased while the combatants waited anxiously to see whether the roof would burst into flames. Thankfully, it didn't, and the battle resumed with renewed vigor. Secret weapons were unveiled, such as buckets of saltwater and streams of water shot from bilge pumps onto the rival crews. In the end, the flares ran out, and the armada, tired from the pitched battle, came to an official truce and retired to the bar to recover and revel in their exploits. The two sides had somehow managed to fire in excess of two hundred flares and numerous rounds of shotgun fire without a single casualty.

It was less than an hour after the last dinghy made it to the safety of the shore that what appeared to be an official Fijian vessel idled into the bay. For some unexplained reason, it pulled up to *Ron of Argyll,* where Peter lay in the netting of the bowsprit. One of the officials called over, "We've had reports of a lot of red distress flares in the area. Do you know anything about it?"

"Not me, mate," Peter replied. "And I've been here all night."

The vessel moved on, querying the other oddly quiet yachties, but receiving the same answer. Finally it motored off, leaving the bay in silence, unaware of the parachute flare that hung from the roof of the hotel, its spent cartridge swinging gently in the breeze.

Chapter 11

———◆◈◆———

Chiefly Traditions

In preparation for the next leg of their journey, the crew of the *Ron* provisioned the yacht with the necessary food and water. Once that was completed, Andrew took charge of the more important task of topping up the stores of beer, wine, and spirits. He and Peter took a taxi to the nearby town and found a store with the capacity to suit their needs. They gazed admiringly around the well-stocked shelves. After a few moments of contemplation, Andrew asked the proprietor, "Do you deliver?" When he was assured that they did, Andrew set to work. It took his practiced eye only about fifteen minutes to complete the order.

After returning to the hotel, Peter joined the rest of the crew, who were settled comfortably around the pool with the few vacationers when they heard a commotion at the bar. Peter went in to investigate and found a slender young Indian lad with a porter's cart loaded with cases of beer stacked nearly as high as him. "What's the problem?" Peter asked the barman.

"We weren't expecting an order today, and there is a whole lorry full outside. This lad is looking for someone named Ron."

"No trouble, mate," Peter replied, and then to the delivery boy said, "This way with those." Peter led the way out the side door from the bar, threaded his way through the deck chairs surrounding the pool, and arrived at the foot of the boarding ramp. The tourists took in this activity but did not stir. The crew quickly removed the beer from the cart and dispatched the lad for another load. He retraced his steps and was soon back with the second load. The tourists did not show any interest, but after the third load, there was some whispering, and by the time the lad had labored with the fifth load, the activity had created genuine curiosity. By the time he had brought the last of the seven loads, the crowd was enthralled. A casual observer would have counted a total of about twenty cases of beer, four cases each of gin and tonic, three cases of rum, and three more cases of a variety of other liquids. A keener observer would have noticed that the *Ron* had dropped almost an inch at the waterline.

The *Ron* motored out from Suva Harbour early the following morning under a low, dark blanket of clouds. Andrew and the three crew—Peter, Don, and a new addition, Ross—were all on deck, seeking a cooling breeze in the tropical humidity. They motored along the channel and out past the skeletal wreck of the coastal freighter on the outer reef before hoisting the sails and setting a course to the northeast to clear the headland. Their objective was to reach Levuka, some fifty miles sailing to the north of Suva, and then go on to some of the nearer islands before heading southeast to the remote Lau Group and finally on to Tonga.

Andrew had been frustrated in his attempts to get permission to visit the Lau Group. Since the prime minister came from the island of Lakemba, which was in this group, they had to visit his office to fill out forms to get the proper authorization. After repeated visits and delays, they had learned from other yachties that permission was never granted, but the officials were just too polite to say so. Undaunted, they determined to carry on with their plans anyway.

Two weeks after leaving Suva, the *Ron* approached the island of Totoya in the Lau Group. It was late afternoon when they sighted the island, and happy hour was eagerly anticipated for an unusual reason: ten miles off the island, they would cross longitude 180 degrees, the international dateline. The crew had convinced themselves that as they gained a day, they were entitled to a double ration of their favorite beverage. There was a suitably rambunctious celebration of the crossing and a few words from the skipper before they returned to their task and prepared to make landfall.

With three days of sailing hard on the wind into bumpy seas behind them, they were relieved to pass between the foaming white breakers that flanked the break in the reef and slip into the relative calm of the lagoon. The sudden transition in the motion of the boat was remarkable. Instead of pitching and rolling about, the boat now stood up and sailed on an even keel, with very little motion, as they moved into the deep azure water of the quiet lagoon. It was about three miles across to the crescent-shaped island, the remnant of an ancient volcano.

Sailing toward the island, Peter thought it was like sailing back in time. As they approached the beach, several small fishing boats and dugout canoes full of islanders paddled out to meet them. Laughing and chattering as they came alongside, a number of them clambered aboard with gifts of coconuts, bananas, and other fresh fruit. The young children peppered them with questions in their limited English, all talking at once. Their enthusiastic greeting made it obvious that the crew was welcome. Peter turned to Andrew. "This is amazing! I wonder if this is how they treated Captain Cook."

"Maybe, but I reckon the women would have been more pleasing to the eye before the missionaries talked them into covering themselves up!"

One of the men, who spoke reasonable English, told them that they had not seen a yacht in almost a year and that the only contact they had with the rest of the world was a freighter that brought supplies every six months.

The anchorage was close to the beach, in a steeply sloping, sandy bottom. After the crew had squared away the boat, they went ashore to visit the chief of the village to ask his permission to stay in the lagoon. They were welcomed on the shore by a boisterous group of children and a few only slightly less-enthusiastic men and women. The villagers surrounded them, accompanied by several barking dogs and the odd supporting rooster that had gotten caught up in the fervor of the occasion. The happy throng led the ship's emissaries along a short coral path through the fringing coconut palms to the village.

There were about thirty homes scattered under the umbrella of several huge trees. Pigs foraged around the trunks, and cooking fires sent a mask of smoke among the tops. The entourage trouped toward the village, past a stream where women worked at washing clothes. Several of the young ladies chatted and giggled as they walked by, averting their eyes shyly. It was not long before the crew approached a home that stood out from the others, being slightly larger and more decorated.

This house was an oval, open-walled structure about twenty feet by fifteen feet, with a dome-shaped roof supported on a ring of evenly spaced wooden posts. Suspended between the posts were rolled blinds made of a woven mat, which were apparently pulled down to protect the house from wind or rain. The roof was clad in corrugated iron sheeting, although others nearby were thatched with the more traditional coconut palm fronds. The roof extended down past the top of the posts so that Andrew had to duck under as he entered. The chief stood, accompanied by several of the senior men of the village, and gestured his welcome, offering them a place to sit on the ornately woven pandanus-leaf mat that was laid out over the floor of broken coral. He was an elderly man by Fijian standards, probably in his fifties but looking nearer seventy. His hair had turned a weathered, silvery gray and was close-cropped. He had lively dark eyes and a steady gaze that revealed an inner wisdom. In stature, he was slightly shorter than the other villagers, but he stood straight and proud.

According to local custom, Andrew had taken along several gifts. When the chief was seated, Andrew offered him the gifts and asked through one of the men for the chief's permission for the *Ron* to stay in the lagoon for three days. The gifts were gratefully received and deserve description. In a place where fresh fish was so plentiful, the gift of tins of New Zealand mackerel in tomato sauce was a most sought-after delicacy. The three large tins that he received made the chief's eyes light up. To the *Ron's* crew, this was a marvel. The other gift was a two-foot-length of rope tobacco. This is a crude tobacco that is formed by twisting the leaves and weaving them

Children row out to meet the yacht at Totoya Island, Lau Group, Fiji

Andrew Clubb going to see the chief, bearing gifts

Ron of Argyll at anchor in Totoya Island lagoon

into a dense sausage the size of your thumb. It had the consistency and the taste of tarred rope. The chief's almost toothless grin indicated that this too was greatly appreciated. He bowed slightly from his seated position, and then turned and dispatched one of the men to the village.

The man soon returned, accompanied by two younger men, who carried between them a heavy carved wooden bowl almost three feet in diameter. They set the bowl down on the floor to one side of the chief. The bowl was filled with a muddy, gray liquid, which Andrew and Peter recognized as kava, the traditional ceremonial drink of the South Pacific. The drink is made from a root that is a relative of the pepper plant. Small pieces of the dried root that look like bits of gray driftwood are crushed and infused in water. The result is a liquid that looks and tastes like dirty dishwater. Kava has a mild narcotic effect that produces a slight numbing of the lips and throat and is an acquired taste, but some men get addicted to it and as they grow older, their voice goes hoarse and their lips harden.

One of the men scooped a small amount of the kava into half a coconut shell and passed it to the other helper. He offered it to the chief, who took the shell in both hands, put it to his lips, and drank it down in one continuous motion. He then took the rim of the coconut shell between his thumb and forefinger and spun it across the mat back to his helper. He gestured to Andrew. According to custom, Andrew clapped his hands once to accept, and the helper passed him the cup. He took it in both hands and followed the chief's actions. The process continued until all of the men had had a drink. At intervals, the chief delivered a short oration in Fijian to express his pleasure in having them as his guests and to offer the friendship of his village during their stay. Andrew responded by offering his thanks for their hospitality and their generosity. It then started all over again, the ceremony lasting for over two hours.

Once the kava ceremony had concluded, Andrew took his turn to introduce the Australian custom of offering a toast with Johnny Walker Black Label whiskey. Once additional coconut shells had been obtained, he poured everyone a shot. Following his custom, he wished the chief and his family good health. Everyone around the circle raised their coconut shells, clunked them together, and with a little coaching, said in unison,

"Cheers!" With that they all tossed back the whiskey. That toast being well received, Andrew offered a second toast for a successful harvest. The chief appeared to be pleased with this custom, but before the full combined effect of the kava and the whiskey was realized, Andrew offered their thanks and they were escorted back to the dinghy.

At daylight the next morning, Peter, feeling groggy from the night before, climbed up the companionway to the deck and walked to the port side for a leak. He was joined moments later by Andrew, and the two of them stood quietly for a few moments, the *Ron* sitting motionless beneath their feet.

"Quite a night, wasn't it?" mumbled Peter.

"Yeah. I still can't feel my tongue properly," replied Andrew. After another moment, Andrew raised his head and with a puzzled look exclaimed, "Hang on—where's the bloody village?" He swung his head back and forth across the horizon quizzically.

"What the hell's going on here?" said Peter, unable to get a familiar bearing. He felt a moment of bewilderment until he looked over his shoulder and cried, "There's the bloody reef! Right behind us!"

Now fully awake, Andrew bolted down the companionway and started the motor. Peter leaped to the tiller, knowing instinctively what to do, and shoved the gear lever into forward and maxed the revs. It took only thirty seconds to get the twenty-eight tons moving, but it seemed like a lot longer before they were able to edge the *Ron* away from the reef and out of danger. Casting around them, they could see the island several miles in the distance. Peter went up to the foredeck and looked over the side to see the anchor hanging straight down, suspended in the deep water of the lagoon. Andrew motored the *Ron* back across the lagoon, and this time after they set the anchor, Peter dived down to double-check it to ensure that they would not have a repeat performance.

Chapter 12

———◈———

"And You Said It Was Only Superstition"

The crew of the *Ron* spent several enjoyable days on and around the island. As they began their preparations to depart, the chief sent word inviting them all to a farewell feast in their honor. At midday the crew eagerly went ashore in their best gear, taking with them more gifts and refreshments. The feast was being set up in the village on the seaward side. The sounds that welcomed them came from a mixture of the women chatting and laughing as they prepared the food and from the music of the ukulele.

Preparations were well under way. A pig was skewered on a spit and set over a low fire, with one of the men inspecting the progress and turning it from time to time. Every half hour or so, he directed a young girl to fetch seawater from the lagoon to baste it. The salt made the skin very crisp, and the water that spilled onto the fire sent up a cloud of smoke that helped to flavor it.

There were more delicacies as well. Lobster and fish were wrapped in taro leaves and nestled into the hot coals to cook for about an hour before the pig was done. While that was cooking, girls squeezed fresh limes and marinated chunks of fish in the juice with a little saltwater. Some of the young men grated coconut meat and wrung out the coconut cream, which was then added with a little more juice to make a succulent dish. Added to

Totoya Island women dancing at the farewell feast

that were taro and breadfruit roasted in the fire and a mountain of fresh fruits from the plantations, including mango, papaya, and banana.

The chief delivered a farewell speech, to which Andrew responded with thanks for the chief's hospitality. It was a jovial atmosphere, and everyone ate, drank, and danced until late in the evening. Only after an hour of good-byes was the crew able to roll themselves into the dinghy and make it back to the boat.

The *Ron* had made plans to leave Totoya lagoon by a narrow passage through the reef on the east side of the island. Taking this route would avoid having to go back to the entrance and sail around the outside of the fringing reef, thus shaving six miles off their trip east to the island of Oneata. While this seemed a practical saving, the village fishermen who came for daily visits to the yacht warned Andrew not to use the pass. They described the legend of an historic battle between the Fijians and the Tongans that had taken place near there. The ferocious battle had lasted for days and cost hundreds of lives. According to the legend, the Fijians had eventually repelled the Tongans, but as the Fijians had chased them through this passage, a final spear hurled from a fleeing Tongan canoe had struck and killed the Fijian chief. The fishermen believed that his spirit guarded the passage and that if anyone tried to go through it, the spirit would throw up a wall of water and destroy them.

Despite these dire warnings, the crew decided to take the shortcut anyway, but to take every precaution due to the narrowness of the passage. They chose their departure so that the sun would be overhead for the best visibility. For additional security, they would send Don to the second set of spreaders to keep watch, dispatch Peter to the bowsprit to keep a lookout, and place Ross on the top of the doghouse with a pair of binoculars. With these preparations in place, the *Ron* departed the village with confidence.

The sun beat down harshly as they motored across the glassy lagoon toward the passage.

"Shit, it's hot!" Peter said and pulled the bucket from the lazarette. He scooped up a bucketful of seawater and dumped it over his head to cool off.

"I'll take one of those as well!" Andrew called to him. Peter retrieved a bucketful for him, and after a quick dousing, Andrew laid out the plan. "We'll run past the entrance first to take a look at it and get our bearings. Don, you give us an idea of what we're in for when we find the entrance and shout out if you see any coral heads. Tell me how far you think it is to the outside of the reef. Pete, you give us a read on the width of it, and once we're inside the passage, watch for any dead Fijian chiefs!"

Following that plan, they skirted the opening. Don called out, "About eighty to a hundred feet to the outside, Andrew, and only a few small coral heads. It's about twenty feet deep, I reckon."

"And about thirty-five or forty feet wide," Peter added. "No visible warriors!"

"There's no room to turn the old girl," called Andrew, "so once we're in, we're in for keeps! I'll run by to double-check, and then we'll go for it!" He turned the *Ron* back and ran past the opening. The water was dead calm in the passage. He brought her around and headed in, keeping to the middle of the channel.

They entered the passage cautiously, maintaining enough speed to keep steerage way, but slow enough to react to any surprises. Peter peered down into the crystal clear water, the colors of the coral vivid in the direct sun. There were no surprises as they passed the midway point. It was a mesmerizing sight, so he was brought abruptly back to reality by the sound of Andrew's warning.

"Hang on!" he bellowed, and Peter looked up in time to see the wave rear up ahead of them. It closed on them in seconds and the bow rose high to ride over it, but the wave was so forceful that it took almost all the way off the boat. Andrew cranked up the motor to full throttle to compensate as they came over the crest, and the bow of the *Ron* dug down deep into the trough. Don, Peter, and Ross clung to the rigging for their lives on their precarious perches.

Andrew Clubb enjoying a deck shower

Without warning, a second wave appeared, bigger than the first, creating a trough that seemed to suck the water out of the narrow channel and left only a few feet of clearance beneath the keel. The motor raced as the vessel crested the wave and the stern was lifted clear of the water. Again the *Ron* dove down, this time burying the bowsprit and pouring water along the decks as it rose up again. They were almost out of the passage and into the deep water when, unbelievably, a third and even bigger wave hit with a force so strong that it lifted the yacht above the level of the surrounding reef, again almost stopping its forward progress altogether. The wave was near breaking and it seemed for an instant that the yacht would be flung on its side onto the reef, but the momentum of its twenty-eight tons just managed to overcome the force of the wave and it surfed down the face the last few desperate feet to clear the passage. The *Ron* rocked from side to side a little before slowing and chugging away into the regular seas. The crew looked at one another in disbelief.

"How close was that?" breathed Andrew, a look of astonishment on his face. "We were within an ace of being another wreck on the reef!" He looked over his shoulder for the passage, but it was now indistinguishable in the foaming surf on the reef. "I think we'd better have a toast to celebrate our good fortune."

Chapter 13

"Wood, Yes, But Will She Float?"

Oneata Island is a remote atoll in the eastern Lau Group. The sea breaks heavily on the eastern end of the fringing reef, and the resulting waves in the small lagoon can make the anchorage very uncomfortable. The *Ron* spent three days at anchor in these conditions. The swell caught the yacht on the beam, causing it to roll severely from one side to the other like a huge pendulum. This constant motion made cooking difficult and any form of enjoyment on board impossible. Sleeping was made doubly difficult because of the grinding noise caused by the twisting of the anchor chain that emanated throughout the yacht.

After paying their respects to the kindly village chief and getting his permission to anchor, the crew had taken every opportunity to go ashore and to spearfish in the abundant lagoon. These islanders welcomed the crew since, like the inhabitants of Totoya, they had not seen a yacht in over a year and enjoyed their company. The village even invited them to participate in a Fijian cricket match. As an additional courtesy to the visitors, the chief hosted them every afternoon in the ceremonial *bure* for the kava ceremony.

The island was completely self-sufficient, with an abundance of coconuts, bananas, taro, and limes, as well as scattered pigs, goats, and chickens, plus

Peter and friendly villagers of Oneata Island, Lau Group, Fiji

the bounty of the sea. It was easy to see how the ancient explorers had been so taken by the purity of this existence. But as much as the crew was enjoying their stay there, the life aboard the rocking yacht became unbearable. The only alternatives appeared to be either to move ashore and take a Fijian wife, raise a dozen children, and never leave this idyllic island, or to pick up the anchor and carry on the 240 miles to the Vava'u Group of islands in the Kingdom of Tonga. Peter considered an offer from the chief to stay, enticed by the lush and fertile island and the hospitable people, but after realizing that he could be there for as long as six months before the next supply ship arrived, he thought better of it. Reluctantly, he chose the latter option. After heartfelt farewells and exchange of gifts, Peter and the rest of the crew picked their way back through the break in the reef marked by a weathered wooden post and into the open ocean.

The normal route taken by sailing ships in the tropics was to follow the prevailing winds and travel from east to west. The route chosen by the crew of the *Ron* ran counter to the prevailing conditions, and this course put the boat hard on the wind into short, steep waves, causing the bow of the yacht to punch into the oncoming seas with a great jolt and the waves to cascade over the deck. To make matters worse, the seas and wind increased, and soon the water began to rise in the bilge to beyond its normal level, requiring the bilge pump to work overtime.

On the afternoon of the second day, Peter had just taken over from Andrew at the helm. Andrew climbed down the companionway, and seconds later Peter heard him cry out. "Shiiit! We've got a problem!" he called up to Peter.

"What's happened?" Peter called back in alarm.

"Nothing much, except that we're sinking!" said Andrew, managing to retain his deadpan humor even in the face of this crisis.

"What?"

"Yeah. The water's up over the cabin sole. Looks like the automatic bilge pump's shot."

Peter tied off the tiller and rushed over. Looking down the companionway, he could see the water sloshing back and forth with the motion of the boat, with two hatches that covered the bilges floating in the main saloon. He watched as Andrew stepped down into the water and with an air of resoluteness splashed his way forward.

"Don! Ross! Get out here! Quick!" called Andrew. He pushed one of the hatches to one side and dropped to his knees, peering into the bilge to look for the source of the leak.

"What you doing down there, Clubby? Trying to catch a fish?" asked Don dryly as he splashed up behind him and peered over Andrew's shoulder.

"Nothing but tins of mackerel here, mate. Now get on that manual pump in the head and let's try to get some of this water out of the boat."

"What do you want me to do, Clubby?" asked Ross, who had appeared from the aft cabin.

"Go up on deck and get one of those plastic buckets out of the aft lazarette. We're going to have to bail the old girl," he said sympathetically.

Peter returned to the tiller while the rest of the crew quickly set up a bucket brigade. There was no time to waste or worry. Peter had been in life-threatening situations before, like the time he was lost with two Swiss alpinists in a blizzard near the 19,348-foot summit of volcanic Cotapaxi in Ecuador in 1976. He knew that the priority was to focus totally on the job at hand—survival. The adrenalin would take care of that. There would be time later to reflect.

With one person bailing the water out of the bilge and passing it up the companionway, a second person at the top of the companionway picked it up and poured the water onto the deck, where it flowed out through the scuppers, before returning the empty bucket back down for another load. This process continued for an hour before rotating the crew. All this time, one person continued to work the manual pump in the head, and the fourth stayed at the helm.

Two hours later, Peter finished his turn at bailing and set the bucket down. He turned and called to Andrew, "I don't know about you, Clubby, but I'm as dry as a dingo's donger!"

"Yeah, me too," replied Andrew. "Go up to the galley and get a big jug of water and throw some of that powdered orange in it."

When Peter returned, he said, "The bloody stove is rooted!"

"What d'ya mean?" asked Andrew with surprise.

"We've taken so much water over the deck—the water's come in and saturated the bloody stove. It must have come in through the porthole overhead."

The crew stopped for a break in the cockpit and took the mugs of water appreciatively. Andrew took a gulp of the drink and immediately convulsed, spewing the mouthful of liquid across the deck. "That's saltwater!" he cried, grimacing.

"Bullshit!" said Peter. "It came straight out of the freshwater tank!"

The others took tentative sips and spat it out.

"Clubby's right," declared Don, pouring the rest over the side.

"We'd better take a look at the water tanks," said Andrew.

They inspected the two tanks located in the bilge under the main saloon and found to their alarm that the hose joining them together had separated, allowing the bilge water to contaminate the freshwater.

"Well, that's the icing on the cake!" said Peter. "You know what this means, fellas. We're gonna have to survive on beer and the water from the canned fruit and vegetables until we get to Tonga!"

"What's wrong with that?" asked Andrew with a smile.

This exhausting work continued for the next twenty-four hours, with breaks only for navigation and adjusting sail. Their efforts kept them just ahead of the incoming water, and when Flat Top Mountain eventually came into view, they were relieved to know that their predicament was nearly over. It took another six hours to reach the shelter of the islands, and as the wind and seas diminished, the flow of water was mysteriously reduced to a trickle. They motored into Neiafu Harbour, restowing the remaining cans of mackerel and beer in the bilges as they went, and finally came to anchor in the shadow of the Paradise International Hotel.

Chapter 14

A Little Bit of Paradise

The Paradise International Hotel, Vava'u Islands, Kingdom of Tonga

Peter climbed down into the Avon dinghy and rowed toward the dock about fifty feet away. Looking back, he saw the *Ron* peacefully at anchor in the perfectly still water of the bay. He had been alone on the boat for several weeks now, doing maintenance and taking care of the boat until new crew arrived. Before he left, Andrew had determined that the water was coming in between the planks when the boat was pounding into rough seas or sailing upwind, but stayed fairly watertight when sailing off the wind or sitting at anchor. The crew had recaulked the bow above the waterline as best they could and taken her out for sea trials to confirm that they had stabilized the situation. They knew that they hadn't fixed the problem but thought that they could manage it by not working her too hard before they got her to Pago Pago in American Samoa, about three days' sailing away, where there were facilities to slip the boat and make proper repairs.

Now Peter had time to go exploring and diving, including making about twenty dives on the three-hundred-foot wreck of the *Clan McWilliam* at the southern end of the harbor. The combination of the warm, clear waters, ideal climate, wonderful people, lush tropical forests, and the abundance of coconut groves and fresh fruit and vegetables convinced him that he was in paradise.

He pulled alongside the old barge that had been filled with debris, sunk, and now served as a wharf. He tied up the dinghy, checked his pocket for his shopping list, and then climbed the 130 irregular stone steps that scaled the steep bank to emerge at the Paradise International Hotel. Peter paused to catch his breath, considering for a moment the long walk in to town, and decided that some refreshment would be in order to prepare himself for the day's events. He made his way along the zigzag path between the individual hotel *fales* that served as guesthouses, up the slope past the main entrance, and around the pool to the bar, the center of social activity amid this collection of rustic Tongan buildings.

Carter Johnson, the owner of the hotel, was at the bar when Peter arrived. He was a solid, compact man of about fifty. Dressed in his green work shirt, denim bib coveralls, and welding hat, he had the look of a construction worker but displayed the demeanor of a foreman. "Give me a double brandy!" he ordered the barman in his Kentucky drawl.

"How're you going, Carter?" Peter called as he approached the bar.

Carter nodded a welcome. "Wanna drink?"

"I'll have a beer, thanks," he nodded to the barman. He turned back to Carter. "What are you up to today?"

"Well, I reckon I'll start work on the next *fale*. I just got a new load of iron, so I'll have plenty to keep me busy." He smiled at the prospect. Carter Johnson had made his fortune in Australia building oil pipelines. He had recently bought the Paradise as a retirement project and kept his hand in at his original trade—welding—by changing the traditional construction of the entire complex to a steel, hurricane-proof design. Given the size of the project, it would likely take all of his retirement and more.

"What you doin'?" Carter inquired.

"I'm off to the market and the post office. Then I've got some varnishing to finish up."

Nodding again, Carter finished up his drink and pulled down the brim of his hat. "Well, see ya later, Pete," he said and walked off.

Ron of Argyll at anchor in Neiafu Harbour, Vava'u Islands, Kingdom of Tonga

Carter Johnson at work

Peter took his drink and wandered to a table in the shade beside the pool. The vista down the harbor was spectacular. From this elevation, he could look through the palms one way past the village and main wharf toward the harbor entrance two miles distant, and the other way a mile to the end of the harbor. A light wind had now sprung up and moved across the water toward him, finally disturbing the palm fronds on the trees of the hotel grounds and cooling the early morning sun.

Behind him, he was aware of the hotel staff preparing the bar and restaurant for the few customers that actually came to stay at the hotel. From the kitchen, Peter thought he heard a familiar grunting. Taking a sip of his drink, he wandered back to the bar and said to the barman, "I could have sworn I heard Gunter's voice."

"He come back las' night. Mr. Johnson, he go and get 'im in 'is plane."

At that moment, Gunter walked out of the kitchen. He was a big man, fiftyish, with a drinker's face and a chef's waistline. Draping his front was a chef's apron that covered a T-shirt and extended past his shorts, so that he appeared at first glance to be wearing nothing underneath. He wore rubber flip-flops that scuffed along the floor as he walked across to one of the tables. He bellowed to the waiter in his German accent, "Dis is no goot! Vee are having lunch, not dinna. Take dis avay und do it r-r-right!" He emphasized this last command with a sweep of his hand and turned back to the bar. The three Tongan staff looked at one another, perplexed, trying to determine what was wrong, and better yet, what was right. Giving up, they shrugged indifferently and trudged off in three separate directions.

Gunter had arrived in paradise from South America two years before. He was one of many German expatriates who had responded enthusiastically to the Tongan government's offer of a Tongan passport in return for certain gratuities. Carter had been happy to inherit such a good chef and didn't probe too deeply into his past. It came as a nasty surprise to them both, therefore, when the Tongan police arrived at the hotel one day with a warrant for his arrest. Gunter was whisked away by a waiting plane to prison in the capitol of Nuku'alofa for crimes unknown.

115

This incarceration was not altogether unpleasant. Each day one of Gunter's friends, a fellow German chef who worked at the Dateline International Hotel, brought him gourmet meals, while the rest of the prison population survived on local fare. As the rumor mill worked overtime manufacturing amazing stories of Gunter's sordid past, Carter sought desperately to retrieve his top chef. Seeing no other recourse, he flew his plane the 150 miles south to Nuku'alofa to negotiate his release. After several days of Tongan "diplomacy," Carter returned—somewhat poorer—with Gunter, who was now confined to the hotel under house arrest. Gunter seemed to be back to his usual gruff, overbearing self.

Like everyone else, Peter was curious about Gunter's story, but he knew better than to ask. He had learned that some people preferred to keep their secrets to themselves, while others enjoyed the notoriety. One person who was not shy about his past was Ronnie Biggs, a member of the infamous gang that perpetrated the Great Train Robbery in England, whom Peter had met in Rio. The key was to let the supposed criminal decide for himself what to tell you.

Peter ambled over to Gunter and said, "You're back! How's it going?"

Gunter shrugged noncommittally. "I am here," he offered perfunctorily.

Seeing no future in this discussion, Peter finished his beer and set the empty bottle on the bar. "Well, I'm off to town. See you later."

Gunter made no reply.

Life was peaceful and slow in paradise. In fact, it was so slow that it sometimes gave the appearance of having come almost to a complete standstill. Visitors to Tonga, known to early explorers as the Friendly Isles, had to undergo a major adjustment to adapt to this pace. Those who couldn't adapt would become frustrated—a concept unknown to the Polynesians. This was an ancient, laid-back way of life, where time moved to the rhythm of the earth. Nothing could make them hurry. Peter found that he had adapted very easily to life in Vava'u, and he was glad that very few tourists had discovered these idyllic islands.

He walked the half-mile into town along the winding, dusty road of crushed coral that followed the contour of the shoreline. The ribbon of white contrasted on the right with the dark green undergrowth, which followed a gradual rise up to a height of about a hundred feet through the plentiful coconut groves interspersed with breadfruit, banana, and mango trees. On the left, out of view from the road, a steep cliff fell to a narrow, rough coral beach, which bordered the clear blue water of the bay, its white sand bottom mottled with coral heads. A few yachts were anchored off the shore.

Peter passed a number of houses along the route, and the children playing outside stopped to look, a *palagi* like himself still being quite a rare sight. Continuing down the gradual slope of the road that led into the town, he passed a small collection of clapboard shops and a short distance farther on came to the post office. Tongan stamps were renowned worldwide for their colorful, peel-off images of fruits like bananas, pineapples, and coconuts. Travelers would be sure to write cards and letters, expecting to thrill their family and friends back home with these unusual stamps. Unfortunately for them, the smiling little man behind the wire mesh screen of the post office was one of the earliest Polynesian innovators. After assessing the destination of the mail and collecting the travelers' money, he would assure them that he would put the stamps on for them. In reality, he introduced recycling to the islands. When the customer walked away from the wicket, with the skill of Houdini, the stamps went back into the drawer, the letter went into the garbage, and the money went into his pocket.

Knowing of this sleight of hand, Peter was careful to scrutinize the little man's every move. He gave two postcards to him and then insisted that they be returned to him with the stamps so that he could mail them himself. With this feat accomplished, he continued with his other tasks.

"Any mail for *Ron of Argyll*?" Peter asked. "Or for Robin at the hotel? She needs her magazines." This was the postmaster's other recycling scheme: any interesting magazines that arrived were withheld until he had read them from cover to cover. Really interesting ones never reached their intended destination.

Little girl near Neiafu, Vava'u Islands, Kingdom of Tonga

"Maybe tomorrow," the Postmaster responded with a hint of triumph. He sat back down on his battered wooden stool and awaited his next unsuspecting victim. As Peter left, he thought that the "recycler" looked a little disappointed that things had not gone entirely according to plan.

————————

The nearby market in the main town of Neiafu was an L-shaped collection of thatched-roofed stalls filled with mounds of local produce arrayed on the floor on woven mats. Fifteen or twenty Tongan women sat alongside their wares, shielded from the sun, chatting and laughing among themselves. They were mostly big women, perhaps up to 200 to 250 pounds, and dressed in colorful *lava lavas* made from a single piece of fabric wrapped around them and tied in the front, covering them from just below their neck nearly to their feet. Their happy brown faces were set off by wide, white smiles and finely combed black hair that glistened with coconut oil.

After haggling on a reasonable price, Peter selected enough papayas, bananas, and breadfruit to fill his bag and turned back to the road for the return trip to the yacht. By now it was almost noon, and the sun was intense. Just as Peter reached the Morris Hedstrom general store, a rusty, beat-up pickup truck pulled alongside.

"Need a ride, Peter?" asked the big, smiling Tongan.

Peter recognized the customs man in the government truck and smiled back. "G'day, Seoni. Yeah, I'm as hot as a snag on a barbie! You going as far as the hotel?"

"'Io," he responded, nodding, and gestured to the empty seat.

Peter placed his bag in the back and climbed in. "Any new yachts in today?"

"One. A German boat just came in from Fiji, and that French boat cleared this morning for New Caledonia. How much longer are you planning to stay?"

"Don't know at the moment. I'm waiting for the owner to contact me and send some crew. But I'm not complaining. I'm in paradise!" Seoni smiled, and soon they pulled up in front of the hotel. Peter opened the door and picked up his bag. "Tofa!" he called and waved.

"Tofa!" Seoni replied as he drove off.

....

In the ensuing days, Peter learned more about the nature of the term *house arrest*, from the points of view of both the local police and Gunter. According to the official terms of the arrangement, Gunter was required to stay within the confines of the hotel. For practical purposes, though, Gunter found that he only needed to appear for the policeman when he arrived to check on him at the same time each day. Gunter had one habit that even the local constabulary couldn't disrupt. Not far from the hotel, he stabled three fine Arabian horses that he had somehow managed to bring in from South America. Every day around dawn, Gunter would walk through the trees behind the hotel to the barn to groom and care for them. Then he would select one of the finely tooled Argentinean saddles and take one of the horses for a long ride through the hills. He was a fine sight in all his splendor, dressed in a crisp white cotton shirt, riding jodhpurs, and polished black riding boots. He would always leave himself plenty of time to finish up with the horses and change his clothes before the policeman knocked on the door at ten o'clock. Flinging open the door, Gunter would appear in his T-shirt, shorts, old apron, and flip-flops and proclaim in his heavily accented English, "I am here." And then close the door dismissively.

Chapter 15

Kidnapped

Peter awoke around dawn one morning to a persistent tapping on the hull. As he cleared his head, he could hear the muted voice of a woman. He climbed up to the cockpit and looked around but couldn't see anyone. He was about to go below when he heard it again, but this time he clearly heard a cry of, "Help! Help me!"

He looked over the side and was astonished to find a young island woman treading water alongside the boat. "Swim round the other side," he called and gestured with his hand. "There's a ladder there."

She clambered up the ladder and with Peter's help climbed aboard. The water dripped from the garment that was wrapped around her as she sat down in the cockpit, her head and shoulders bowed forward in exhaustion. She glanced up at Peter with a frightened look. "Please help me," she pleaded.

"What's happened?" asked Peter with concern.

She pointed to the German yacht lying about 150 feet away. Talking rapidly she said, "He wouldn't let me off the boat. He told me we were going sailing around Suva. Then we came to Tonga."

"Hang on, slow down a bit! You've lost me. Now, where do you live?"

"In Fiji. Suva."

121

"Why didn't you just get off?"

"Because he locked me in the cabin every time he went ashore. He's asleep, so I jumped off. I have no money. He told me we were only going to sail around for a couple of days. All my things are on the boat."

"Well, take it easy. You're safe here. Come below and get cleaned up. I'll grab you a towel and find you some dry clothes. Then I'll make you a nice cup of coffee."

This situation reminded Peter of a lost girl back in 1977. He had met two blonde American girls on the flight from Rio de Janeiro to Casablanca and taken the bus with them from the airport into town. The bus station was in a typical chaotic marketplace, with people and traffic everywhere amid the maze of streets, alleyways, and market stalls. They got off the bus to retrieve their bags, and while Peter talked with one of the girls, her friend simply vanished. Three days later when Peter left Casablanca, she was still missing, despite searching the streets themselves and appealing to the police and the American Embassy. The general consensus was that she had been kidnapped.

Peter remembered vividly his frustration at not being able to find the missing girl and the anguish of her friend. It went against everything he had been raised to believe by his mother and his father, a captain in the Royal Engineers, and against the solid principles instilled in him through his English education. He was determined that he would not be thwarted this time.

News of the abduction traveled quickly, and it was only a few hours later that Peter motored over to the German yacht in the dinghy with two recruits from an adjacent American yacht for support. Coming alongside, the two Americans jumped on board, followed by Peter. His American friends took up positions flanking the companionway, and Peter stood behind the wheel in the cockpit. With the three of them spread out this way, the yacht's owner would have little hope of repelling the boarders if he got belligerent. The skipper emerged from the companionway with a surprised look and demanded indignantly, "What do you want?"

The shoreline near Neiafu with visiting yachts at anchor

"I've got a Fijian woman on my boat. She wants her belongings," said Peter angrily.

"Ah, she's a crazy woman!" he replied, holding up his hands and waving them wildly around his head.

"Yeah, we've heard all about it, you arsehole," said Peter. "Now get your ass below and get her gear together in a bag. And make sure it's all there or we'll come back."

The skipper hesitated for a moment. Seeing that arguing would be futile, he disappeared below. The boarding party waited in silence for the few minutes that it took him to collect the items in a bag and bring them on deck; then they loaded it into the dinghy with them and motored away.

The whole village was soon aware of the woman's plight, and in true Polynesian tradition, a local family took her in. The yachtsman's lot was not so easily settled. The yacht was tied to the customs wharf for several days, and rumor spread about his location. Eventually he reappeared, apparently having been in custody in the tidy little chamber at the rear of the customs office, and departed without much notice.

Peter was leaving the Morris Hedstrom shop the following day when Seoni once again stopped to see if he needed a ride. There were two fine pigs in the back, and the truck appeared to have four new tires.

"Hot day, Peter," he said with a smile.

"Yeah," Peter agreed. "How's our young Fijian friend?"

"Good," he replied. "She's going home today. Looks like someone found some money for airfare. New clothes too."

"That's a bit of luck," Peter said, knowingly. "And what happened to that arsehole of a skipper?"

"He left. He was not happy."

Part Three

———✦◆✦———

A Canadian from the North

Chapter 16

---◆◆✕◆◆---

There's a Moose in My Way

Kitimat, British Columbia, December 1981

Alan Boreham stood in the middle of the dimly lit motel room, his lean, athletic frame wrapped from head to toe in different forms of insulated clothing. He looked himself over, taking stock of his gear, before pulling on his well-worn Sorrel snow boots and fitting the elastic strap of his goggles over the heavy wool toque. Once he had pulled the hood of his coat over his head and finally put on the bulky mitts filled with goose down, he turned to look in the mirror for a final check. He sighed, and then lumbered over to the door and reached for the snow shovel propped against the wall. Grasping the doorknob in his mitted hand, he opened the door and pulled it inward. As he did, snow tumbled into the room up to his knees, followed immediately by a rush of minus forty-degree air. He gasped at the initial shock as the first frigid breath filled his lungs. He stood for a moment squinting, in spite of the tinted goggles, at the reflection of the brilliant sun off the snow. Resignedly, he began shoveling the snow out of the room to clear the carpet and doorway.

Alan had followed the advice of the motel owner and done this several times a day for the seven days that the storm had lasted just to keep the entry to his room open. It was a good thing, too, because the dry Arctic air blowing over the ocean and onto the northern coast of British Columbia had picked up enough moisture to dump a total of seven feet of snow on the little resource town of Kitimat before it rushed up and over the coastal mountains behind it. He had shoveled enough to create a snow canyon the short distance from his doorway to the parking lot in front, with snow heaped high on either side. With the coming of the sunshine, he hoped that this would be the end of it. Alan had been up here almost full-time since the summer to build a salmon hatchery. He had expected to see some very wet and extremely cold weather over the course of the year that the project would last, but this was more than he had counted on.

When he had shoveled enough to get the door closed, he stuck the blade deep into the snowbank in front of him, reached back inside the room for his snowshoes, and slammed the door shut. It was difficult to buckle up the snowshoes with the bulky mitts, but he managed to get them on. He then stepped up onto the fresh snow and began plodding his way across the parking lot. It was empty except for the single mound of snow that represented his pickup truck. At the entrance, he looked both ways and saw that the night's snowfall hadn't been cleared yet. He stopped to listen, slowly turning his head back and forth to try to gather any sounds and let them filter through the layers of headgear. Somewhere off to the right, he could hear the roaring sound of the heavy snowblowing equipment and decided that the cross-country route would probably be safer. He clambered about twenty feet up the steep slope of densely piled snow that the plow had pushed to the side of the parking lot and then down the other side and set off on the three-mile hike to the construction site.

As he trudged along, he surveyed the massive expanse of snow, its surface punctuated only by the tops of the power poles that defined the road and the scraggly Douglas firs of the sparse forest. He now understood the reason for the signs slung from the high voltage lines thirty feet in the air that read "Do Not Touch." Anyone walking along the tops of the snowbanks that lined the roads to avoid the traffic would be in imminent danger of electrocution. It wasn't long before the sounds of the equipment were hushed by the snow and he travelled on in silence. His route followed a slight downward slope toward the river, and when he turned to look behind him, the line of snow on the horizon had erased any proof of human existence.

A heavy, reddish-brown beard protected most of his face, providing some protection from the cold, but the frigid air stung his nose and cheeks. With each exhalation, the warmth of his breath washed over his face, providing a temporary relief, although some of the humidity hung on his moustache, freezing instantly so that he had to brush it occasionally to dislodge the big chunks of ice that robbed his body of heat. He kept a slow, steady pace, not wanting to work so hard that he began to perspire. Nothing, in his mind, would be as sad as to be found frozen to death in his own sweat.

In the distance, he saw a movement and wondered what other being shared this frozen world. As he got closer, he saw that it was a moose, buried up to its chest in the light snow, nibbling at the exposed tips of a tree. He stopped to steady his breath and observe the huge brown beast as it struggled through the fresh snow, foraging for its food.

"Poor bugger," he said softly, forcing these muscles to life. As he watched, he resolved that he wouldn't be stuck here in the north like that moose. He didn't rest long, though, before resuming his trek, taking care to give the creature a wide berth, knowing the danger that a startled moose could pose. Even with the potential advantage that the snowshoes gave him over the snow, he didn't want to get into an argument with an angry, 1,200-pound animal.

When he had graduated with a degree in engineering two years before, Alan had never imagined that he would be working in such an unforgiving environment. He had lived farther south, on the west coast of Canada, for most of his life, having immigrated to Canada from England with his family when he was just two, and the sea was a far more familiar and inviting environment than this place. He had grown up around boats, spending a lot of time on the water with his father and friends in powerboats, rowboats, and canoes. He had even helped his father build a wood and fiberglass sport fishing boat in their garage. Alan was introduced to sailing dinghies at university and had graduated to cruising yachts after beginning work, taking every practical training course available since then. With practice, he had become proficient in navigation and seamanship. The one thing that he hadn't done was blue-water sailing—sailing passages out of sight of land—and he longed for that experience. He had first traveled overseas to England and the Netherlands after university, and that had left him with a desire to see more. This project would be finished by the summer, and he had no real ties at home. He had a little money saved up, and he had always wanted to see the South Pacific. An image of coconut palms and sandy beaches danced in his head, and as he plodded on in the relentless cold, he indulged again in his fantasy of sailing off into a tropical sunset. It was a pleasant, if only illusory, distraction that occupied him until he arrived at the building site.

The single-story industrial building covered two acres of ground. The snow drifted up its sides and piled high on the roof, almost concealing it in the monochrome landscape. He walked around the perimeter looking for any signs of failure and happily found none. He would have to wait for the heavy machinery to clear the wall of snow away from the entry doors so that he could survey the interior of the unfinished building. There was no chance of work resuming for several days. The snowplows first had to clear the access road, and then the giant, propane-fired "salamander" construction heaters inside had to make it warm enough to work. He thought enviously of the construction workers waiting out the weather in the warmth of their bunkhouse and turned to make the return trip to his motel.

———

Back in his room, he peeled off the layers of clothing and felt the warmth gradually reaching his numbed fingers and toes. He strode purposefully to the small table, sat down, and picked up the telephone. He dialed a Vancouver number, and a familiar voice replied after the first ring. "Hello, Seawing Sailing."

"Hi, Leilani. It's Alan. How're you doing?"

"Hi, Alan! Good to hear from you. I didn't know you were back in town."

"I'm not, unfortunately. I'm still up in Kitimat, freezing my ass off, but this couldn't wait."

"Well, what's so important that you had to call from way up there?"

"Are there any crew spots left on the trip to Hawaii in July?"

"Hang on a sec'. Let me check." The line was silent for a moment before she returned. "Yes, there are two spaces left on the trip down and just one space coming back."

"Reserve a spot for me on the trip down. I've decided this will be a one-way trip for me. I'm quitting my job and then making my way south to New Zealand. I'll be out of here by Christmas—even if I have to walk—and I'll drop by to see you."

"Great! Look forward to seeing you."

He hung up and, with a feeling of contentment, sat back in the chair and savored the warmth of the room.

Chapter 17

＊

The Way South

The yacht *Second Chance* motored slowly out through the narrow entrance of the False Creek channel, passing under the girders of the Burrard Street Bridge and emerging into English Bay. It was a warm summer day in Vancouver, and the early-morning joggers along the seawall paralleling the channel had kept up with the custom-built, forty-two-foot aluminum sloop for a while. But as it cleared the buoys marking the channel entrance and entered the bay, it increased to a comfortable cruising speed of six knots, leaving the joggers and shoreline behind. A light breeze rippled the surface of the water, giving a muddy appearance to the reflection of the low cloud that concealed the tops of the North Shore Mountains.

Alan and two other crew stood at the stern pulpit and made a final wave to the friends and family members who still stood on the distant dock waving their farewells. It was a beautiful, sunny first of July—Canada Day—and as a tribute, a solitary pilot maneuvered a huge kite, shaped like the red Canadian maple leaf flag, high aloft on the light breeze, trailing a sequence of twelve smaller flags along its long tail. For his five crewmates, this was a sailing trip, a training course to top off their inshore experience with the challenge of an offshore passage. For Alan, it was all of that and more. It was the beginning of an adventure.

Alan (center) and crew wishing final farewells as *Second Chance* prepares for departure from Vancouver

Second Chance leaving Vancouver

With nothing to hold him back, he was launching himself into the world of "no fixed address."

"Give us a hand with the sails here, Al," called the skipper. John had prepared every possible element of the trip that could be foreseen, from detailing the menus for up to four weeks and preparing a storage list for every ingredient to organizing the charts for each leg of their trip in chronological order in the chart table. If anything could be planned for, it was, the lesson being that preparation made it that much simpler to deal with the unexpected situations that inevitably arose. Now John was choreographing the setting of the first suit of sails from the neatly organized sail locker. "We'll start with the main and genny," he instructed. "That should get us out of the bay in these light winds, and then we're probably going to need the number two, so make sure the sheets are on hand."

"You've got it!" Alan responded, hurrying down the companionway, happy to be underway.

Hours later, Alan woke up to the persistent sound of the alarm above his head. As he swam up from the deep sleep to consciousness, he was suddenly aware of the roaring sound that the alarm had somehow managed to overcome. The next realization was the chaotic motion of the boat. He was amazed that he had managed to sleep through it. The noise was like the thundering of a freight train—beside him, underneath him, all around him—and the angle of the boat pinned him into the crevice between the bunk and the hull so that at first it seemed that he'd been trussed up and stuffed into the trunk of a car for a chase through the hills of San Francisco. It was as black as a coal mine and he sat up, struggling to find the clothes that he had so neatly laid out at the foot of his bunk. He managed to find one leg of his pants and grabbed it before hoisting himself up and swinging over the protective lee cloth, avoiding the lower bunk and landing on both feet on the cabin sole.

"One hand for the ship and one hand for yourself," he mumbled, performing a weird dance as he kept hold of the grab rail above the bunk and slipped first one foot and then the other into the legs of the pants and artfully jumped up and down a few times, pulling them up with his free hand. He fastened his pants with difficulty and then grabbed the doorway to stabilize himself. "Whew!" he exclaimed out loud, feeling a little more stable with four points of contact again. "That wasn't so bad."

His eyes were becoming used to the dark now, and he could make out the cocooned shape of his shipmate behind the lee cloth in the lower bunk. He glanced aft to the main saloon and through the hatch to the cockpit, but could make out none of the on-watch crew. The only thing to do was to get dressed and out on deck, so he braced himself and reached back into his bunk and pulled out a sock. Holding it in one hand, he thought for a moment. This was going to be a little more challenging. He realized that getting dressed in this kind of a sea would have been easier to do in his bunk. He would do that from now on, but this time he finished dressing on the floor, putting on his clothes as well as his foul-weather gear, boots, safety harness, hat, and gloves. All prepared now, Alan stood up, knees slightly bent, and moved through the dizzying motion of the cabin, grasping the handholds overhead as he went.

He grabbed the companionway ladder and scaled the first three steps so that he could see into the cockpit. As he did, the noise changed from the echoey din inside the boat to a dynamic battle of distinct sounds outside. Above his head, the uneven wind in the mainsail complained with a constant howl, tearing at the leech in a sharp staccato as it departed. As if in competition, from astern he could make out the low, lioness growl of a stalking wave, growing as it approached until it surrounded the boat in a threatening roar, lifting it on its back and balancing it there for a moment before letting it slide down with a disdainful chorus of hisses into the path of the next one. An accompaniment of goading whistles emanated from the standing rigging, modulating in an eerie chorus in the darkness.

The seas threw the boat around, shaking Alan like dice rattling around in a cup. He had to hold on tightly to the companionway ladder to keep from being catapulted out. He grabbed the clip of his safety harness and quickly reached out and snapped it onto the big stainless steel ring in the cockpit, where three other clips already jangled about. In the meager glow of the compass light, he could make out a white, hooded shape at the wheel. Two others dressed in yellow gradually became visible on the adjacent seats, their heads tucked down to their chests under their hoods against the wind. They all clutched the stout, stainless steel pipe that was bolted to either side of the cockpit sole in front of the wheel and looped up and over the binnacle that housed the compass, gaining a purchase like a cowboy on a tireless bucking bronco.

"You guys had enough?" he shouted over the bedlam. They looked up at his call.

John was on the port side and called back, "Gary's just made some fresh coffee! Get yourself a cup first if you want!"

"Naw, keeps me awake!" Alan replied with a grin. "May as well get at it!"

The shape to starboard relinquished its grip and moved cautiously toward the companionway. It was Scott. His long, matted, straw-colored hair framed his jovial face.

"You won't need coffee to keep you awake tonight!" he chortled. "You can have my seat. I've been keeping it warm for you!"

Alan stepped out into the cockpit to let him by, ducking his head to clear the dodger. He laughed as he stood up. "Very thoughtful—" The shocking cold of the wind took away his breath, cutting off his words, and he swung his face to leeward in an instant reflex. "Christ, that's cold!" he exclaimed, and dropped heavily onto the starboard seat. It wasn't warm.

It was Gary who was standing at the wheel. He had a heavy build and planted himself solidly at the helm, rocking steadily in time with the movement of the boat. Alan looked up at him, pulling his hood forward like the others to shield himself from the wind. "How's she handle in this wind?" he called.

"Not bad," Gary replied, peering at him over his spray-spattered glasses, "but you've gotta keep an eye on the rollers." He stopped talking as he glanced over his left shoulder to measure up the next wave and turned the wheel about two spokes to starboard. He guided her stern smoothly down into the next trough as the wave slid under them, and then he turned the wheel back as she was lifted up on the next crest. "You need to find the track and stay on it," he continued. "It's kind of like skiing through moguls."

"But don't overcompensate!" John called from the port seat, "or you'll broach!"

Broaching meant letting the wind drive the bow around and then holding the bow down, leaving the vessel broadside to the waves. In these conditions, the seas would wash over the side and swamp the yacht, likely resulting in their shipwreck and disaster.

"All right!" Alan called back. "Let's have a go at it."

Gary made room for him to slide in behind the wheel and waited until Alan had braced himself at the binnacle before letting go. "Steering 260. Keep her steady so I can get some sleep," he said in his straightforward manner.

"No problem. You'll sleep like a baby," Alan replied confidently.

Andy was emerging as Gary went below. He clambered out and sat on the starboard side, his perpetual smile spread across his face. "This is great!" he burst out gleefully. "Wow! Look at those waves! Yee-ha!" He swiveled around in his seat to take in the foaming tops of the nearby waves on the seascape. "Boy, some of those suckers are big!" A wave lashed at their side, showering them in spray. "Whew, that's cold!" he said with a chuckle, seemingly undaunted. "How's it going, John?"

John shifted in his seat. He was a tall, lanky man, distinguished by a bushy brown beard and a thicket of unruly hair, both of which fought to expose themselves to the elements from inside his hood, with some success. John came from the east coast of Canada, the land of the Bluenosers, and continued his ocean heritage on the west coast through his work as the chief instructor with the sailing school. A gentle man, he had an exceedingly calm manner. This was comforting when you first met him, but as the crew was coming to understand, became somewhat disconcerting as you got to know him because in contrary or even dangerous situations, his response was the same as if a crewman had spilled his soup. In fact, it was difficult from his reaction to a situation to know if you were going to be merely inconvenienced in getting to your destination or had the potential to die along the way. It appeared that in John's world, if the situation were inevitable, then it was better to accept it and deal with it than put a lot of energy into worrying about it. Alan didn't really understand John's philosophy but figured he had the three or four weeks it would take to get to Hawaii to work it out.

"It's a little rough with this southeaster and the flood tide," John explained in a teacherly way. "Wind over tide—it throws up a bit of a sea. It should settle down in another couple of hours when the tide changes."

The hull of the boat pushed strongly forward through the water under the insistence of the sail. It splashed a cascade of spray to leeward as it crashed heavily into a truant wave, and then rocked to windward in response and dipped its bow below the surface of the trough.

"Hey, take it easy out there!" came the reproach from the cabin.

"Sorry about that!" Alan shouted back. "Missed a mogul!"

The bow rose with a jerk, scooping up an angry torrent of frigid water to surge along the foredeck, splitting as it hit the cabin top, and rush, chattering, in two unequal hordes headlong into the cockpit to molest the legs of the crew before gurgling rudely down the drains and back into the sea.

"Ease her through the waves; don't force it," John said in a level voice. "As long as you're in the groove, the boat will lead you. And always watch for changes in the pattern of the waves. You can't always avoid them, but you can miss most of the big collisions."

Alan wasn't sure exactly what a "big collision" would be like, but thought it better to avoid finding out. He kept a vigilant eye over his shoulder as instructed, and with a rooster tail of spray flying out behind her, *Second Chance* fled the Strait of Juan de Fuca for the open sea.

Chapter 18

———◆◆◆◆◆———

Let There Be Light

Alan and Andy's next turn was the forenoon watch, which lasted from 0800 to noon. Each watch lasted for four hours, except for the two traditional two-hour dogwatches between 1600 and 2000. Working a two-hour watch instead of four had the effect of alternating the watches every day to provide some variety in their day and night shifts.

At sea, the on-watch crew prepares the meal for the off-watch crew, so when Alan awoke, the cabin was filled with the aromas of a hot breakfast. Their first meal at sea was comprised of orange juice, coffee and tea, steaming hot oatmeal with plenty of brown sugar and fresh milk, scrambled eggs, and toast with strawberry jam. Gary was the cook for this morning, and he displayed both pride and assertiveness in his serving of the crew.

"Grab a bowl and get it while it's hot," he called as Alan shuffled sleepily into the cabin, listing to compensate for the angle of the boat. Gary gestured first to the table where the bowls were spread out among the condiments, all corralled by the raised edges of the tabletop, and then to the stove, which imitated the motion of the boat as it rocked on its gimbals. A pot of oatmeal sat steaming politely on one burner, and a covered skillet accompanied it on the other. Alan steadied himself against the galley table. He gathered up a bowl and hovered by the stove as Gary

140

ladled in the oatmeal, swaying in time with the outstretched hands, until the bowl was half full.

Alan stared at the bowl for a moment, and a sudden vertigo overtook him. He looked up and out of one of the large port lights at the horizon to try to get his equilibrium. A chill slowly crept over him, accompanied by a clammy sweat. From his hundreds of hours afloat in small boats, he knew that the growing nausea was the result of the conflict between the motion that his body was feeling and the apparent stillness of the inside of the cabin, heightened by the barrage of smells. "Think I'll have mine topside," he said casually, still staring outside.

Gary's head jerked up, and he squinted at him through the smoked lenses of his glasses. "What about the eggs and toast?" he demanded.

"No, just oatmeal, thanks," Alan replied wistfully and reached over to carefully place the bowl on the table. He was embarrassed at feeling seasick and didn't want the rest of the crew to know, hoping that it would soon disappear.

"And the tea. You said you wanted tea," Gary added emphatically.

"Yes, well, I suppose I could take some tea," said Alan, clearly not caring about tea at this point. He quickly climbed the first two steps of the companionway to take a few gulps of fresh air and try to orient his brain to the surroundings.

Scott was on the wheel, and John was in his regular seat to port. "You're looking a little pale!" Scott called to Alan through teeth that were clenching the stem of a pipe.

"Must be the heat!" Alan forced a smile. "Need some company out there?"

"Finish your breakfast first. I've got a little while to go yet."

Alan looked over his shoulder at the forlorn bowl of oatmeal and then turned back to the cockpit. "Maybe I'll give breakfast a miss. I'll just get my gear." He took a couple more deep breaths and retreated quickly to his bunk to gather up his foul-weather gear and harness. The nausea returned as he darted back through the cabin to the companionway. He took a few more breaths, like a skin diver seeking life-giving air at the surface, and dressed as quickly as he could.

"And what about this oatmeal?" Gary inquired suspiciously, holding the abandoned bowl.

"Ah, yes, I'll take it with me. Thanks. Looks good," Alan said unconvincingly and grabbed the bowl as he hurried up the steps. He placed the bowl on the cockpit sole, not daring to risk the wrath of the cook by letting it slide around on the seats and topple into the cockpit, and then snapped himself onto the ring and clambered out into the fresh air. Clutching the frame of the dodger with both hands, he stood and thrust his face directly into the frigid wind, as if the cold would somehow suspend the queasy sensation.

"It sometimes takes a day or two to get used to the movement of the ocean," said John in a level tone. "It's a lot different from sailing around the straits."

Alan nodded but didn't reply.

"You should try to eat a little food and have some water just to keep something in your gut," he added.

Alan glanced down at the bowl as it slid along the cockpit sole and came to rest against his boot, as if nudging at him like a lost puppy. He pushed it away, and it slid a few inches before returning. He stared out at the horizon again, ignoring it, but when he looked down, it was still there, a hazy skin now forming on the chilled surface. He ducked his head down and looked into the cabin. Andy was busily slathering a heap of jam onto a piece of toast. "Say, Andy, would you toss me up a spoon please?"

"No problem. Catch!"

The silverware flew neatly within reach, and Alan was able to grab it without incident. He plunked himself down on the starboard seat, leaned over, and picked up the bowl. The cold, gelatinous mass stared up at him, the surface shrunken into goose bumps. Alan looked away, uninterested, but then looked back. He lifted the bowl and sniffed at it for inspiration, but the wind swept away any aroma. He lowered the bowl into his lap and queried his stomach, which responded that it had no appetite. Then he rolled his tongue around his mouth and lips to see if this foreplay would elicit any interest. It didn't. He took the handle of the spoon between his forefinger and thumb and slapped the bowl of the spoon down onto the surface. And again. Nothing. He looked over at John, who just gave a slight nod. So this was to be his first meal at sea. Normally Alan loved his food. Now he dug the spoon into the oatmeal and took a mouthful, eating mechanically, out of necessity, and without joy.

It was halfway through their shift when John emerged from the cabin with a fistful of tools.

"What's up?" asked Andy.

"The compass light went out last night. Made it hard to see. I want to get it fixed in plenty of time for the evening shift."

"Hmmm …," Andy calculated quickly, "that would be us. Sounds good to me!" he said with a laugh.

John took off his gloves and passed the tools to Alan. He selected them one by one as needed, being cautious to keep a good hold on each one so that it would not fall and go skittering around the cockpit and make the inevitable escape down one of the drains. His bare hands were cold and that reduced his dexterity, but with the care of a surgeon, he proceeded to dismantle the shrouding around the top of the binnacle to expose the bulb. He carefully extracted it and held it up with his chilled fingers to inspect the filament. "There you go; it's burned out," he declared. "I've got one of the spares here." He pulled it from his pocket. "You can never have too many spares." He inserted the bulb, tested the light to make sure it was working, and with equal care reassembled the pieces. "That should last us for the rest of the trip," he concluded with satisfaction. And with that little bit of maintenance out of the way, he returned to the cabin.

It didn't last, of course. Or at least the compass didn't continue to light up as it should have. It was five days later, just after midnight, when the seas had settled somewhat and the wind had subsided to a manageable twenty to twenty-five knots. *Second Chance* was making good time on its track to Honolulu, running about 350 miles offshore, steering a course of 185 degrees true, when the light went out again. Scott was at the helm and had to make do with shining a flashlight on the compass from time

Alan on watch off the coast of British Columbia

to time to check their heading. This created a problem, though, because the intensity of the light ruined his night vision, blinding him until his eyes could adjust to the darkness again. Gary tried stretching two pieces of duct tape across the lens of the flashlight, leaving just a narrow slit of light, but it didn't reduce its intensity. What it really needed was a red filter. They improvised by taping a piece of blue rag over it, which diffused it somewhat. The light needed to be fixed.

Alan, Andy, and Margaret took over at four in the morning local time. Margaret was making a valiant attempt at standing watch after having been disabled by seasickness and then by the side effects of the seasick patches since leaving Vancouver. One of the other crewmen still hadn't made it out of his bunk due to seasickness. Compared to them, Alan didn't feel so bad about his own short bout of queasiness. He checked the log while Andy prepared to relieve Scott at the helm. "Any problems?" Alan asked Gary.

"Naw. We made about thirty miles. That's 180 over the last twenty-four hours. The wind's fairly steady and—"

He was interrupted by a call from the cockpit. It was Andy. "Hey, Al! Bring up another flashlight when you come. This one's almost gone, and the darned compass light's out again!"

Alan looked back to Gary, who added plainly, "and the compass light's out again."

"Thanks," Alan replied with a smile. "Better note that in the log."

It was almost four bells—6:00 a.m.—before it was light enough to deal with the compass light. The weather was still overcast and cold, so the work on the compass light was another chilling experience. They checked the fuse first and it was okay, so, going by the principle that when something goes wrong, check the last thing you fixed, Alan dutifully dismantled the binnacle as John had done and inspected the lightbulb. The filament was intact, and when he tested it using a piece of wire and a flashlight battery, the light shone brightly. "Looks like this is going to be a little more work than last time," he sighed.

It took them the rest of the watch to find the problem, and Alan was just finishing the reassembly of the binnacle when John stuck his head out of the companionway.

"How's it going up here?" he asked. "I heard you guys tinkering with something."

"Good," Alan replied. "The compass light was out again. Turns out one of wires has been rubbing against the edge of the fiberglass cutout in the cockpit sole where the binnacle attaches. The wire was worn through—only being held together by the insulation. We couldn't see it, of course, until we took the whole thing apart. We spliced it and taped it up. Should be okay now."

"Let's hope. Gary'll be right out. You guys look like you could use some breakfast."

This time Alan agreed.

Chapter 19

———◆━━◆◆━◆———

The Love Boat

The route to Hawaii can vary depending on the position of the North Pacific high. This is an area of high pressure in the North Pacific that generally establishes itself off the west coast of British Columbia, Washington, and Oregon in the summer months. It protects the coast from bad weather by deflecting low-pressure systems that bring rain and strong winds. With the high in this position, a sailor would head offshore from Vancouver and then generally head south, skirting the calm at the center of the high by traveling around it in a clockwise direction to take advantage of the favorable winds. Somewhere north of San Francisco, the route ducks below the high and out to the west before leaving the influence of the high to curve away to the southwest in search of the northeast trade winds. Depending on the latitude of the trade winds at the time, the route then follows roughly a west-southwesterly direction to reach the islands.

When the high oscillates unseasonably to the north or south, it allows low-pressure systems to move in close to shore as intense, intermittent storms. In this circumstance, it is often better to head west from Vancouver and travel farther offshore to stay well clear of the coast and avoid these weather systems before heading south. It was one of these lows that had bounced *Second Chance* around on its departure. Now, after a period of relatively moderate conditions, a new low had developed and begun another assault.

Sailors of the day followed the weather by observation and by monitoring the regular updates on the single sideband radio. These broadcasts indicated the location of the highs, lows, and troughs, along with wind strengths and directions, so that sailors could plot the weather systems and plan their course. *Second Chance* was approximately six hundred nautical miles west of San Francisco and following a course south-southwest when the weather began to deteriorate. The low-pressure system was developing quickly and the pressure was dropping fast, indicating the approach of strong winds and rough seas. It didn't take the broadcast to tell them that conditions were going to get bad. From the cockpit, they had watched as the southern horizon darkened and the clouds dropped to the surface of the water. Then, as the winds rose and the seas began to grow, the midday light seemed to dim, as if someone had turned down the houselights in a theatre, and a uniform dullness descended.

The crew had double-reefed the mainsail and bent on the storm jib in preparation for the worst. Now it was just a matter of waiting. It didn't take long. Within hours, the wind had reached gale force, and *Second Chance* resumed its hectic ride south. Even with these conditions, though, the crew, now ten days into the voyage, were accustomed to the manner of the yacht and stood watch unbothered by the weather. Sailing on a close reach, they were making between eight and ten knots and managing like old hands.

The temperature had not improved, however, and the helmsmen switched every half hour, partly for a rest but mostly to warm up as the temperature at this latitude was still cold. They were into the second dogwatch when Scott went below for his break. A pork loin roast was in the oven, and it filled the main cabin with a delicious aroma. Alan was busy updating the log at the galley table. He carefully made the entries for the watch: Course 170 magnetic, 192 true; Wind WNW 40 knots, estimated; Speed 9 knots; Conditions overcast, alto cumulous, mist, rain, visibility 2 miles; Barometer 28.5; Bilge dry; Engine on at 0200 GMT.

"Boy, that sure smells good!" said Scott. "I kept getting whiffs of it in the cockpit. How long 'til it's ready?"

"Should be done in twenty minutes or so. In time for the change of watch," Andy responded brightly. "We're sure roaring along, aren't we?" he added happily. "I can almost hear the surf on Waikiki Beach now!"

They had started the engine to recharge the batteries, and Alan got up and made his way forward to the navigation station to check the charging rate. He frowned and tapped the gauge, and then called over to Scott, "What've we got the battery selector set on?"

Scott went over and stooped to look under the companionway steps, where the switch was located. "Uhhh … number one," he replied and straightened.

"That's what I thought. Try switching it to number two." Scott did, and Alan watched the other gauge. The needle did not move.

"What's up?" asked Scott.

"The batteries aren't charging." Alan went back to the table and made the entry. "Batteries are at about ten and eleven volts," he said.

"Better tell John," Scott suggested.

John brought his usual practical approach to the problem. "Let's have dinner first. It'll give us something to do afterward," was all he said.

Troubleshooting took all the first watch, with John, Alan, and Andy crawling on their hands and knees around the cabin following wires, removing panels to expose the engine from various points, and testing the various components. It all ended with no solution in sight. John announced his plan at the change of watch.

"It looks like the alternator's not working," he said. "We could carry on, but it's going to be at least twelve more days to Honolulu, maybe fifteen or eighteen depending on the weather. We could reserve one of the batteries to start the engine and for emergency communication, but we still need a house battery for navigation lights and some interior lights at a minimum. With that kind of use, the house battery would last for about eight days." He paused to let that sink in before continuing. One additional consideration for John was Margaret's condition, and she was showing no sign of improvement. "It's about five days to San Francisco. We're going to head in there and get the alternator fixed, let Margaret off the boat, and then see what you guys want to do. Anyone who wants to carry on to Hawaii from here on their own can leave now," he added dryly.

There were chuckles and laughter, and everyone understood that his decision was probably the right one, especially Andy, who was getting married as soon as he got back. Even at that, he was not to be denied his trip to Waikiki. "You know, if we get to 'Frisco and get the alternator fixed in one day, we can still make Waikiki in twenty-eight days," he enthused. "No reason why we can't!"

There was general agreement with this.

"The one small problem that we'll have," John continued, "is that we don't have any charts or tide tables for the area. That's where we'll have to depend on our seamanship and cunning." A small smile appeared at the corners of his mouth. It was obvious that he was looking forward to the challenge. This had all been too easy so far.

The ride into San Francisco was as intense as any they had endured so far. The low moved north to intercept the path of their retreat, resulting in frequent trimming of the sails and creating rollers bigger than the ones they had experienced leaving the Strait of Juan de Fuca, requiring constant vigilance at the helm. They kept two people in the cockpit at all times and had one dressed and ready down below in case of emergency. It was during the morning watch in the midst of all of this when they were reminded of the ultimate power of the ocean.

Alan was at the helm and Andy was on deck with him, holding onto the binnacle and hunched over with his head tucked down into his hood in the now-familiar posture. With each wave, Alan would look over his shoulder, squinting against the cold and spray, searching for the foam that outlined the crest that guided his hand on the wheel. Over and over this scene played out, the dark, ominous waves rising up and then passing under them as he steered a course to ease the pounding on the yacht. His turn on the helm was just about up when he looked over his shoulder and saw nothing but black. He peered harder, searching for the crest, puzzled by this total absence of light. Then the stern started to rise, and he saw a flicker, a reflection of the stern light, and something made him look up. He had no time except to shout, "Hold on, Andy!" before the towering crest of the wave crashed down on them, pummeling them onto the cockpit sole and inundating the whole aft section of the yacht, immersing them in the frigid seawater and halting all forward motion of the yacht.

For the few seconds that it took for the oversized cockpit drains to clear the cockpit, Alan didn't know if he was on board the yacht or not. One second he was being churned about in this black, turbulent water, and the next he was left cold and sputtering on the cockpit sole, his hands gripping his safety line. He realized that he was safe for the moment but knew that he needed to see what damage had been done and the status of the crew. He bumped against the binnacle as he got to his knees, but with no headway the motion of the boat was chaotic and he was knocked over again. He scrambled up and grabbed the wheel, as much for stability as control. He saw Andy get up and make a similar plunge for the helm, and between them they got their bearings. The giant wave had rushed on in a mass of seething foam, and the boat was suddenly underway again, answering the helm and apparently undamaged.

Alan and Andy were looking at each other in dripping disbelief when one of the pair of companionway doors opened to expose a hint of miserable light from below that framed John's furry face. "You guys okay?" he inquired casually.

"It was," Alan sputtered, water still draining from his hood as he reached up with one hand to indicate the wave's size, "huge!" The water from his extended sleeve immediately ran down inside his foul-weather jacket, inside the bib of his foul-weather pants, and exited from the left leg, the boot being too full to accept this late addition.

"Yeah!" Andy confirmed, nodding to emphasize his statement and throwing a similar spray. "And wet!" he exclaimed nonsensically, and then he paused for a second to gather his thoughts. He puffed absently at the water that dripped from the end of his nose. "I mean," he added shrilly, "we were underwater!"

Second Chance was regaining speed now, and Alan looked apprehensively over his shoulder.

"I'll get someone to relieve you so you can dry out," John offered, and the door closed.

"Your turn," Alan suggested to Andy, the tension draining away as well. "Remember to look up."

Early on the fourth day of the trip in to San Francisco, they sighted a light through the ragged cloud and fog. They watched it for a while to confirm the characteristics: one white flash every five seconds. From the *Pacific Coast List of Lights, Buoys, and Fog Signals*, they knew that it was Point Reyes Lighthouse, located just north of the Golden Gate Bridge. As they saw their first landfall in thirteen days, they were excited that they had arrived right on target, but the exhilaration was somewhat subdued by the fact that they had landed about 1,500 miles short of their intended destination. They were further deflated to find that the battery was too weak to start the engine. They were going to have to do this the hard way. John kept three people on deck now to steer and stand watch. The seas had subsided to about six to eight feet and the winds had dropped to a less strenuous twenty-five knots, but San Francisco was a busy port and in their compromised condition, he wanted to avoid any complications.

The Point Reyes light is visible in good conditions for over twenty miles, much less through the cloud that now clung to the surface of the sea. As they approached the coast, all the crew were on deck, watching and listening intently for other vessels and infused with the excitement of having to depend on their wits to make it into port safely. Visibility was about a mile—seemingly lots of time to maneuver if they encountered another boat—but the cloud and fog seemed to breathe, moving in and out with an almost audible sigh and leaving them at times obscured from the world in a wind-whipped cloak. From the intermittent flashes of light, they

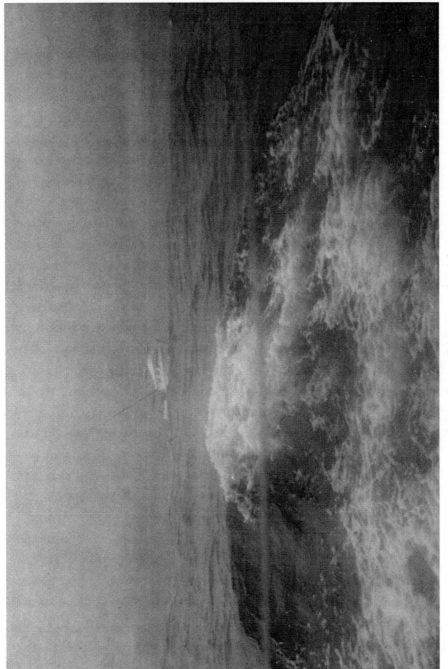

A fishing boat off the coast of California

thought that they must be about three miles from the point. They took bearings to the light as the opportunity presented itself and were able to plot their location on their chart of the Pacific Coast, but it was just a tiny dot in the vast ocean—meaningless for coastal navigation. They conversed in whispers, straining to hear a sound of any kind as they headed toward what they thought was the entrance to the harbor.

It happened suddenly. The cloud parted, as if walking through a curtain, and they emerged into sunshine, the totality of the light reduced only by wisps of mist overhead. That surprise was welcome, but the next was not. While their navigation had been impeccable, their timing was terrible. Dead ahead, not more than three hundred yards off, was a huge white shape, glistening like an iceberg and framed by the orange expanse of the Golden Gate Bridge. It was a cruise boat, making about ten knots straight for them. There was an instant of silence when everyone seemed to blink in unison at the brightness and shield their eyes—and then total mayhem. Seven people in the cockpit and on the rails had been manageable when they were keeping watch, but now that they were required to maneuver the boat, it was about four people—and four safety lines—too many. John sat calmly on the windward side of the cockpit, watching them as they tried to move to handle the lines and sheets, tangling themselves in the process.

"All right," he interceded, taking control, "off-watch crew below." There was a rapid untangling and retreat of three bodies, leaving Alan, Scott, and Andy on deck. "Let's bear away to a beam reach," John continued, and the on-watch crew eased the sails and turned south onto a course roughly perpendicular to that of the big ship.

The rest of the crew were glued to the port lights down below, watching as their fate was determined. Gary was one of the few who had the presence of mind to take a photograph. There were a few anxious minutes while they cleared the navigation channel, running parallel to the coast, before they were sure that they were safe.

Andy took a seat beside John and leaned back to help reduce the heel of the boat. "Wow! I've never seen a cruise boat before. It's huge!" he enthused, unbothered.

He was right when measured by the standards of cruise ships at the time. From their vantage point, only fifty yards away as it passed, the size seemed magnified a hundred times. The ship soared about ten stories above them, and as it slid by, the lines of portholes on the massive white hull seemed to extend like a string of dots on a blank page.

"Hey! It's the *Pacific Princess*!" said Andy. He held up his hands, waving them in time as he swayed from side to side with an imagined tune as he crooned, "The Looove Boat!"

It was indeed the cruise ship made famous by the weekly television program *The Love Boat*. There was a roar of laughter as the off-watch crew, assured now of their safety, tumbled up to have a closer look. They were all a lot more relaxed after their close encounter and waved at the few hardy souls on deck.

"Can you see Captain Stubing on the bridge?" asked Scott.

"No, but I'm sure that's Gopher by the rail!" Alan chimed in.

The banter carried on this way until they were well clear, and then they got back to their task of sailing safely into port. They headed up, tacked cleanly, and then bore away to retrace their course. Gauzy cloud dashed by from time to time, snatched from the nearby fog bank like spray blown from the top of a wave, but otherwise the visibility was excellent.

As they reached up the coast, Gary asked, "Ever been in here before, John?"

"Nope," he replied simply, "but there's quite a current that runs in and out of here."

"How do you know that?"

"No boats."

Gary looked toward the bridge and then up and down the coast. There were no vessels in the channel or anywhere near. "You're right." He paused, and then added, "I guess the cruise boat wasn't bothered much by the current, either flood or ebb."

"Probably not," said John, "but smaller vessels will wait for slack. So will we."

Second Chance traversed up and down the coast within sight of the bridge for over five hours, like a ship of the line laying siege to the harbor. The crew made use of the time to retrieve mooring lines, fenders, and ground tackle in preparation for their arrival, and then they hoisted the United States courtesy flag and yellow quarantine flag up the flag halyard that was strung from the port spreader down to the deck. When John was sure that they were all set, they amused themselves by taking sightings with the hand bearing compass and calculated the maximum flood current, which they determined to be about three knots at the approach to the harbor. As the current began to decrease, a tugboat appeared from somewhere south, making its way toward the bridge. *Second Chance* turned to follow, and soon several small commercial ships began to motor out of the harbor. A freighter emerged from the fog and overtook them as they were approaching the bridge.

The wind began to increase as it funneled between the headlands, causing the yacht to heel over more and send a spray along the deck as it ploughed forward. John kept them as near to the center of the channel as possible, seeking clean air, but the winds, reflecting from the rock cliffs that formed the abutments of the bridge, buffeted them and sent them repeatedly dashing for the sheets to maintain their heading. Alan was grinding in the jib sheet and looked up as they passed under the bridge. "It's bigger than it looks on TV," he called back to Scott at the helm. "I'm amazed at how high it is."

"I'm more amazed that the Love Boat made it underneath," Scott called back. "I guess that's why they went out at the end of the ebb."

Andy struck up a helpful rendition of "Do You Know the Way to San Jose?" and they entered San Francisco Bay in good spirits.

———

It has been said that when you don't know where you're going, any road will take you there. This was indeed the case for the crew of *Second Chance*, with the one additional qualification that their road had a mind of its own. Once they were inside the protection of the bay, the wind dropped

Pacific Princess leaving San Francisco Harbor

Second Chance approaching the Golden Gate Bridge

Second Chance at the St. Francis Yacht Club in San Francisco

to about fifteen knots and the tide turned to ebb. With increasing speed, the current nudged them back toward the bridge so that their search for a safe moorage became more urgent. Their task seemed easy enough: look for a bunch of masts and a dock, and then sail there as fast as possible and tie up to it. In practice, it wasn't that easy, but after an hour of scouring the coast through binoculars and several unsuccessful forays close to shore, they finally found a suitable spot. At four in the afternoon, *Second Chance* sailed silently toward the prestigious St. Francis Yacht Club, turned her head to wind, luffed the sails, and stopped with a gentle bump against the dock. Their first offshore adventure had ended.

Chapter 20

---◆◆✕◆◆---

Taking a Second Chance

Andy had been right. It took only a day and a half to get the alternator repaired and the batteries charged, so their objective of reaching Hawaii still seemed achievable. By a vote of six to zero, with one abstention, the crew voted to continue. The abstention was Margaret, who had reluctantly chosen to return home. So it was that, by nine the following morning, they had refitted the equipment, enjoyed their last hot shower and cold beer at the very hospitable St. Francis Yacht Club, topped up their water and fuel, taken on another two weeks' worth of provisions, and were heading once again toward the Golden Gate Bridge. They had tied a reef into the mainsail and hoisted a working jib, so they felt a bit conspicuous when a beautiful, tanned, blonde woman skimmed by them on a sailboard, wearing only a light blue bikini and a Sony Walkman.

Down below, the crew was stowing everything away and updating the provision list and menu. They had the local radio station playing in the background, enjoying the last few hours of civilization before they were out of range and left to their own entertainment. As they worked, a news update interrupted the music. One item caught their interest.

"The Coast Guard is warning swimmers to stay out of the water at Bay area beaches since a fisherman caught a twelve foot great white shark in his net this morning. More news, weather, and sports at eleven."

"That's it. My morning swim is off until further notice!" Andy exclaimed decisively.

"I hope that pretty blonde is tuned in to this," said Scott. "She'd look a lot like shark bait out there on the bay!"

"Hmff," Gary snorted. "You'd have to be crazy to get into the water out here. Don't know what's down there."

They all agreed.

The cloud consumed them again by late afternoon, and the off-watch crew turned in for some sleep. It was a rough ride. They sailed into the same gale they had encountered on the way in to San Francisco, and it persisted for almost three more days. After making a sail change one night in these rough seas, using the engine to help bring them up into the wind, the engine suddenly stopped. Since it was too dark and dangerous to fully investigate, it wasn't until the morning that they could see that the coiled jib halyard had come loose and washed over the side, catching in the propeller. The halyard was still tied to the cleat on the mast and pulled as tight as a bowstring over the side, where it angled back toward the stern and disappeared underwater. The crew tried pulling it off, tried repeatedly to unwind it by putting the transmission into reverse, and finally admitted that it wasn't going to come off voluntarily. Apart from the embarrassment of having caused this to happen, there was the problem that they couldn't lower the jib and they certainly couldn't use the engine for propulsion.

John had them heave-to at the change of watch at noon and convened a crew meeting in the main cabin. "We've got a little problem to solve," he began and laid it out in simple terms. "We can't get the halyard off from here, so we're going to have to dive for it." The crew looked around at one another in silence. The wind and seas had died down considerably, and hove-to the boat rocked gently in about five-foot seas in the relative quiet.

Scott at the helm, with Gary on watch, as *Second Chance* leaves San Francisco

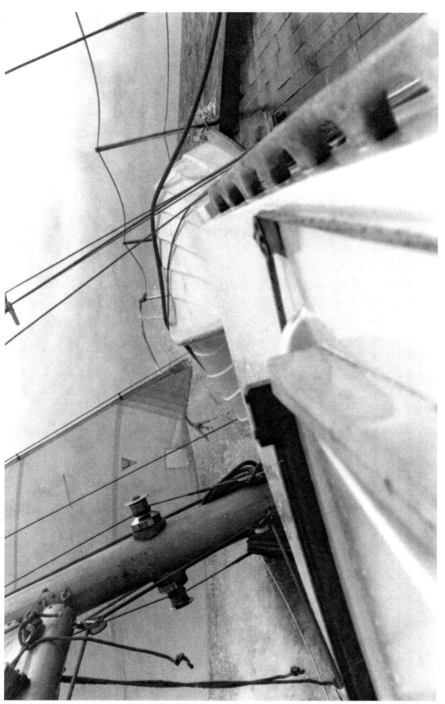

Second Chance in the North Pacific en route to Hawaii

"We're going to have two people in the water for security," he continued, "wearing their safety harnesses, which we'll tie off up here on deck so they don't drift off. The water's going to be cold—about fifty degrees, I'd guess—so they won't be able to stay in too long because of hypothermia." He paused and looked around. "Any volunteers?"

There was some uneasy movement among the crew, but no one spoke for a few seconds.

"Well, I've got my short wet suit and snorkel gear here that I was planning to use when we got to Hawaii," Alan thought out loud, "so I'll do it."

"I'll go too," Gary added quickly.

There were no arguments from the rest of the crew. Alan and Gary put on their masks, grabbed their knives, and strapped on their safety harnesses. They double-checked everything and were ready to go.

Andy raised one final detail. "Ah, John," he started uncomfortably, "what about the, uh, great whites?"

"Hmmm ... yes," said John. "The crew on board will be on shark watch while they're in the water."

Alan and Gary looked at each other. Alan was slim, and the light blue wet suit seemed to emphasize his sinewy physique. Gary, on the other hand, wearing only a brief swimsuit that failed to fully contain his stout midriff, appeared even bigger than his adequate girth deserved. "If I was a shark, I'd go for you first," Alan remarked glibly.

Gary just shrugged dismissively. "Let's go," was all he said and jumped in.

Alan was right behind him. The cold water was a shock, but it was probably the prospect of voluntarily jumping into rough seas two miles deep that really made Alan question his decision. He shoved any concerns aside. He just wanted to get on with the job and get it done as quickly as possible. He ducked his head below the surface and instinctively did a quick 360-degree check for hazards.

Gary bobbed in the water about ten feet from him. "What're you looking for?" Gary called over.

Alan spat out his snorkel and called back, "Sharks."

"You don't really expect to see one, do you?"

"No, but if a shark does get me, I wouldn't want anybody to be able to say that I should have seen it coming."

With that formality out of the way, he and Gary surveyed the situation and made their own plan of attack. The halyard was tangled in the propeller as they had expected, but en route it had somehow wrapped itself tightly around the short section of the propeller shaft between the hull and the skeg, the narrow strut that extended down from the hull and supported the shaft just ahead of the propeller. Their plan was to try to unwrap the halyard first, and then to cut it off if that failed.

The propeller was located about five feet short of the transom and about four feet below the waterline, not much of a swim in a calm sea, but a challenge with the hull rising and falling in these rough conditions, as there was a danger of the hull bonking a diver on the head. Their system was to have one of the swimmers watching from the surface while the other held his breath and dived underwater to work on the halyard. The rounded, spoon-like step formed by the extension of the bottom of the hull past the transom served as a good place for the one on watch to hold on, even though the yacht's more violent lurches hauled him out of the water almost to his knees. The one on the surface kept watch on the one underwater, ready to dive down to help him if he became tangled or was knocked unconscious.

Gary was the first one underwater. It wasn't as easy as they had thought to pull on the halyard, since there was nowhere to brace himself save for hanging onto the smooth shaft, but he managed to unwind one wrap on the propeller on the first try. Alan went next and had similar luck. They continued this way for about fifteen minutes, sometimes making progress, sometimes not. In between dives, they rested on the surface, standing by to help. On board, the remaining crew kept a diligent watch in a futile attempt to detect marauding sharks below the obscured surface of the rough sea.

Once Alan and Gary had freed the line from the propeller and around the skeg, the only task that remained was to unwrap the line from the shaft. Of course, it was not going to be that easy. The line remained tight, the tension on the line having reduced its diameter to half its original size, just small enough for one wrap to override the next and jam the two together into the tube that housed the shaft bearing in one rock-hard, knotted mass. They cut and nipped and sawed at the line for another fifteen minutes before they were able to cut it free. It was none too soon for Alan, who had begun to shiver with the cold, while Gary, protected by his natural insulation, seemed as yet unaffected. They swam back to the boarding ladder, and Alan was barely able to pull himself aboard.

Back in the cockpit, there were congratulations for the swimmers. Scott handed Gary a big towel to dry off, and with trembling hands, Alan began to undo the zipper on the wet suit. He had experienced mild hypothermia once before, in the fog and rain of the mountains where he had been on a backpacking trip with a friend. He had gotten wet and cold and was only able to stop the shivering by making a fire in the stove of an old prospector's cabin they had been using. He felt the same now and thought that a warm meal would do the trick.

"Hold on a minute, Al," Scott said with a smile. "John's got a treat for you."

Alan was puzzled but stood there shivering as John stepped into the cockpit with a big bucket of steaming water. "Put your head forward," he instructed, and as Alan did so, Scott pulled the neck of the wet suit back and John slowly poured the warm water into the wet suit. It was an instant relief as the water chased down his back, surrounded his waist, and ran down to his legs before filling the lower part of the suit and backing up to immerse his entire trunk and then overflow into the arms. Alan closed his eyes in ecstasy as John poured some warm water over his head and then dispensed an equal amount over Gary.

"Ahhhh!" Alan breathed as the water seeped out of the suit and his temperature began to return to normal. "Better than hugging an Eskimo!"

Chapter 21

Has Anyone Seen an Island?

It took four days before they escaped the influence of the low and found themselves ghosting along at three or four knots on a slowly undulating sea. They were on a southwesterly course and had entered the zone between the turbulent weather systems of the northern Pacific Ocean and the more predictable conditions of the northeast trade winds, which began just north of the Tropic of Cancer. What wind there was finally disappeared half a day later, and they were becalmed. It was midafternoon, and the sun cast a broad halo through the high, gauzy cloud that veiled the sky. This cloud extended to the far distance, melding with its own reflection in the surface of the sea and obscuring the horizon. Both the air and water temperatures had warmed considerably, and the crew took full advantage of this pleasant change, taking turns sitting on the stern step to have a wash in the crystal-clear water or swimming off the stern. On deck, the wool sweaters were gone, and for the first time the weather was warm enough to wear shorts. The aroma of suntan lotion filled the air.

By the end of the second dogwatch, everyone had collected in the cockpit to watch the sunset. Remarkably, after three weeks at sea, this was the first approximation of a sunset that they would have the opportunity to see, and nobody wanted to miss it. The surface of the sea was flawless,

Andy at the wheel as *Second Chance* emerges from the storm

Alan having a wash during a calm mid-Pacific

Some of the crew going for a swim during the calm

unmarked by a ripple, a splash, or a seabird. It was as though the whole world was holding its breath along with the crew in respect of the moment. They sat reverently in silence as the soft glow of the sun, still masked by the screen of cloud, disappeared discreetly, gradually illuminating the horizon in a palette of light pastel colors that seeped across the sky toward them. The colors were reflected in the glassy sea, the two images extending like delicate pincers above and below, encompassing them, until the yacht and its crew were finally absorbed by a starless night. Reluctantly, the off-watch crew turned quietly to their bunks, leaving Alan and Andy on deck.

Over the previous few days, they had been blown a long way south by the storm. John decided that the crew had enjoyed enough of this soft living and was determined to take advantage of the calm to make up some of their westing under power. After prudently checking that the halyards were properly secure, they started the engine and got underway to the unfamiliar thrumming of the diesel.

Alan and Andy took the next watch. "I'll take the first turn on the wheel if you like," offered Alan.

"Fine with me," Andy agreed. "I'll make some coffee."

The wind returned halfway through the watch, in small gusts at first but becoming more steady and requiring more attention at the helm. By the time Gary and Scott came to take over from them, a few stars had become visible through the breaking cloud layer. Alan was completing the log while Gary put on his safety harness.

"Feels like the wind's back," Gary commented.

"Yeah, just started. About seven to ten knots from the east-northeast," Alan replied. "Not really enough to shut down the engine yet, but if it keeps up, it won't be long."

"Any problems on your watch?"

"Naw. Piece o' cake."

"Good. Coffee hot?"

"Yup."

Gary poured himself a cup—black—and headed up the companionway.

"Oh yeah," Alan called over his shoulder, "we fixed the compass light again."

Gary turned on the steps, ducked his head to look back into the cabin at him, and gave a hint of a smile. "Good," he said again, and continued out into the cockpit.

Alan began to wake up and smiled with satisfaction when he opened one eye to look at his watch and found that he had slept for a full seven hours. He felt more relaxed and refreshed than anytime during the trip. He lay there for a few minutes, taking in the sounds and the regular motion of the boat, knowing that he had an hour before he had to be on watch. As his mind began to work, the first thing he noticed was that the engine was off. This meant that the wind had picked up, and from the steady motion of the boat, it seemed like they were getting close to the trade winds. Then he noticed several voices, both in the cabin and in the cockpit, and recognized one of them as Gary's. He puzzled with this thought for a moment, wondering why Gary wouldn't have turned in after his watch. But it was the persistent sound of the electric bilge pump that suddenly wrenched him from his half-sleep and caused him to tumble out of bed to investigate.

The scene was shocking. The removable panels down the centerline of the cabin sole had been pulled up, and the provisions that they had so carefully catalogued and stored in the bilge had been unpacked and piled up along the leeward side of the cabin. Gary was on his hands and knees, head in the bilge, peering about with a flashlight. Alan looked past the clutter of the cabin and out the companionway. From this perspective, he could only see the legs of the helmsman and, at the same level, the head and torso of John, situated beside the legs and facing him. In this bizarre scene, it looked as if John had been chopped in half, with the bottom half at the helm and the top half resting beside him in the cockpit. Alan closed his eyes and shook his head, and then opened them and looked again.

John's top half called to him. "Hey, Al, would you bring me that bucket out of the head please?"

"What?" he called back to the apparition in amazement.

"The bucket in the head," he said again. "I need it." And the top of John disappeared straight down and out of sight.

Alan hesitated for a moment, and then went forward to the head, grabbed the bucket, and returned aft to the companionway. He stepped over Gary on his way and cautiously climbed up the companionway steps. He was relieved to see Scott—both top and bottom parts of him—at the wheel. But as he looked apprehensively into the cockpit, he was both relieved and disturbed with what he saw. The engine access panel in the sole of the cockpit had been removed, and both John and Andy were down below, wedged into the narrow gaps on either side of the engine, with water sloshing back and forth in this confined space. Alan didn't mention his nightmarish vision.

"I wondered when you'd wake up," Scott chuckled. "You're missing all the fun!"

"What's going on?" Alan asked, dangling the bucket down to within John's reach.

"Oh, thanks, Al," John replied, contorting his right arm around and over his head to take it from him. "We seem to be taking on some water. Gary's looking for the source up forward, but I think we've discovered where it's coming from." He had a plastic mug full of water in the other hand and dumped it into the bucket. He continued bailing. "Tell Gary we've found it."

Gary appeared beside Alan at the companionway as Andy's head popped up from the other side of the engine. "Hi, Al!" he greeted him. "Looks like we've got something else to fix!"

"That's a relief," Alan returned, smiling. "I was afraid we'd have nothing to do."

"There's water seeping in right under the oil pan," John explained.

"It looks like there's a hairline crack in the hull about three inches long," Andy added.

"A crack?" said Gary. "How far back?"

Andy did a quick estimate. "Oh, I'd say about five or six feet ahead of the transom."

"You know what?" asked Gary, and continued without waiting for an answer. "That's right where the skeg is. We heard a rumbling sound start when the engine was running last night. I bet that damned halyard's bent the prop shaft."

"And it's worked the skeg back and forth until it's cracked the aluminum weld at the hull," John finished the thought. "You could be right." John peered under the oil pan again with a flashlight to take another look at the source of the problem. "Well, there's not much that we can do with it," he said. "There's only about an inch of space." He thought for a few seconds. "The bilge pump will keep it under control for now. It'll probably be okay as long as we're not motoring, but we'll check the level in the bilge twice a watch anyway. If it gets any worse, we'll have to deal with it. It's too bad we can't lock the prop shaft to stop it moving, though."

The winds were to rise and fall over the next few days as they maintained a course of about 200 degrees true, trying to work their way down into consistent trade winds without sacrificing their westerly progress. The leak didn't appear to be getting any worse, so the watches were mundane and uneventful, a high point coming seven days after leaving San Francisco when they finally gybed from a port to a starboard tack. A long passage typically follows three phases: novelty, routine, and endurance. It had now been twenty-five days since leaving Vancouver and, allowing for a two-day stopover in San Francisco, a total of twenty-three days at sea. Novelty had long since passed. The watches had survived the routine phase, and now the withering of the fresh vegetables was reflected in the mood of most of the crew (except, of course, the irrepressible Andy), indicating that they were most certainly moving into the endurance stage.

When the trade winds eventually filled in at about twenty-five degrees north latitude, they brought regular, six- to eight-foot waves and produced speeds of seven to eight knots. With a reasonable guarantee of consistent

Second Chance under full sail in the trade winds

Anybody want flying fish for breakfast?

winds for the duration of the trip, the crew began to take bets on when they would sight land. Their estimates were made to the half hour and ranged between two and a half and three days. This was a good—if temporary—distraction, but one that was overwhelmed by the brief excitement of sighting dozens of flashing white lights across the evening horizon. It was a mysterious spectacle since no vessels were visible nor any running lights and no radio activity accompanied them. The crew reluctantly steered *Second Chance* south of the strange flotilla, giving up the westing but wanting to stay clear of any unknown hazards and hoping to find a clue to their origin at dawn. But daybreak revealed nothing, and the only reasonable explanation was provided by Alan.

"It was probably drift-netters," he said. "I hear they operate at night so they won't be detected." He explained that a single boat could set hundreds of miles of nets every night that trap anything that gets in their way, including dolphins, seabirds, and even whales. Environmentalists called them "walls of death." "The ends of the nets have long poles attached to them," he said. "What we saw were probably lights on the poles so they can go back and find them."

"Someone oughta do something about those guys," Gary said sternly.

"Lots of countries are trying. Some just don't want to know. Vigilante groups have been chasing them down for a while." Alan squinted at the empty horizon. "Guess we'll never know for sure."

That morning the sky became overcast and the barometer dropped by almost half an inch in an hour—an indication of a rapid change to bad weather. The deteriorating conditions produced a heavy downpour for a few hours before the clouds thinned out to a patchy, irregular pattern and the wind died to fickle, varying gusts, leaving them almost dead in the water. When they heard the 0800 weather report, they understood why. Hurricane Gilma, one of the many tropical storms to be spawned in the eastern Pacific, was gathering strength southeast of the Hawaiian Islands and threatened to brush past them as the crew approached Honolulu.

"At this time of year, the storms typically head west, swinging south of Hawaii and blowing themselves out near the equator," John explained, "so I'm not too worried about being overrun by the storm."

But that didn't mean they were in the clear. As Alan sat at the galley table and plotted the projected storm track, he could see that even if it did what John said, the leading edge of the storm, about three hundred miles from its center, was packing sixty-knot winds and advancing quickly toward Honolulu. At its present speed and direction, the front would reach land within thirty-six hours. They hadn't had a sun sight that day to fix their position with the sextant, but from their dead reckoning position, they were about 250 miles from Honolulu. Every hour they sat there increased the potential for them to encounter the dangerous quadrant of this hurricane.

Everyone realized the danger. The crew talked over the situation and their options: they could turn away to the north to get more sea room and try to avoid the effects of the hurricane altogether, or they could carry on, using the engine to motor through the calm until they reached the trade winds again, and hopefully get into port before the worst of the storm arrived.

Racing the hurricane front to shore appeared to be the better option, so in spite of the risk of increasing the crack in the hull, John made the decision to motor through the lull in the wind. As if to signal a turn of bad luck, when the crew dropped the sails, they discovered a rip in the genoa. At the same time, the number one battery was found to be too low to start the engine. They switched to the number two "house" battery and were happy that it had enough power left to do the job. They kept on motoring until late in the evening in a building sea, all the time accompanied by the *thump, thump, thump* of the bent propeller shaft. They continued to monitor the water level in the bilge closely and found that the water had not increased significantly all day. When the wind finally increased enough to make a reasonable speed under sail, they shifted the engine into neutral and kept it running at idle, not trusting the batteries to start it again.

Overnight the weather deteriorated further, with thickening cloud and moderate seas. In the morning, Alan was sitting at the galley table with the off-watch crew when the electric bilge pump kicked in and hummed away under his feet. He glanced at his watch. It was only a little over four minutes since the last time it had been called to duty, much shorter than the eight- to ten-minute interval earlier in the day. He looked across the cabin to John, who seemed to be listening too, and thought about the crack in the hull.

"Let's take another look at that leak before the weather gets out of hand," said John. It was clear that he had been thinking about a solution in the event the situation got worse because he added, "And pull out a couple of life jackets and a roll of duct tape."

When they opened up the access panels and again squirmed down into the recesses of the hull, the situation was obviously much worse. Water gushed up under the oil pan, splashing out from all sides like a geyser, and had accumulated to such a depth that the spinning pulley at the forward end of the engine was partly submerged. It threw a constant spray of water up against the underside of the cockpit sole so that it rained down upon them as they bent down to inspect the damage.

After a few minutes of poking about with a waterproof flashlight, John straightened up to report, "It looks as though the crack has followed the weld around the shape of the skeg. The crack is roughly oval in shape by the look of it, about four inches by an inch and a half," he said analytically. "The piece of metal that's left in the middle is moving from the force of the water going past the prop, and water is coming in around it. I can see blue water through the crack."

The crew looked at one another. Gary was the first to ask the question. "What do you want us to do?"

"Ever see the inside of one of those life jackets?" John asked. They all shook their heads. "Well, they're full of kapok—it's like cotton batting but denser—and wrapped in a watertight plastic bag. I want you to cut them open and make up a bunch of small packets. Wrap the duct tape around a handful of kapok. They need to be no smaller than two inches thick and not too tightly packed. We're going to stuff them under the oil pan from all sides to make a dam. Andy, you'll work from the port side, and I'll work from the starboard. Any questions?"

There were none, and they set to work quickly, with Alan at the wheel as they raced the storm toward Hawaii in the ten- to fifteen-foot, irregular seas.

As the work progressed, the decision had to be made to turn off the engine as the alternator was in danger of being shorted out from the constant rain of seawater. This was a risk since the batteries had proven unreliable and the crew didn't know whether they would be able to start the engine again. Aside from this uncertainty, the real downside was the need to preserve what electricity they had left, which meant manually pumping the bilge. This task was accomplished by using a two-foot-long pipe handle to operate a diaphragm pump located under the cabin sole. With the amount of water that was coming in, the water in the bilge was up to the underside of the cabin sole in about twenty minutes. To overcome the inrush of water and empty the bilge meant pumping hard for about ten minutes, or about five hundred throws of the handle. It was tiring work, and with all hands on deck, the crew took turns steering, pumping, wrapping the peculiar little packets, and resting, while John and Andy persisted with the temporary repair.

Alan wondered how long they would have to keep up this routine. They were still about seventy miles from Honolulu, and the crew was already starting to look fatigued. During one of his spells on the pump, he noticed that the water was becoming yellow. He pointed that out to John.

"That's dye from the life raft," he said. "You deploy the dye into the water if you have to abandon ship. It's used to help aircraft find the raft during a search. When we pulled the raft out of the locker so we could get at the crack, the dye pack started to leak."

Alan hadn't thought about abandoning ship—like the rest of the crew he was focused on managing the problem—but now he did. What would the loss of the dye pack mean to their chances of survival, he thought, if they had to use the raft? They were so close to their goal. It didn't seem right that they would not make it. So close. Horseshoes and hand grenades. That was the only time *close* counted. He decided to put that out of his mind and kept on pumping. John didn't seem worried. This was just one more thing to fix. They would find a way to stop the leak.

The damming of the water was not easy. Several times they had almost sealed off the inflow when the pressure of the water blew out the little kapok packets, leaving them to bob around the engine compartment like tiny lifeboats in the resulting flood of water. Over and over again, the crew refined the size and technique of making the packets until after almost three hours of work and a roll of duct tape, the water appeared to be reduced to a moderate flow. Andy extricated himself from the cramped space and stretched. "Duct tape," he declared, "the force that holds the world together! How's the pumping going, fellas?"

"Not bad," Scott replied nonchalantly. "With your dam installed, it only takes about three hundred throws to pump 'er dry. It's a walk in the park now."

The seas and wind had been building while they toiled away, and as the occasional waves began to splash over the deck, they were glad to be bolting the hatch cover down. But the situation did not look good. Over the next hour, the clouds dropped to the surface of the sea, and visibility was reduced to about half a mile. The seas grew to an incredible forty feet and were pushed into sharp crests by the increasing wind, creating short troughs between them. As before, they had to steer the boat up the side and cross the crest perfectly to prevent tumbling down the other side, and then surf down the backside at over fifteen knots and into the next trough. The winds had increased to something over forty knots, and as warm as it was, the helmsman had to wear rain gear to protect himself from the bullet-like raindrops and wind-whipped spray that assaulted him. It was demanding work, and they rotated helmsmen about every thirty minutes to prevent the fatigue that could result in a fatal mistake.

They needed to reduce the size of the jib, so they took their smallest sail, one that had had several hanks ripped out in the gale south of San Francisco, and jury-rigged it by folding the head down to the tack. They

Jury-rigged storm jib after upper hanks tore out in the gale

lashed the sail to the forestay to create an improvised tack, hoping it would hold long enough to get into port.

Down below the scene was no better. The violent motion of the boat had apparently dislodged their kapok dam, and the bilge was again filling quickly—much more quickly than before—requiring constant pumping. As Alan climbed below from one of his turns at the wheel, he found Gary at the pump, Andy and Scott sprawled out asleep on the cabin sole, and John sitting wearily on the port settee maintaining his silent vigil. They all wore their foul-weather gear and safety harnesses.

"There's coffee there if you want some," said John.

"Thanks," said Alan through a hazy consciousness.

Andy stirred at the sound of the conversation. "I was just getting up, dear," he said, wriggling around in his yellow rubber pajamas. He opened his eyes and stared up blankly, gradually realizing where he was. He sat upright and smiled. "Are we there yet?"

"Not quite," Alan replied, returning the grin, "but Wilf's at the wheel, and you're the next one to try."

"Speaking of next, your turn on the pump," said Gary and slumped into a sitting position on the cabin sole beside Andy.

Alan took the handle and started counting the strokes. With each one, about a pint of water would be shooting out the hose on the port side of the hull. He visualized this tiny amount disappearing into the vast ocean. He repeated the ancient saying "Many hands make light work," as much to convince himself as anything, and kept pumping.

"I've updated our position," said Gary. "I figure we're close—somewhere in the channel between Oahu and Molokai, which would account for these waves—but it's hard to say just how close."

The twenty-six-mile-wide Kaiwi Channel that separates the Hawaiian islands of Molokai and Oahu is one of the most treacherous and unpredictable channels in the islands, even in good weather. The trade winds blowing into this relatively shallow, narrow area commonly create thirty-foot swells. It was conditions like those that now combined with the opposing swell and winds of the approaching hurricane to produce these wild conditions.

"He's right," said John, nodding slowly. "Visibility is less than a mile. We don't want to get onto a lee shore in these conditions. On the other hand, we can't wait around here too long, or the conditions will just get worse."

"What do you suggest?" asked Alan.

"I'm going to see if there's anyone out there," he replied and moved over to the navigation station. He switched the radio over to the US Coast Guard frequency and called: "Honolulu Coast Guard Radio, Honolulu Coast Guard Radio, Honolulu Coast Guard Radio, *Second Chance, Second Chance, Second Chance*, Over." They all waited in silence for half a minute, the only sound the metronome of the bilge pump in the background. John repeated the call. There was no reply. "Could be we're too far away. Or maybe the batteries are too weak." John looked at the faces of his weary crew and then flipped back the pages of the log. He ran his finger down the page before pausing and then looking up. "Well," he said resolutely, "I guess we're going to have to do this the old-fashioned way and just discover Oahu ourselves." There was an instant brightening and smiles all round, as well as a few chuckles. "And my guess was to sight the island in …" he paused to consult his watch, "just over four hours!"

"No way!" Alan responded quickly, "two and a half!"

The debate started afresh until they were interrupted by Wilf at the helm. "Hey! I think I see it!"

There was a stampede for the companionway, a hasty untangling and clicking on of lifelines to safety harnesses, and they all emerged on deck. Sure enough, there, just a mile or two off through the mist, was the unmistakable crashing of waves on the shore. And what a sight it was! The forty-foot waves were detonating on impact with a towering cliff face and exploding extravagantly a hundred feet into the air. It was a welcome but potentially fatal sight.

"Bear away to run parallel to the shore 'til we know where we are," John ordered.

The on-watch crew trimmed the sails and steered south-southwest, while the off-watch crew went below and pored over the charts. The cloud lifted a little to reveal more of the coast, and it wasn't long before they could recognize the landforms and take some bearings to plot a position about three miles off Koko Head on the northeast side of the island of Oahu. They kept on their course down the channel until they cleared the southeastern tip of the island, and as they did, the waves subsided considerably and the cloud lifted to reveal patches of blue. They gybed and cleared the point off Diamond Head crater by about five miles, sailing westerly and coming into the lee of the ancient volcano. More of the shore became visible, and all hands were on deck to witness their "discovery" of the island.

As they turned the corner, the air suddenly became much warmer, and they were overwhelmed by an unfamiliar aroma. It was land—land and all its trappings. There was soil and water and trees and strange flowers—and, Andy insisted, cold beer. This seemed like a reasonable time to break out the champagne to toast their success and claim this foreign land for Canada. At least it seemed reasonable at the time. An extra ration of bubbly went to Wilf, who had the double distinction of sighting land and being closest in his estimate of the time of sighting it.

It took almost two hours for them to reach the entry to Ala Wai Harbor, and all of that time to prepare the boat for arrival. They were all weary, but they turned to the work enthusiastically—even the nonstop pumping—until the leak was staunched once more and the boat was cleaned and shipshape, the lines and fenders were at the ready, and the anchor was retrieved from the lazarette and secured at the bow, just in case. The remaining battery did its duty and started the engine as they approached the channel, saving them the task of sailing into the harbor.

Second Chance pulled alongside the fuel dock in the bright sunshine that fought its way through the heavy clouds. Scott and Gary stepped onto the dock with the bow and stern lines, swaying a little unsteadily on the unaccustomed terra firma. Alan and Andy followed with the spring lines, Andy laughing at the strange feeling. Wilf joined them to plug the electrical cord into the shore power to run the bilge pump, and then they all stood on the dock, each rocking slightly, still wearing their foul-weather gear so that they appeared like a flock of scruffy, flightless birds on their rookery.

John enjoying champagne to celebrate the discovery of Oahu

Second Chance on arrival in Ala Wai Harbor

Andy indicating the hole in the hull of *Second Chance*

"What's the first thing you're going to do when we go ashore?" asked Andy.

"Shower," Alan replied. "A two-hour, soak-to-the-bone, hot, delicious shower."

"Thank Christ!" Gary responded sarcastically. "It's about time. Me, I'm going to find an ice-cold beer or two and a large pepperoni pizza."

"Can't stand all the healthy food, eh?" Scott teased. "I'm going to have a short nap to restore my strength and then head down to Waikiki Beach and see the sights."

"I will get a hotel room with clean sheets," said Wilf. "What about you, Andy?"

"Well, first I'm gonna call my honey back home, and then I'm going straight up to that yacht club there and order a jug of mai tais."

John stepped off the boat wearing his going-ashore clothes and carrying a briefcase, looking very businesslike. "Well, you characters are going to have to wait to live out your fantasies until I've gone up to the office to clear Customs, Immigration, and Health," he proclaimed. "They're going to want to go through the boat, so don't go anywhere until I get back."

The crew loafed about on the dock, enjoying beer from the cooler. The thousand pounds of ice in the forepeak had all but melted, leaving only enough slushy residue to keep the beer slightly below tropical temperature. They relived exciting moments from the trip, all the while shuffling about uncomfortably. It took awhile before the full effect of the fatigue and the land sickness, with its creeping nausea, took hold of some of them.

"I think I'll wait for Customs on the boat," Alan suggested idly and climbed back aboard.

"Yeah, me too," said Andy.

"Hmff," Gary responded. "Took us a month to get here and now you want to go back aboard."

But before long, he and the rest of the crew were back in the cockpit, more comfortable with the motion of the boat, and the happy banter continued. Very soon the exhaustion of the past twenty-four hours and the effect of the beer overtook them, and one by one they succumbed to sleep. The pleasures of the tropics would have to wait.

Part Four

The Professionals

Chapter 22

―◆―✦✦―◆―

All Roads Lead to the Waikiki Yacht Club

Waikiki Yacht Club, September 1982

The halyards rattled against the masts of the two hundred or more yachts moored at the Waikiki Yacht Club in Honolulu. It was a hot day, in spite of the fresh breeze, and Bob was finishing up work on the forty-six-foot yacht *Red Witch* and looking forward to a cold beer. He had done a lot of work on this elegant Peterson-designed ketch for its owner, "Slim" Lambert. When Slim had met Bob, he had found both a kindred spirit and a friend who could give the care and attention to his beloved boat that he had given her himself. Slim was well known around Hawaii as a self-made millionaire. Then in his seventies, he'd given Bob a blank check to maintain the boat as he saw fit, and Bob returned this trust by keeping it in Bristol fashion. The real payoff for Bob, though, was joining Slim and his family on their Sunday sails off Waikiki Beach and trips around the Hawaiian Islands. He and Slim had developed a firm friendship and mutual respect.

A gruff old dude, Slim started his career as a cowboy in Arizona in the early thirties. He had looked forward to making his life in the ranching business there, but he told Bob that life changed for him when he was falsely accused by the foreman of the ranch of making inappropriate advances to his wife. Deciding that discretion was the better part of valor, Slim chose to move on. With a taste for adventure, he headed north to Alaska and got a job at a salmon canning factory. There were workers from all over the world there trying to make their fortunes, with Chinese immigrants forming the largest ethnic population. They were fast and efficient and dominated the processing lines.

Being handy with equipment, Slim was assigned the job of keeping the machinery going. This was no small feat. When something got jammed, the whole rig would seize up and spray fish parts all over the place. At that point, the drone of the machinery was replaced by the bedlam of curses, which he knew were not complimentary since the crew was paid based on their production.

Slim soon discovered how expensive it was to live in Alaska, so to save money, like most people at the cannery, he lived on canned salmon. By the time he left, he had three forty-five-gallon drums outside his bunkhouse full of empty salmon cans. He often said that he couldn't look a salmon in the eye after that. Besides the cost of living, Slim just didn't see a career in the salmon business with the way it was run. At times the catch far outstripped the capacity of the processors, and the company just took whole barges full of salmon out to sea and dumped them. Slim saw this terrible waste and realized that he wouldn't make his fortune there.

After working just long enough to set aside some "running money," Slim headed back south to San Francisco. He found a job there as a high-steel rigger, first on the construction of the Bay Bridge and then on the Golden Gate Bridge. From the vantage point of this famous landmark, Slim saw the sailing vessels and commercial ships coming and going. It was then that he decided that one day he would sail his own yacht to Tahiti.

The construction of the span over the Golden Gate Strait took just over four years, and for most of that time the project had an impressive safety record. *Timelines of History* provides information that this was largely due to the chief engineer on the project, who "... was determined to use the most rigorous safety precautions available. Protective hardhats and glare-free goggles were required and special diets were developed to combat dizziness. But it was the safety net strung under the bridge during construction that saved the lives of nineteen men who became known as the 'Half-Way-to-Hell' Club." In fact, as the San Francisco *Chronicle* reported, until February 17, 1937, just months before it was complete, only one life had been lost.

On that day, Slim was heading up a crew that was working on a movable scaffold suspended under the bridge deck. This platform was used to strip the formwork from the underside of the concrete roadway, one of the last jobs that remained for them. Slim told Bob that without warning, the ten-ton scaffold broke loose, and he dived off it into the safety net below, followed by the plunging platform. The stout rope used to make the net was intended to hold the weight of a man, but it couldn't support this huge weight. The platform tore the whole safety net from the bridge, sending Slim and eleven others plummeting with it 250 feet into the bay. Slim clung to the net until he got close to the water and then somehow got clear of it and hit the water feetfirst. He was one of only two men that survived the fall.

Floating there in the ice-cold water with breaks to a collarbone, a couple of ribs, and several vertebrae, as well as a dislocated shoulder and two injured ankles, he spotted one of his crew, alive but also badly injured, and managed to grab hold of him. He collected some bits of timber from the shattered scaffold as they floated by him and used them to keep the two of them afloat. Then he saw a body floating vertically with its feet in the air. He recognized by the boots that it was one of his close friends and somehow managed to swim over to assist him. It was too late, but forty-five minutes later, when a fisherman who had seen the accident and gone searching for survivors finally found the three of them, Slim was still supporting the body of his lifeless friend. The injured man died on the way to shore, leaving Slim as the only survivor of the tragedy.

After the accident, the company gave Slim twenty dollars for his troubles and told him that if he wasn't back to work in ten days, he'd be out of a job. At this point, he decided that it was time for another career change, so when he had recovered, he set his sights on Tahiti. He only got as far as Hawaii because he met a girl.

Her name was Eleanor, but everyone knew her as "Cotton." She was engaged to someone when they met, but Slim convinced her to marry him instead. He was working for the Hawaii Electric Company at the time but didn't have much beyond his charm and his reputation to offer her. Fortunately for him, he was a pretty good cardplayer, and when times were tough, he would make some extra money playing poker. Some nights he would call Cotton and tell her that he wouldn't be home for a while and he'd play poker all night, showing up the next morning with a pocket full of cash.

Cotton was a pretty good cook and Slim was a natural entrepreneur, so they decided to set up their first business, a small hamburger stand on a street where the Ala Wai Canal is now located. It was hard work and long days, but they persevered. Things were cheaper back then, of course, and they'd go home to their apartment every night and count the nickels and dimes on the bed. They saved their money until they could make a down payment on a small apartment building. It wasn't long, however, before Slim found out that he wasn't cut out to be a landlord, and he went looking for other opportunities.

The attack on Pearl Harbor forced a change of thinking for him, but whether it was a reprieve for surviving the fall from the bridge or because his steel-working skills were valuable on the home front—he was never sure—he wasn't accepted into the military. Instead, he spent the duration of the war fabricating huge steel fuel tanks that still mark the western waterfront near the Aloha Tower. At the end of the war, he and a friend got one of the contracts to clear out the debris and hulks from the west lock of Pearl Harbor. They worked long and hard to complete it, and when they finished, he'd learned an enormous amount about ships and the ocean and had over ten thousand dollars in the bank, more money than he had ever seen.

Slim was a visionary and recognized the potential for tourism in Hawaii, particularly on the water. Having now developed some experience in that area, he saw the opportunity for tourist boats. Before long, he was awarded the first commercial license to take tourists inside Pearl Harbor. His company, "Hawaiian Cruises," led the way in the offshore tourist industry in Hawaii, offering glass-bottom boat rides and dinner cruises off Waikiki beach and in Kaneohe Bay. Some of the early boats were converted navy boats, but when he was able to afford it, he had purpose-built boats constructed on the US mainland. He sailed them across to Hawaii himself, sometimes with his family. Slim told Bob that these boats were as ugly as sin, but they carried lots of paying passengers.

True to his dream, Slim bought a series of small sailboats and finally made his voyage to Tahiti in one of them. This, too, was a learning experience, as the leaky old boat required the constant exercise of the bilge pumps. He later reported that it was a pretty impressive sight to stand below and watch the water squirt through the seams between the planks like fire hoses when she punched through the big waves. This taught him an important lesson, and he soon acquired *Silver Sword*, a solid seagoing sloop. Strangely, he lost this yacht not by misfortune but by integrity. Slim was a shrewd businessman, but prided himself on his honesty. One day he was messing about with the yacht at the dock when a man walking by stopped to admire it. After exchanging a few pleasantries, the man told him that he'd like to buy the yacht and inquired how much Slim would take for it. Without giving much thought to it, Slim named a price that was far more than he thought he would ever get, thinking that this would put this trifler off. It was a rude surprise when the stranger agreed and extended his hand to seal the deal. Well, Slim was stuck because he was always as good as his word, so *Silver Sword* was sold. Slim said that this was ironically the only boat he ever sold that he got the price he asked.

The Waikiki Yacht Club was a playground for sailors, both young and old, and even with four children of his own, Slim gave generously of his time to help them. His various yachts were often used at the start or finish lines for races, although Slim preferred to be at the second mark with the boats bearing down on him, spinnakers flying, to watch them rounding the mark, some professionally, some not so professionally. He especially liked the club's program to take out mentally handicapped children, providing them with an experience that was often only available to tourists.

As Slim aged, he had naturally become less agile, aging being one challenge that even he could not beat. He expressed the problem to Bob in his straightforward way: "The worst thing about getting old is that you get as weak as a chicken." Still, he had done everything that he had set out to do, even owning his own ranch. He was almost sixty when he fulfilled his dream by founding the 6L Ranch on Oahu to raise horses and cattle, and went on to promote rodeos and travel around the circuit with them.

It was with these memories in mind that Bob sauntered up the dock to the bar of the yacht club. This had been a thirsty day, and he settled himself in at a table to recuperate. He was on to his second cold beer and just starting to relax when he happened to glance across to the main door as it opened and found himself looking straight into the face of Andrew Clubb. Bob stood up as Andrew approached. "Shit! The last time I saw you was aboard the *Ron* in Suva. I didn't expect to see you here!" exclaimed Bob with a smile, shaking hands.

"I was looking for you!" Andrew replied with a grin.

"Well, come and sit down. How the hell'd you find me?"

"It wasn't too hard," replied Andrew sarcastically.

Bob smiled again and laughed. "Well, what are you doing here?" he asked.

"I'm on my way home. I've been down in Taiwan. I'm having a new boat built—a Holland 51—and I wanted to check on how it was going."

"What are you doing with the *Ron*?"

"You know how I love that boat," Andrew said with a sentimental edge to his voice, "but I just can't see keeping the two of them. I want to get it up to Los Angeles to sell it."

"Where is it now?"

"Peter's sitting on it down in Vava'u." He leaned forward, placing an elbow on the table, and lowered his voice, as if sharing a secret. "What about you going down to Tonga and bringing it back here?"

"I could," Bob replied in a speculative tone. He turned and gazed out across the forest of masts, the high-rise hotels, and the busy waterfront, contemplating for a moment. He had been ashore for a while now, and he knew that this would be a chance for him to renew his association with the sea. He turned back to Andrew and looked him in the eye. "Cross my palm with silver, and I'm sure we can come to an agreement," he said, smiling broadly at the prospect of the negotiation.

Andrew brightened and pushed himself back from the table. "Good!" he said. "I'll get us a couple of drinks, and we'll see if we can't work something out."

Over the next couple of hours and a good deal of alcohol, they hammered out the terms of the agreement. Bob was left with the task of finding more crew to help with the delivery.

———

The next boat basin over from the Waikiki Yacht Club was the Ala Wai State Marina. It was early the next morning that Alan approached the dock where his friend Michael's yacht was moored. Alan had sailed over to Maui with Michael and another friend and spent two weeks anchored off Kaanapali Beach. They had a great time there, snorkeling off Black Rock and meeting lots of people on shore. Among the fun-loving people Alan had met was a girl who, unbeknownst to him, was the girlfriend of a New York mobster. Alan had suddenly found himself in grave danger when the mobster back at home discovered what his girlfriend was up to and sent one of his lieutenants to deal with them. Alan had to make a very quick departure from a discotheque late one night and swim back to the yacht. He spent the final days of their trip on board. He didn't know how far the angry gangster would go to get even and didn't want to find out.

The yacht was three slips along on the left, moored bow-to, and he had a clear view of it as he walked down the ramp. Michael was talking to someone in the cockpit. The other person's back was to him, but the broad shoulders and a head of white hair were unfamiliar, making Alan hesitate for a moment. He had not imagined that the gangster would pursue him from Maui, but seeing the stranger made him wonder. Before he could reconsider, Michael spotted him and waved, so he continued apprehensively toward the yacht. He passed around the bow and along the finger that ran beside it.

"Hey, Al. Howzit?" Michael called out in Hawaiian slang as he approached.

"Okay, Michael," he replied, stopping at the boarding gate. "What's up?"

The stranger was sitting on the starboard side of the cockpit, facing him now. He wore a faded red T-shirt with a discrete white script where a breast pocket would be that read "Paradise International Hotel." Alan looked into the noncommittal stare of the ice-blue eyes.

"Come aboard. Meet a friend of mine, Bob Rossiter."

"G'day, mate," said Bob, standing.

"How are you?" replied Alan, slipping off his flip-flops and climbing aboard. He stepped down into the cockpit and shook the large, calloused hand. He sized Bob up, estimating him to be about six-foot-two, 220 pounds. He looked fit but probably not fast in a foot race. He hoped he wouldn't have to find out. Alan sat himself down beside the boarding gate. "Where are you from?" he asked.

"New Zealand. But I live in L.A. most of the time."

Alan looked steadily into the emotionless eyes, searching for a hint of this man's intent.

Bob continued, "Michael was telling me that you've done some sailing."

"Yeah, some. I guess he told you about our trip to Maui."

"Yeah, he told me about your escapade." Bob smiled and the eyes twinkled.

Alan relaxed a little. "Don't believe everything you hear," he replied guardedly.

"Well, *one hand for yourself, one hand for the ship*, as they say. It sounds like you came out of it all right."

More at ease now, Alan gave his version of the story, leaving out some of the more incriminating details. Bob chuckled at the conclusion. "Sounds like you're lucky to have evaded the polyester-suited land sharks!"

"It's certainly something I won't forget in a hurry, that's for sure!"

They exchanged more stories for a while, and Alan had the feeling that he was being quietly evaluated. Then Bob got down to the point. "Ever been to Samoa?"

"Nope. Don't even know where the hell it is!"

"Want to come down and deliver a boat up to Hawaii with me and a couple of other guys?"

Alan thought for a moment. The mob was still very much on his mind, and surely they had never heard of Samoa either. "Sure," he said, and then added decisively, "when do we leave?"

"Real soon," Bob answered. "I'm leaving tomorrow for Tonga to pick up the boat. I'll call you with the details. Where can I get hold of you?"

Alan gave Bob the number, and he scribbled it into a well-worn notebook. "Morning is best."

"Good. I'll arrange a ticket for you. You can pick it up from S.P.I.A.," he said, pronouncing this acronym *spee-ah* like a commonly understood word.

"Who?"

"South Pacific Island Airways."

Alan thought for a moment. "Where is it?"

"Down on Nimitz Highway."

"No, I mean Samoa."

"It's about a five-hour flight south-southwest—in the middle of nowhere. Now," Bob changed the subject to matters of more importance, "I need you to pick up some gear I've ordered from Ala Wai Marine. Don't leave without the engine-driven bilge pump!" he said emphatically. He tore a page out of the notebook and handed it to Alan.

Alan read it over. "Anything else?"

"I'll give you a list of some other small shit, but that's the guts of it."

Back in Vava'u, Peter had been alone on the boat for about three weeks. One afternoon, as he was making his way up the steps from the jetty to the bar for happy hour, Carter Johnson spotted him from the roof. He took off his welding visor and called out in his deep southern drawl, "Pete, there's a telegram for you. I left it with the barman." This had apparently seemed the most reliable place that Peter would be found during the day—quite correctly, as it turned out.

"Thanks, Carter!" he called back with a wave. Peter continued around to the bar, and as he walked in, the barman gestured to him.

"Peter," he said with a big smile, "I've got a telegram for you."

"Yeah, I just saw Carter on the way up. He told me." The barman handed an envelope to him across the bar. Peter took it and looked at it inquisitively. "Thanks, mate," he said. "You'd better give me a double gin and tonic while you're at it." He smiled back. "Keep the malaria away."

Peter held the small, square envelope flat between the thumb and forefinger of one hand and spun it absentmindedly with the flick of the other hand, chatting with the barman while he mixed the drink and set it down in front of him. He knocked back half the drink before regarding the telegram again. Peter put down the glass and tore open the side of the envelope. He pulled out the small piece of paper that was inside and unfolded it to see that it was addressed to him, care of the Paradise International Hotel. A smile spread across his face as he read: "EXPECT HOLLYWOOD BOB SOON STOP ANDREW."

Chapter 23

The Grave

Bob and Peter finished up their dinner onboard the *Ron* and were sitting around the main saloon having a coffee. They had begun to prepare the yacht for the trip to Samoa and had put in a full day's labor. Weary, Peter stretched and contemplated, "I think I'm going to have an early night tonight, Bob."

Bob mused for a moment and then replied, "In that case, I reckon I'll pay my respects to the chief and maybe take a stroll over the hill to the next village to visit a friend."

Peter raised his eyebrows, knowingly. "Ah yes! And should I expect you back tonight?"

"Probably," he replied with a smile, "but don't wait up!"

Bob cleaned himself up and was soon ambling along the road past the Paradise International Hotel toward the local village. It was a balmy evening, with a light tropical breeze that sweetened the air with the aroma of frangipanis and jostled the palms lining his route, causing the shadows cast by the moon to dance along the road. The cheerful sounds of the hotel bar dropped away as he went and finally disappeared. He walked on in silence until he reached the village. The chief greeted him warmly, and Bob expressed his pleasure at being in Vava'u again. They talked briefly, and before leaving, the chief invited Bob to join the village men for their kava ceremony the following night, which Bob graciously accepted.

The route to the neighboring village took Bob a little farther along the main road to a junction where he turned into a narrow grass track. It was cut from the lush tropical undergrowth and worn from the footsteps of the villagers. It ran straight for about half a mile between towering coconut trees, giving the impression of a long tunnel, and it took Bob a few seconds for his eyes to become accustomed to the diminished light. Overhead the moon filtered through the palm fronds, creating tiger-striped patterns on the ground that trembled before him in the breeze. It was quiet, except for the occasional disturbance in the bushes as he walked by and the rustling of the banana leaves where the breeze managed to penetrate the cloak of the undergrowth. The dank smell of the decomposing vegetation rose with the fall of the night and filled his nostrils. As he strode along, a flock of fruit bats emerged from their hiding place, making their strange intermittent squeaks and screeching sounds as they swarmed through the treetops in search of their food, the beat of their broad wings creating a choir of gasps in the dark.

Partway along the path, there was the village graveyard set off to one side. The moonlight peeked down into the clearing, casting still shadows across the graves farthest from the track. There were a few dozen graves there, widely spaced and consisting of mounds of coral stones. Each was decorated in a personalized way with sand and shells by the surviving families. The graves of some of the more prominent occupants were also circled with brown beer bottles, upturned and pushed into the ground. The oldest ones had been built up by dutiful relatives over generations, reaching a height of over six feet and standing like sentinels of the dead.

As Bob approached the graveyard, he was surprised to hear the sound of distant voices behind him and turned to see the faint silhouette of what appeared to be two villagers entering the track. This was unusual since Bob knew that the Tongan people were very superstitious, the missionaries having instilled in them a fear of the dead. Since the missionaries' arrival,

Graveyard near Neiafu, Vava'u Islands, Kingdom of Tonga

many stories had developed, including that of restless spirits emerging from the graves at night. There were tales of ghosts drifting in and out of the surrounding trees and terrifying anyone who happened to pass by, so it was very rare for the villagers to pass a graveyard at night. Inspired, Bob quickly stepped off the path and looked around at the newest graves that were nearby. He selected the closest one, about two feet high, which was easily seen from the track. With a devilish grin, he lay on his back on top of the grave with his arms by his sides.

As the two villagers approached the graveyard, he could hear them raise their voices and pick up speed to bolster each other's confidence against the dreaded "deovolo." When they came abreast of him, Bob let out a low, bloodcurdling wail. The two startled young men looked over, and as they did, Bob slowly sat up, appearing to rise from the grave, his arms and crooked fingers held out threateningly in front of him. The moon glinting off his platinum hair illuminated his head like a specter. He turned in their direction to see their reaction, but they had already fled at an astonishing speed. Swinging his legs around and standing up, he dusted himself off, paid his respects to the incumbent, and chuckling to himself, strolled over to the track. By the time he got there, the young men were nowhere in sight.

When Bob finally sauntered into the village, he found it eerily quiet. There were no dogs, pigs, or people in sight, and he thought for the moment as he walked among the *fales* that he might have caused such fright in the village that he had scared them all away! He was relieved when he arrived at his friend's *fale* to find that she was indeed at home.

The sky was just beginning to lighten as Bob walked back down the track. Despite having had little sleep, he had a spring in his step. He smiled as he passed the graveyard, remembering the reaction of the two lads to his hoax, and wondered what tales they would tell about the event.

———

Bob returned to the local village that evening for the kava ceremony. Sitting on the woven pandanus mats for the traditional "fai kava," Bob spoke idly with the village men. After a time, the talk turned to the misadventure of two young men who were visiting from the neighboring village. As they began their tale, it dawned on Bob who they were. The two told of a harrowing experience the night before, where they had narrowly escaped the clutches of the deovolo. Bob sat in silence while they told and retold their tale. He hadn't realized that he would inadvertently find himself at the Tongan academy awards, where he was the only candidate, and hoped he wouldn't receive it posthumously.

With the flow of the kava, the young men's embellishments of the story increased. In their final telling of it, the deovolo had risen out of the graveyard and pursued them down the path. He had come so close that one of the lads claimed that he had felt the devil's fiery breath so hot on his back that it had singed his T-shirt. Bob decided not to make them aware that the devil himself was in fact seated among them, for fear of raising their ire and becoming a permanent fixture in the same graveyard. Instead, before he left, he thanked the young men for the warning and told them that their telling of the tale made him feel as though he had actually been there.

Chapter 24

━━━━━◆◇✕◇◆━━━━━

Do You Smoke?

Peter and Don Coleman stood side by side on the foredeck and leaned forward together to take a fresh grip on the heavy, five-eighths-inch anchor chain. Over the throbbing of the engine, Peter called, "Heave!" With that, they pulled together on the chain, arms straight and lifting with their legs, straightening as they did so. The chain rattled over the bow roller and turned the drum of the anchor windlass, the slack falling behind them through the spillpipe and into the anchor locker below deck. After repeating this procedure three more times, the chain was taut. Bracing himself and pulling hard on the chain, Peter grunted to Don through clenched teeth, "Can't get any more! Put the brake on!"

Don quickly reached forward and pulled back on the long lever to lock the anchor windlass. This electric windlass was the only "modern" equipment on the yacht and had been installed by a previous owner. Unfortunately it wasn't strong enough to pull you out of bed, so its sole use was to lock the anchor chain in place when raising or lowering the anchor.

Peter relaxed and stood up to look over the bow to see the direction of the chain. He extended his arm in front of him and about twenty degrees to port to indicate the direction of the anchor. Bob was at the

208

helm and put the engine into gear. He nudged the throttle and turned the tiller, easing the *Ron* in the direction of the anchor. He eased back on the throttle, knocked the engine out of gear again, and let the *Ron* coast forward as Peter and Don heaved in the slack chain again. After fifteen minutes of this backbreaking work, the anchor hung directly below the bow, and Peter waved to indicate that they had broken the anchor free. Bob threw the engine into gear and swung the bow away from shore. With five steady heaves, Don and Peter retrieved the last three fathoms of chain, and the stem of the sixty-pound CQR anchor slid over the bow roller. They removed the chain, and together they carried the anchor to the stern and stowed it in the anchor locker. With the ground tackle stowed, they were ready for sea.

As the *Ron* made way down the harbor, Don sat down in the cockpit to rest after the exertion, sweat dripping down his face and into his bushy black beard. He rubbed his swollen ankles and looked over his shoulder to the shore. His wife and daughters stood outside the Paradise International Hotel, waving their farewell. He climbed out onto the aft deck to wave and then returned to the cockpit.

Bob looked over to Don and asked, "How's the legs feeling, Don?"

"A little sore, but boy, do I feel great!" he said with a grin, the white of his teeth revealed from behind the beard. "It's good to be at sea again."

The swelling in Don's knees and ankles resulted from the close call that he had with death several years earlier. He had been working as a commercial scuba diver in the Marshall Islands in Micronesia and had suffered the bends while returning to the surface. The nitrogen gas remaining in the "slow" tissues like the bone marrow can form bubbles when a diver surfaces too quickly and causes excruciating pain unless the victim can be quickly repressurized. Even worse, bubbles that form in the blood can lodge in the brain, causing an embolism and resulting in a painful death. With no recompression chamber nearby and days away from a medical facility, he was lucky to have escaped with his life, but the damaged joints were a painful reminder that would continue to restrict his movements. An accomplished shipwright, Don now made his home in Vava'u, and this was his first return to sea since the accident.

"There's no breeze, so let's get the main up, and we'll center it until we get out of the harbor," Bob said.

Peter and Don moved up to the mainmast, Peter taking the throat halyard and Don loosening the peak halyard on the pin rail.

"Ready!" Peter called back to the cockpit.

"Anytime, fellas!" Bob called back.

Raising the mainsail on a gaff rig has to be closely coordinated. The two halyards have to be hauled simultaneously, with the gaff on an angle to prevent jamming the throat of the gaff into the mast. "Ready, Don?" asked Peter.

"All set. I'll take it up a few feet." Don reached up with both hands and hauled down the halyard.

"That's good, Don. Now, together!"

They hauled the halyards in unison, lifting the four-inch-diameter gaff and the heavy sail up in stages. When the gaff neared the top, Don tied off the peak halyard around his belaying pin with a figure eight and then came around to help Peter sweat up the throat halyard. Don secured the free end of the halyard around the belaying pin for extra purchase, and then Peter grasped the halyard at shoulder height and pulled the halyard like a bowstring away from the mast, using the mechanical advantage this maneuver generated to make some slack. This action raised the sail a little and lifted the end of the eight-inch-diameter Douglas-fir boom from its crutch. Don took up this slack, and they repeated this motion twice more before the luff of the sail was taut.

"That's it, Don," Peter puffed. "Let's finish off the peak."

Bob eased in the mainsheet to stop the movement of the boom while Peter and Don moved to the port side to take up the last of the slack in the peak halyard, and then they set to coiling and securing the halyards. When they had finished, they returned to the cockpit.

"Nice work, boys," said Bob. "Take it easy for a few minutes. We'll get the foresail up when we get farther out."

The breeze had come up by the time they passed the main wharf. From below, Peter heaved the bag with the number two sail through the hatch onto the foredeck and scrambled out after it. He pulled the sail out of the bag, hanked it onto the forestay, and secured it to the lifelines with a short piece of line to prevent it from blowing over the side. He tossed the sail bag down the forward hatch, turned aft to remove the sail cover from the staysail, and sent it below as well. Next he picked up the jib sheets that they had run from the cockpit down the port and starboard sides of the deck and rove through the heavy blocks secured to the deck. He quickly tied them to the clew of the foresail using bowline knots and checked that all the running rigging was in place.

"All set up for'd skipper!" he called.

"Stand by, mate!" Bob replied. "Ready, Don?"

"You bet, Bob!"

"All right—hoist away!"

Peter stood by with the foresail halyard free from its cleat on the mast, and at Bob's order, reached over and pulled the slipknots securing the foresail to the lifelines. He clapped onto the halyard as high as he could with both hands and heaved down to the level of his knees. The sail responded by shooting up the forestay an equal distance, the bronze hanks making a metallic "zing" sound against the wire stay. Without pausing, he reached up hand over hand to his maximum height before hauling down again. The hanks repeated their song, louder now as the sail rose, and more of them joined in, with the exposed luff of the sail flapping a happy chorus. After the next heave, Don began to take up the slack on the sheet in lengths, edging the heavy foot of the sail along the wooden deck with a baritone scraping sound. This orchestra continued in rhythm, Peter and Don alternating their tones and the luff approaching a crescendo as the sail reached toward its apex. With the bow of the *Ron* just off the wind, the bulk of the sail stretched out behind Peter, undulating in a lazy wave. The full weight of the sail was now bearing on the halyard, so he took a quick wrap around the wooden cleat to jam it from moving and Don stopped hauling in the sheet.

Peter began the next musical movement by sweating up the halyard, pulling outward with one hand and then taking up the slack with the other. The sail inched up each time, the halyard squeaking in its soprano voice as it was pulled around the wooden cleat. With a steady tempo, he sweated the sail up, finally finishing the composition when the halyard would no longer respond.

"That's it, Bob!" he called. He tied off the halyard, coiled it up, and secured it. Don took up the last of the slack of the sheet and cleated it off. With everything secured, Bob eased the *Ron* off the wind, and the luffing sound was replaced by the smooth flow of the wind over the surface of the sails.

The *Ron* slid past the distinctive flattop mountain, Talau, which marked the entrance to Neiafu Harbour, and headed down the passage lined each side by the small, steep-sided islands of Lotuma, Utungake, Kapa, and Nuapapu. As they passed Swallows Cave, they adjusted course to leave Nuapapu and Hunga Islands to the port. They could clearly see the rusted remains of a large, corrugated metal church roof on Hunga Island, where it had been unceremoniously dumped by a hurricane several years before, over two miles from the village church that it had sheltered. They emerged from the islands after a couple of hours, hoisted the mizzen, and set their course for American Samoa, some 350 nautical miles to the north-northeast. The crew trimmed the sails for a beam reach and settled into the shipboard routine, which included checking the bilge every hour. They were happy to find that the amount of water coming in was easily handled by the new automatic bilge pump that Bob had brought with him from Hawaii.

Later that night, the sky clouded over and darkened in an ominous boiling motion. As the system approached, flashes of lightning lit the horizon. The rumble of thunder woke Bob. He rolled out of his bunk and climbed the companionway to the cockpit to see Peter at the tiller.

"What's going on, Bucko?"

"Have a go at the lightning! It looks like World War III!"

Bob studied the horizon for a moment. "It looks like it's not going to slip down the side of us. We're going to have to go through this shit."

"I reckon. If we have to sail through the middle of that shit, we're liable to come out the other side looking like a couple of burned potato chips."

"We'd better get some sail off the old girl. Give Don a call, and we'll take the main right out of it and just sit here quietly under the jib and mizzen." Bob took the helm while Peter went below.

Peter returned a few minutes later with his foul-weather gear, and just in time too, as a tropical downpour descended on them. It was curiously not the kind of conditions that you might expect from the foreboding darkness because, although the rain was heavy, there was not much wind. Peter hunched forward and drew his hood down as far as he could to protect himself, one hand on the tiller and an eye on the compass.

Don climbed up the companionway, sleepy and rumpled from being roused out of his bunk. Peter didn't see him as he stepped into the cockpit until a flash of lightning suddenly illuminated him, reinforced by an almost simultaneous, bone-rattling clap of thunder. Peter was startled at this image of a demon with messy hair and huge bushy beard.

"Holy shit!" Peter exclaimed, agape. "You look like a messenger from hell, Don! I hope you're not an omen of what's ahead!"

The crew worked quickly to shorten sail and secure the deck. The system approached fast and a rain continued to fall, but surprisingly the state of the sea and wind still didn't worsen appreciably. As the system descended upon them, Bob turned to the other two. "Christ!" he exclaimed. "Have a look at those clouds. They're as black as the inside of a cow's guts!"

Within minutes, lightning and thunder crashed around them, surrounding the boat like the Normandy invasion. It was everywhere, huge daggers of lightning stabbing through the sky. Less than a quarter of a mile ahead of the boat, a lightning bolt with a jillion megawatts blasted from the sky and erupted in a geyser sixty feet high. The concussion from the thunderclap shook the boat from end to end. In unison, the crew unconsciously tucked their heads down between hunched shoulders and closed their eyes.

Bob called out, "That last flash was so bright it lit up the inside of my eyeballs!"

"Holy shit!" exclaimed Peter again, in what seemed like the only appropriate expression.

Don cast an eye aloft at the lightning rod at the masthead, which was, in theory, designed to direct any lightning strike through a heavy cable that ran down the mast and over the side of the hull into the sea. He turned and gave Bob a quizzical look, as if to say, "Do you think that damned thing will do any good?" His unspoken question was answered only by a shrug of the shoulders.

"Why don't you two go below, and I'll finish my watch," called out Peter. "If you come up for your watch and see a black crust burned to the tiller, you'll know it's me!"

"Might as well," said Bob, "but let us know if you get hit. Give us a bit of a scream or something."

"I don't know if I'll have time! You'll probably smell me!"

Don climbed down the companionway and tried to get some sleep amid the pandemonium. Bob decided to sleep in the doghouse at deck level and put on his foul-weather gear and a big orange sou'wester in case he was needed on deck.

"Shit, Bob, you look like a gigantic orange mushroom!" said Peter with a laugh.

Bob checked on Peter from time to time over the next two hours. Each time, he found him hunched over the tiller, shrouded in his foul-weather gear, looking like the Ghost of Christmas Past, but with no obvious smell of smoking Aussie. Finally, when the worst of the storm had passed over them, Bob came back on deck.

"Well, you still smell normal, mate. Thank Christ the lightning rod didn't attract anything!" he declared with a smile.

"What do you think would have happened?"

"It probably would have turned the mast into toothpicks! You hungry?"

"Yeah!"

"Good, because Don's below whipping up some grub."

"What's he making?"

"One of my favorites—canned corned mutton and mashed potatoes."

Peter groaned, "Well, even that sounds good to me right now."

"We'll rip into it, and then put some more sail up on this old girl and get moving."

On the following day, there was very little breeze, and the sea was calm. The *Ron* was ghosting along under spinnaker and a mizzen staysail, making barely three knots. Peter was dozing on a sail bag on the foredeck in the shade of the spinnaker, immersed in the comforting sounds of the workings of the boat. There was a low babbling sound as the bow cut through the water, the blocks lifting and falling on the wooden deck with each puff of the wind, the low groaning of the sheets from the tension of the sails, and the gentle rocking of the boat from side to side.

Bob was in the cockpit, leaning back against the combing with his foot on the tiller, watching ahead. Something in the distance caught his eye, and after staring at it for a moment, a perplexed look crossed his face. He stood up to get a better look, but still wasn't able to make it out.

"Hey, Don," he called out. "Bring up the binoculars, will yer? I want you to check something out!"

A few moments later, Don stepped into the cockpit. "What do you see, Bob?"

"I can't work it out. There's some sort of shit in the water about half a mile ahead. See what you can make of it, will yer?"

Don looked through the binoculars and said, "I can't make it out either, Bob. There's a bit of a smooth patch, like an oil slick with some kind of debris."

"That's fucking weird," Bob said, frowning. "Maybe a boat went down in the lightning storm last night. Let's take a closer look. Get Pete to give you a hand to sheet in the sails, and I'll head up a bit."

Don stood with one arm hooked around the aft port shroud and stared through the binoculars while Peter climbed up the ratlines to get a better look. As they drew closer, Bob called out to them, "I'm going to just run down the side of it. What do you see?"

"It looks like oil all right!" Don called back. "It's about fifty yards across."

"And it looks like big chunks of fish floating around in it!" added Peter. "Some are pretty big, and boy, does it smell!"

They came abeam, about thirty feet from the edge of the oil. The closest chunks were still twenty or thirty feet farther off, spread throughout the oil.

"I'm going to take us in a little closer," Bob called to them. As he did, they could just make out the detail of the lumps. "That's what's left of a giant squid!" said Bob in astonishment. "Looks like this was a battlefield."

"A giant squid?" Peter called down in surprise.

"Yeah, you could go your whole life out here without seeing something like this. The oil is from a sperm whale. That's the only natural predator for the giant squid. Looks like this one was a draw!"

"I can see the suckers on the leg!" called Don excitedly. The suckers were as big as dinner plates, rimmed in large claws.

Peter said, "If one of these ever comes aboard, I'm going to sleep with the door closed!"

"I don't think that'd help," Don replied. "He'd suck you out of there and chew you up like Australian spaghetti!"

"Apparently the bastards can grow up to a hundred feet," Bob said, "but very few people have ever seen 'em! There's enough bait there to last a guy a year!"

Strangely, there were no birds.

The southeast trades filled in that evening, and the next two days proved to be uneventful. Each morning the crew collected the flying fish that had landed on deck during the night. These slender, bluish fish were about twelve to fourteen inches long, with large winglike fins. With a quick flick of their tails, singly or in schools, the fish launch themselves out of the water and can glide up to fifty feet to get away from underwater predators. Their escape was thwarted in this case by the untimely passage of the *Ron*. The cook of the watch tossed them into a frying pan with a bit of oil for a hot breakfast. These made a delicious meal, despite the tremendous number of fine bones.

On the afternoon of the third day, the island of Tutuila came into view; and toward evening the lights of the villages began to appear, dotting the hillsides. The boat ran along the coast during the night, and by dawn was within sight of the headland of Pago Pago Harbor. Smoke was beginning to rise from the cooking fires as the first light reflected off the corrugated metal roofs of the cooking huts. When the *Ron* was within three miles of the shore, the crew was able to distinguish the traditional thatched roofs of the village *fales* and the shapes of the coconut and banana trees.

By the time the boat turned to bearing 342 degrees to follow the leading light beacons into the harbor, the wind had dropped so that it barely filled the sails. As they passed slowly over the reef and through the entrance, they looked over the side and could see the shadow of the boat sixty feet down on the sandy bottom. They were sailing into the heart of an ancient volcanic crater, whose remaining walls formed in part the dramatic Rainmaker Mountain, which rose vertically from the harbor to a height of almost 1,800 feet. Ahead, against the lush green rain-forest background, a brilliant white Catholic church stood in stark contrast.

"The channel is well marked," said Bob, standing behind Peter at the tiller. "Let's stay in the middle. No shortcuts." To emphasize the point, he gestured to a battered and rusty wreck of a fishing boat perched on a reef off to their right. On the left, a small but deadly circular reef was marked by a green floating buoy. They sailed slowly along, and the vaulted roof of the famous Rainmaker Hotel came into view on Goat Island Point to their left. They waited until the hotel came abeam before they started the engine, lowered the sails, and made a gentle turn to port.

As the commercial harbor opened up ahead of them, the water turned gray, and there appeared a floating graveyard of derelict Asian fishing boats, rafted up two and three abreast and leaning against one another for mutual support. Each group of rusting hulks hung off one of a series of massive ocean buoys by a single cable. Alongside the wharves bordering the harbor lay the remainder of the neglected fleet. Their rust-streaked cabins and hulls indicated the lack of maintenance.

The crew was suddenly assaulted by the putrid smell of fish, in complete contrast to their initial impression of this scenic paradise. Looking over to the right and upwind, they saw that the source of this offensive product was the belching stacks of two fish canneries on the shore.

Peter looked over to Bob and sputtered, "It's not exactly frangipani blossoms, is it?"

"I'm going to turn her head to weather," called Bob. Don and Peter moved to the foredeck, ready to release the anchor that they had prepared at the bow. Bob signaled with his hand and called, "Let her go!"

Peter knocked off the pawl on the winch, and the chain rattled over the bow roller as the anchor splashed into the dark, rainbow-hued waters of inner Pago Pago Harbor.

Chapter 25

---◆◆◆◆◆◆---

Flight to Samoa

From somewhere above deck, Alan heard a faint call, but try as he might, he couldn't make out the words. He turned over in his bunk, ignoring the sound and leaving the activity to the crew on watch. He heard the sound again, this time much louder, and a hand nudged at his shoulder. Pulling himself up in his bunk, he opened his eyes and looked into the face of an attractive, dark-haired woman. Alan blinked, puzzled by how she could be on board the boat. He looked around at his bunk, gradually bringing his surroundings into focus in the early morning light that seeped through the windows and realized that they were in their Waikiki hotel room. He looked back at Kerrie, the vivacious young lady he had saved from drifting out to sea on an inflatable mattress off Kaanapali Beach the week before.

"Alan, wake up! It's for you!" Kerrie called to him insistently, holding out the telephone.

He took the telephone from her and mumbled, "Hello."

"You sound like you're still asleep, you lazy bastard!" boomed the Kiwi voice on the other end.

"What time is it? Is it morning?" Alan murmured stupidly.

"Can't handle the pace anymore, eh? Well, get yourself out of bed, mate," Bob responded, "and into a cold shower! But before you do, start your brain up and get a pen and paper. I've got a list of some more shit for you to pick up at Ala Wai Marine."

"Where are you?" Alan queried, fumbling for the shopping list and still not quite awake.

"We're in Pago Pago—sailed in yesterday morning. Where do you think I am—Outer Mongolia?" said Bob with a laugh.

"How was the trip?" Alan asked, sleep now slipping away.

"Pretty good, but not without incident. The boat didn't take on much water. Not more than the bilge pumps could handle anyway," said Bob, "but we're going to have to haul her out and do some serious work on the bottom. We're anchored off the main wharf, just up from the raft of Taiwanese rust buckets. Now, I want you to write these things down and then get yer ass on the next plane. You might get the plane this afternoon if you're lucky; otherwise, you'll have to wait until Tuesday. Now listen, I've only got a few minutes left on this call before my nickel runs out, so here's the list." Alan scribbled down the items on the reverse of the original list that he'd left on the table beside the bed. "All right, Bucko!" concluded Bob. "I've got to go. See you soon!"

The plane banked to make its final approach, and Alan looked past the large Polynesian woman sitting beside him and out the window for his first glimpse of Samoa. At first, the tops of the trees of the dense tropical rain forest and the corrugated steel roofs of the simple buildings nestling among the coconut groves were all that he could see. Then, as the plane descended over the apron of the runway, the foaming surf that pounded on the reef paralleling the airport came into sight for a few seconds before the plane touched down. Alan was excited by the unusual and amazing sights. He'd been dreaming about experiencing the remote parts of the South Pacific for years, and now here he was. This was living his dream.

While the plane slowed to taxi to the terminal, the passengers, mostly more large Samoans, started to get up and gather their belongings, oblivious to the "Fasten Seat Belt" signs. Alan thought it safer to stay where he was until they came to a stop, although his modest weight would likely not have added much to the huge mass of the current melee. Fortunately his seatmate didn't object.

Alan descended the stairs to the asphalt and was overwhelmed by the hot, humid air and the earthy fragrances. He walked toward the small building that served as the terminal, savoring the exotic perfumes of the tropical flowers. The airport building was designed like a Samoan house, he would discover, with a concrete floor and a domed roof of plaited coconut fronds attached to wooden beams, which were supported on posts arranged in an oblong shape. The baggage was brought in from the plane on a cart and deposited in a pile in the center of the floor. Alan rummaged through the various suitcases, sacks, boxes, and bags amid the happy chatter of the other passengers and the numerous members of their families who were there to greet them. He was startled to find that the box of parts that he had spent all day searching out, including the all-important engine-driven bilge pump, was not part of the heap. After forty-five minutes and the help of the airport staff, Alan finally located the parcel mixed up with the mail. With a sigh of relief, he gathered it up along with his seabag and strode out of the building.

He was disappointed to find that there was no form of transport in sight. Alan stood there debating what to do when a small, rusty, blue pickup truck pulled up in front of the building. A huge Polynesian man was jammed into the cab of the truck, his enormous gut wedged against the steering wheel. One bare, fleshy arm swung out of the window, and a cigarette stub hung smoldering from his lower lip. A middle-aged woman of only slightly smaller proportions came out of the terminal and approached the truck. Alan intercepted the woman. "Can you please tell me how far it is to the yacht harbor?" he asked.

"Sure," she replied in a good American accent. "It's about a twenty-minute drive. We're going right by. Jump in the back, and we'll give you a ride."

"Thanks!" said Alan cheerfully.

The woman beckoned in Samoan to three giggling children who were riding in the back of the pickup and wagged her hands at them to move to one side. Alan lifted his baggage into the back and climbed in, squeezing himself in between the children and three large, lumpy sacks of what appeared to be vegetables. The truck pulled away and bumped along the rough asphalt the mile or so to the main road, and then they turned right and followed a winding route that hugged the coastline.

As they drove along, Alan could see and hear the waves breaking on the fringing reef not more than a hundred yards offshore. On the other side of the road, the lush undergrowth grew from the top of the hills right down the hillside until it encroached on the asphalt. They passed a number of small, brightly painted shops along the road and groups of villagers walking in twos and threes. Closer to the town, they passed the Rainmaker Hotel before turning toward the harbor and continuing to a small town square and market. Here the truck stopped and Alan jumped out, retrieved his seabag and package, and thanked the couple for the ride. He waved good-bye to the happy children and then shouldered his bag again, tucked the box under his other arm, and walked the twenty-odd yards to the harbor wall.

From here he saw a number of yachts at anchor at the head of the harbor. Among the various styles and designs, a classic ketch matching the description of *Ron of Argyll* stood out. Taking up his gear again, he made his way a few hundred yards along a rough path that followed the shore to a jetty nearly opposite the *Ron*. The jetty was made of piled-up rock the size of washing machines topped with smaller rocks and then crushed stone to give it a flat surface. This rough structure, often referred to as a rock mole, protruded about a hundred feet into the harbor and then extended to the right an equal distance to create a breakwater. There were ten or twelve yachts tied to the jetty, and several dinghies were pulled up along its shore.

He dropped his bag and set the box on top. His T-shirt was wringing wet from the exertion in the heat and humidity. The yacht was moored about three hundred yards out, so he cupped his hands to his mouth and called out, "Ahoy, *Ron of Argyll*!" After a minute, he called again, but seeing no dinghy or any activity aboard, he dug a hat out of his bag to protect him from the intense heat and sat down on the edge of the mole to wait.

Alan gazed across the harbor and was struck by the spectacular mountain opposite him and the lush undergrowth that clung to its nearly vertical face. The harbor that lay at its base stretched about two miles long by about a mile at its widest point, narrowing to about half a mile where the yachts lay. The waterfront opposite was populated by industry. A power plant clattered away, spewing out its diesel exhaust, while two factories pumped what appeared to be steam into the air. A wind shift would soon tell a different story. Tied up in front of the factories were rafts four and five deep of rusted, aging Asian long-liners. These contrasted with the two larger, modern-looking, American deep-sea seiners that were anchored in the roadstead. The seiners were about two hundred feet long, and each held a small helicopter on a platform above and just behind the wheelhouse.

Alan looked around him. On the left side of the mole, eight or nine rundown yachts were anchored by their sterns and tied to the mole from their bows with long mooring lines that dipped slowly and repeatedly into the dark, rank water of the harbor, trailing long, slimy black tendrils of algae. The hulls of the yachts themselves were filthy, and the decks were strewn with old broken-down equipment, flowerpots, and assorted building materials. Everything wore the bleached pallor caused by long exposure to the sun. None of them appeared to have moved for years. On the right side, more exposed to the wind coming down the harbor, there were four more yachts similarly moored, as well as two larger yachts tied alongside the mole. The larger yachts didn't appear to have been there as long.

Behind him, the road was busy with local traffic. The buses looked as though they had been constructed in someone's backyard. Starting life as Datsun or Toyota pickup trucks, they had been transformed by the addition of a wooden box behind the cab with about five rows of bench seats and open windows. This whole assembly was attached to the chassis and painted with brightly colored custom designs. These vehicles were a tribute to Japanese engineering, because nobody would ever have anticipated the enormous weight of Samoans that these vehicles would be expected to carry. Every bus seemed to be finished off with an ear-shattering boom box that announced its appearance well in advance of it coming into sight.

American Samoa International Airport

The Rainmaker Hotel at the entrance to Pago Pago Harbor, American Samoa

Ron of Argyll anchored near derelict fishing vessels in Pago Pago Harbor, American Samoa

Aerial view of yachts tied up to rock mole in Pago Pago Harbor

Aiga buses at the market in Pago Pago, American Samoa

As Alan took in the local scene, he heard a voice from behind him. "G'day, mate. Rattle yer dags and give us a hand to load this shit in the dinghy, and we'll get it out into the big boat." Alan turned to see Bob and two other guys. They were unloading boxes from one of the buses. "This is Peter from Oz and Don, who's come up with us from Tonga."

They greeted one another, shook hands, and then carted the boxes of goods down to the shoreline.

"Put your bag on your knees," advised Bob, "or the water sloshing around the bottom will soak everything. You've got the supplies?" Alan gestured to the well-trussed box at his feet. "Good, let's get el diablo fired up and get out of here. I need a beer."

They bundled themselves and their goods into the Avon dinghy and with barely six inches of freeboard putted off for the *Ron*.

Chapter 26

—◆◈◆◈◆◈◆◈◆◈◆—

Rosie

It was September—spring in American Samoa—but located only thirteen degrees south of the equator, that didn't really matter much as far as the heat was concerned. Every day was either hot and humid or very hot and humid, and even with the hatches open, by midday the sun had warmed the inside of the boat like an oven. Along with the coming of spring came the onset of spring rains. Most days the clouds came over Rainmaker Mountain anytime after eleven in the morning, and the rain would bucket down for a quarter to half an hour. Afterward, the hot decks would steam in the sun and were dry no more than fifteen minutes later.

Working in those conditions required acclimation and taking some precautions. The crew of the *Ron* set up the custom-made sun covers over the length of the deck to keep the sun off both them and the boat. These covers were made up of a jigsaw of pieces that were designed to fit around the masts and rigging, being tied off in a peaked shape along the centerline of the yacht to also drain the inevitable daily rains. The crew started work early in the morning to avoid the heat and knocked off for a couple of hours at midday, resuming again after the day cooled a bit and worked until the sun was low in the sky. They consumed gallons of water a day that they hauled from shore in the dinghy in five-gallon plastic jerricans.

Alan joined the crew in the established routine to get the yacht ready for the trip to Honolulu while they waited for the date that had been set by the marine railway for their haulout. Early on, Bob proclaimed the crew's rating. Peter, because of his thorough familiarity with the running and sailing of the vessel, was rated first mate. Don, who was a temporary helper, was rated ordinary seaman. Alan, with his skills in carpentry, ropework, and navigation, was rated bosun. Bob assigned the work each day from a long list according to some arcane system of priorities and the crew's skills. They worked hard and there was plenty of work to go around, but curiously, as the days went by, the list didn't seem to get any shorter. One Saturday morning, about two weeks after Alan's arrival, Bob arrived back from town in the dinghy with good news.

"Since we've made such good progress on the boat, I've decided to give you guys the night off," he joked.

"With pay, I hope," laughed Peter.

"And a chauffeur-driven dinghy," added Alan.

"Just as long as you make it home by ten!" Bob agreed. "Actually, I'm not letting you two characters out of my sight. Don's going off to see some friends, but I've made arrangements for the rest of us to go see a Samoan cultural show at Herb and Sia's. But we've still got a day's work to do, so keep at it, fellas!"

Alan and Peter worked with renewed enthusiasm for the rest of the day, and by five o'clock, they were ready to knock off and get cleaned up. The crew showered at the rock mole and put on their cleanest shorts and T-shirts. It was a ten-minute walk into town, but it took another ten for the crew to navigate their way up the hills and through the potholed, winding streets to find the building above the town. This little Polynesian suburb held some new features for Peter and Alan. In contrast to the villages they had seen here so far, these houses were much closer together, and most of them had electrical power. They were all built up about two or three feet on stilts at random levels to accommodate the irregularly sloping hillside. A rough ribbon of asphalt wove between them, bordered by a fairly uniform blanket of crushed volcanic stone. As they walked by, the children playing in the streets regarded them with a mild curiosity, but shyly avoided making eye contact. Inside, the women could be heard in their domestic chores, while the men, often gathered in small family groups, talked quietly, sitting or lying on woven grass mats.

Herb and Sia's Guest House was a local institution. For about twenty years, Herb and Sia had been providing accommodation, good local food, and a special Polynesian meal with live entertainment every Saturday night. The guesthouse had a small bar that would seat up to a dozen people comfortably, and the adjoining area was arranged to seat double that number for dinner around rustic wooden tables on a combination of sturdy wooden chairs and benches. At the end of that room was a space that served as the stage and dance floor. The décor was authentic Polynesian. Interlaced palm fronds sheathed the supporting pillars, while tapa cloth, made from the bark of the mulberry bush and decorated with local designs, adorned the walls. The floor was covered by woven mats, and from the roof beams hung strings of fresh, fragrant flowers.

When the crew arrived, they joined about ten others, but within half an hour—time enough to consume two or three cold beers—the place was bursting at the seams and it was standing room only. Besides the *Ron*'s crew, the crowd included the guests of the house—two American couples, a Dutch woman, and six English aid workers—a dozen or more yachties from neighboring boats, and a number of Samoans dressed in traditional Polynesian attire.

The meal was a treat of roast pig, fish, taro, and cassava, combined with a host of fresh fruits and lemongrass tea. During dinner one of the waiters stood out from the rest by paying special attention to Bob. He was a somewhat effeminate lad of about twenty-five, and was distinguished by his immense size, weighing at least three hundred pounds. He was excited to see "Captain Bob" and introduced himself as "Rosie." Bob was puzzled by this familiarity.

"Who's your little friend?" asked Peter.

"Fucked if I know, but he's sure big. I wouldn't want to piss him off!" Bob replied with a laugh.

Rosie continued to pay particular attention to Bob, which reached its limit when he ceremoniously shook open a napkin and spread it out on

Bob's lap. At the touch, Bob recoiled like a striking rattlesnake in reverse. He snatched the napkin away. "I'll take care of that, mate!" he blurted. Rosie smiled coyly and walked away.

Peter laughed. "I think your little friend likes you, Bob!"

"Watch it, mate," Bob replied irritably, "or you'll be swimming back!"

With the meal underway, the crew forgot about Bob's close encounter and set about enjoying the entertainment. The show began with a group playing Polynesian music. They included a delicate young woman playing the ukulele and a woman strumming an old guitar, along with a man beating on a skin drum and two others pounding on what appeared to be lengths of wooden logs. These last instruments, one longer than the other, were laid horizontally and struck with two-foot-long sticks. Only a slit appeared along the length of the log, but the sound indicated that they had been hollowed out to some degree. These drums made a primitive sound that created a subtle, mesmerizing mood.

The first performance was a dramatic show of Samoan warriors dancing in time to a thunder of drums and the flash of flaming torches. They were dressed only in colorful *lava lavas* tied around their waists, with their faces marked with streaks of war paint that gave them a fearsome appearance. They stomped and grunted guttural cries meant to intimidate their enemies. It was a powerful show of might that left the *Ron*'s crew very impressed.

The next performance began with a group of five beautiful Samoan women dancers. Their long black hair shimmered from the coconut oil that was combed through it, and as they danced, their dark brown skin glistened in the heat, contrasting with the startling white of their broad, happy smiles. Around their heads they wore strings of small white flowers like a tiara, and around their necks hung fresh flower leis, accented by a single flower behind either their left or right ear. They were dressed in long grass skirts and coconut shell brassieres, and as they danced, their languid movements told a story of life in the village. Their arms and hands moved in a fluid motion to describe how the fishermen pulled in their nets while the women eagerly awaited their happy return. The drums beat a slow, hypnotic rhythm as the women wove their sensuous tale.

"I would think the fishermen couldn't wait to get home!" Alan whispered to Bob.

"I can see what you're thinking, bosun, but be careful," Bob replied with a smile. "See those flowers behind their ears?"

"Yeah."

"The flower behind the left ear means they're single, but when it's behind the right ear, it means they're married."

"That's a valuable piece of information!"

"Yes, because they're all related in the village, including those big guys with the clubs!"

"An important point. Thanks."

The tempo picked up for the next performance, and both the women and men took to the floor in a fast, happy rhythm. After a few minutes of this, the dancers stepped into the audience, and each led someone back to dance with them, some voluntarily and some not so voluntarily. Peter and Alan were in the former of the two groups and joined in eagerly. Some started somewhat apprehensively, but egged on by the crowd, before long everyone was laughing and doing their best to imitate the steps. It was a humid evening, and before they finished, all of the volunteers had worked up a healthy sweat.

"Christ, those women can move their hips!" exclaimed Peter.

"Darn right!" agreed Alan as he sat back down in his chair. He turned to Bob and added, "And they have excellent taste!"

The dancing finished, and the performers disappeared behind a tapa-cloth curtain. Moments later, the small group of musicians emerged again, but this time with a very large woman in the center playing the guitar. She was dressed in a floor-length muumuu and decorated with a massive flower lei and a large hibiscus flower in the middle of her hair. It took a minute, and then Peter leaned over to Bob and said, "That big sheila in the middle looks like your little friend Rosie, Bob!"

Bob ignored the jibe and squinted at the musicians with a slightly puzzled look. He exclaimed, "Shit! That looks like my bloody guitar!"

"What are ya on about? What guitar?" said Peter with surprise.

"*My* guitar," Bob repeated.

"You're kidding! How did she get it?"

"It's 'he,' you moron. And I don't know. I lost it last time I was here with Hal."

"Well, you'd better ask her for it back," suggested Alan with a grin.

"I don't know," replied Bob uncertainly. "Look at the size of *him*," he emphasized.

"She's pretty good," noted Alan, trying to change the subject, "but why is the flower in the middle of her hair and not behind her ear?"

"Because he's a *fa'afafine*. It means 'ladylike' in Samoan. They say that when they have a big family and the older kids are boys, they sometimes raise one of them like a girl to help the mother. They grow up spending most of their time with the women and end up like that."

"Are there many of them?" Peter asked.

"Quite a few. All over Polynesia. And they're treated with a lot of respect in the villages, so mind your manners," Bob insisted.

"Then you'd better treat her right!" teased Alan.

Bob only glared at him, and they sat in silence as the performance continued. There was a short interval before the next performance, which was signaled by a dimming of the lights. When the lights came on, there was Rosie in the middle of the dance floor, dressed in an enormous grass skirt big enough to thatch a roof and wearing nothing else except another large flower lei. As Rosie began to dance slowly to the sound of the ukulele, the audience was amazed at how light he was on his feet. The crew was impressed with his skill. "I expected him to sound like a hippo in hobnail boots, but he's very good," Bob commented respectfully.

Rosie approached the job with professionalism and soon had the audience cheering in approval, a big smile spreading across his face as he executed his performance. In contrast to the more slender, shapely women dancers, Rosie shifted his bulk with a more determined motion, his mass sometimes trailing behind his hips by a fraction of a second, but he demonstrated an amazing talent. After the end of the first dance, Rosie circulated through the adoring crowd while the music continued, finally reaching the table where the *Ron*'s crew was seated. He leaned heavily on Bob's chair. "Did you like my show, Captain Bob?" Rosie asked.

"It was good, Rosie," Bob complimented him awkwardly.

"Good, come dance with me!" Rosie said decisively, and without waiting for an answer, clamped a huge, fleshy hand onto Bob's wrist and with a lurch pulled him from his chair. Bob resisted valiantly, his deck shoes skidding along the floor, but the simple physics of the situation sealed his fate.

As the music started, the passionate look in Rosie's eyes appeared to strike a certain fear into Bob's soul. With the crowd roaring their approval, Rosie began to dance in a slow but dogged pursuit around the dance floor, while Bob did his best to politely turn the dance into a Polynesian version of "catch me if you can." The dance ended with Bob's dignity barely intact, and he hurried to rejoin his crew.

"My money was on Rosie," said Peter as Bob regained his seat.

"Mine too," said Alan. Bob glared at them. "No offense," continued Alan, "but he seemed to have the inside track on that last turn."

"Where's the guitar, Bob?" prodded Peter with a grin. "Didn't you ask him for it?"

"Forget it. It's gone. I need a beer," stated Bob flatly. "Better make it two."

Chapter 27

---◆※◆---

Heartbeat

B ob maneuvered the dinghy slowly between the yachts and approached the rock mole, timing the arrival carefully. He gunned the motor as the lines rose out of the putrid water, and the dinghy slipped narrowly under the slimy mooring lines to nudge gently against the rocks. Alan grabbed hold of the handiest rock as Peter steadied himself and stepped onto a large, flat chunk of concrete, taking the painter in his other hand. He tied it to an overhanging tree, allowing the dinghy plenty of slack to prevent it rubbing on the oyster shells that caked the rocks below the waterline. Bob shut off the motor and tipped it up so that it would clear the rocks as it drifted at its mooring. He looked down at the Avon.

"Looks like she's going flat again, fellas. We'll have to give it a couple of squirts with the bellows when we get back."

"Geeez, I just pumped it up before we left!" said Alan with surprise. "Needs another patch, I guess. I'll have a look at it again when we get back to the boat."

They clambered up to the top of the mole, shower gear in hand, to the roughly constructed cubicle of plywood and boards that was plumbed to serve as a shower. The crude facility was occupied, and from the black-haired form that towered above the shower wall, they could see that the occupant was Leonard the Aztec, a tall, fine-looking young man who was supposedly a distant relative of the lost Aztec race.

"Shit!" cursed Bob. "It's Leonard. We'll be here all fucking day." Alan and Peter groaned and turned to take a seat along the stone wall that bordered the mole. "Don't take all the cold water, Leonard!" called Bob. "Leave some for the rest of us!"

Leonard turned and beamed at the crew and ducked his head under the nozzle to continue his languid washing routine.

"I don't know how he can spend so much time in there," declared Alan. "Doesn't he get cold?"

"He'll be in there for an hour or more if you let him," said Peter. "You'd think he liked it. Come on, Leonard!" he chided.

When Leonard finally emerged, Bob asked, "Is Gary on board?"

"Sure, he's working on the motorbike," he replied.

"Tell him we'll stop by for a beer after we've cleaned ourselves up a bit."

Leonard beamed again in response, nodded, and strode away.

"Doesn't talk much, does he?" commented Alan.

The crew approached the white-hulled yacht tied up to the wharf. Along its side was painted in red the distinctive sawtooth ECG image and the name *Heartbeat*. On the wharf alongside, a figure hunched over an old blue 90 cc Honda step-through motorbike. This was the latest in a succession of motorbikes that Gary Green had picked up for nothing. The master of innovation, Gary would pick up a discarded machine and coax it back to life, piecing it together only well enough to meet the local regulations. This model had a beer can improvised as a muffler, and although it didn't take long to wear out, Gary had an endless supply of them. Due to past abuse and his abuse of a motorbike once he got hold of one, its life span was very short. It wasn't out of the range of possibility if it crossed his mind for him to haul a fifty-gallon barrel of diesel fuel on the back. Because of this, his motorbikes were always under repair, but when they finally expired, Gary

Gary Green aboard his yacht *Heartbeat* in Pago Pago Harbor

abandoned them and went in search of another one. There was always one to be found since the islanders were not the best of mechanics.

Gary straightened as they approached. He was a six-foot tall, wiry Kiwi with thick brown hair. He tossed a filthy rag to the ground and looked up at the crew. He declared dryly, "Give me a dollar, and it's yours!" He took an idle kick at the offending machine and turned away in mock frustration. "Leonard said you were stopping by. Come on board for a drink," he beckoned with a smile.

The crew kicked off their boat shoes and stepped onto the wooden deck. Alan took note of the heavy stainless steel stanchions, the massive sheet winches, and the oversized stainless steel cleats before following the rest down the companionway and into the main saloon. The deadlights, high along the topsides, provided good light; and the forward hatch, hinged open to catch the wind, allowed a pleasant breeze to waft through the boat. Gary's partner Coral greeted them as they entered. "Hello, lads. Can I offer you a drink?"

"Let's have a few Steinlagers from the cooler, thanks, Coral," Gary replied.

"This is a pretty sturdy boat, Gary," said Alan.

"Too right it is!" Gary exclaimed. "I've had my fill of half-assed, shit-pot, Taiwanese rip-off fiberglass boats!" he added exuberantly.

"Yeah, Bob and Peter told me something about your experience in the South China Sea. Must have been an absolute nightmare!"

Gary grunted and handed each a beer. "I'll roll myself a smoke and give you the guts of it." He pulled a football-shaped pouch out of his pocket, unzipped it, and pulled out a pinch of tobacco and a rolling paper. He skillfully rolled the cigarette between his thumbs and forefingers, pinched off the ragged end, and poked it into his mouth. Then he scratched a match on the underside of the galley table, lit the cigarette, and inhaled deeply, expelling it completely and leaning back before beginning.

"It all started when this cow-cocky mate of mine decided to give up farming and go cruising around the world. He'd heard that they built cheap boats in Taiwan, so he got in touch with this shifty-eyed Chinaman up there to contract to have a boat built. After at least twelve months and a lot of shenanigans, he got a call that the boat was ready to pick up. He said to me, 'What about going up with me to bring the boat back?' Since the cows had dried off at that time of year, I thought it was a bloody good idea. So we packed our bluey and flew out to Taiwan. We eventually found the boatyard, and even without knowing much about boats, we knew that the mast was way too fucking long. We tracked down Mr. Chee or Mr. Wee or Mr. Pee or whatever his name was—a joker with a mouthful of gold teeth who never stopped smiling—who was the boss of the yard. We spent a day or so going through the boat and had a list as long as your arm of shit that wasn't right."

"The problem with Taiwan is that there's hundreds of boatyards there ready to take your money," said Bob, "and most of them aren't worth two bob. There's only half a dozen top-notch yards. Your mate must have picked a dud."

"Yeah, we figured that out. Whenever we told Mr. Chee about something, he just smiled and nodded his head. Work seemed to be getting done, but nothing seemed to happen. Finally we decided that the only way to see what we had was to take it for a sail. It was immediately obvious that the mast hadn't been shortened. After several more rounds of smiling with Mr. Chee, we decided that we had to get the hell out of there."

"But how did your mate settle up with this Chee asshole?" asked Peter.

"He managed to negotiate a better price instead of him fixing all of the remaining fuckups, and we headed out."

Gary described how they picked up two more crew and took off for New Zealand. They had one problem after another for the first two weeks, and the rest of the crew was seasick. Then the weather started to go to hell as they unknowingly sailed into the track of a typhoon. It was then that water started to come into the boat.

Gary's voice took on a serious tone. "I was lying on me guts underneath the cockpit, and I could feel the hull moving underneath my hands. This was the place where the skeg that supported the rudder was attached. I thought, 'Holy shit, if this lets go, we'll be in deep shit.' I got back out and told the others what I'd found and impressed on them that if this thing broke, we were in shit street and that we'd better get the lifesaving gear ready. A few hours later, we started taking on water and the bilge started filling up. I crawled back underneath the cockpit and found that we had a hole three feet long and two feet wide opening up."

"Shit!" exclaimed Alan. "That's exactly the kind of problem we had on our boat coming down from Vancouver, only ours wasn't so severe!"

"Well, this was very fucking severe, because at that point it was 'good night nurse' and obvious that we were going to have to get off." He leaned forward, gripping the edge of the bench and staring into the distance, as if reliving the event. "We tethered the life raft to the boat, and just as we were getting the provisions aboard, a thirty-foot wave took the raft and flipped it over, tipping the entire contents overboard. We managed to get it on its feet again, but by now the boat was on its way down and we only had time to grab what was handy, get in, and cut the line before the boat sank completely."

Gary collected himself and craned his neck around to call over his shoulder to Coral. "Get us another beer, would you, Coral?" He rolled another smoke and inhaled deeply before beginning again.

The audience sat in silence.

"For the next twenty-four hours the ocean roared, and several times the sea picked the raft up on its end, almost turning us over. By the next day, the sea had calmed down a bit, and only the occasional wave would stand us up on end. Then in the afternoon, one wave that was bigger than the rest stood us up and catapulted me out the door into the sea. By the time I came to the surface, the raft had passed me, so I desperately swam after it. I saw immediately that the raft was moving away faster than I could swim and I realized that I wasn't going to catch it. It was bloody terrifying," he almost whispered, looking down and slowly shaking his head back and forth.

Looking up, he continued, "Then something brushed by my face and I grabbed it. It was the fishing line that we'd been trailing behind the raft. I managed to tie it around my wrist and hoped to Christ that it wouldn't break. By now the rest of the crew in the raft realized what was happening and began slowly pulling in the line. They couldn't hear me shouting to take it easy, and I just kept hoping that the fucking line wouldn't break. They finally got me in."

He paused for a few seconds in reminiscence.

Gary told them that they had next to nothing to eat on board and only two containers of water. They tried everything to catch something to eat, but the fishing gear that came with the raft was useless. He even unraveled a piece of rope and spent an entire day making it into a net, but still couldn't catch anything. He was convinced that a speargun is the only way to survive in a raft. They quickly ran short of water and were getting down to a biscuit and half a cup of water each a day. This got even more meager, and after a week, they were down to a tablespoon of water each. Two of them started to drink seawater and were getting delirious.

"I told myself, 'Greeney, you're never going to give up, as long as your heart's beating.'" Looking intently at them, he said, "I'll tell you, mate, you've got no fucking idea what it's like to start to die of thirst. No fucking idea."

On the ninth day, they finally saw a pretty big boat coming in their direction. Everyone wanted to shoot off the only flare they had left, but Gary told them to wait until it was right on top of them to make sure they'd see it. Things were looking good, and then the boat started to veer away from them. Gary fired the flare, and the boat continued to change course until it was stern-to and headed for the horizon.

"My heart fell into me boots, and I thought, 'Greeney, you're fucked,'" he said as he slouched forward, deflated. "We watched in silence as the boat kept on. Then gradually the ship began to turn until it was pointing back toward us. We sat there and couldn't believe our eyes," he said, sitting up straight and his eyes brightening. "They'd seen us! When they got near us, they lowered a boat and came over and pulled us out and took us back. It turned out to be a Russian fishing boat. I've never been so happy in my life as when that bloody great Russian seaman wrapped his arms around me and pulled me out of that fucking raft."

Alan muttered, "That's some story."

"Shit yeah," agreed Bob.

"That's enough of that," Gary said, slapping his knees with his hands to lighten the mood. "What have you jokers been up to since you left Fiji?"

They shared more stories until the banter was interrupted by the sound of a fire-alarm bell going off somewhere within the boat. Everyone jumped and looked at Gary, whose eyes had narrowed. The alarm stopped, and Coral stepped from the galley. "It's only the pressure water system. The alarm goes off if the water is left on. Gary gets a bit sensitive about water use."

"I can't bloody well blame him," said Peter. The others nodded in agreement.

Chapter 28

And He Didn't Even Get His Feet Wet

Bob climbed up the side of the *Ron*, ducked under the sun awning, and dropped a box of spare parts onto the deck.

"Here y'are, fellas," he called to Alan and Peter.

"Did you manage to get the diaphragm for the bilge pump?" asked Peter, popping his head out of the companionway and climbing into the cockpit.

"Yeah," he replied. "But there's no glue for the dinghy in any store on the island."

Alan lifted himself up through the forward hatch and walked back to the cockpit. "I've patched up the dinghy bellows as best I can, but it's going to need a major overhaul if we don't have the glue."

"We'll fuck with that later. Let's take a union break. I'll make some coffee," said Bob as he climbed down the companionway.

"Grab those biscuits as well while you're at it!" Peter called down after him.

When Bob returned, they sat together in the shade under the awning.

"I ran into the harbormaster in town," said Bob. "He gave me the whole box and dice on that loser who claimed he lost his yacht in a storm a few weeks ago."

"Who was that?" asked Alan.

"He's a typical Pago deadbeat loser," Bob replied. "One of the low-rent crowd down by the rock mole. Lives on that black heap of shit with his girlfriend, that fat, gray-haired fading hippy."

"I don't think I've noticed it."

"Oh, yeah," said Bob brightly, "it's a real asshole of a boat. More like a floating contrivance. It has definitely seen better days."

"How big is it?" asked Alan.

"Ah, it's about thirty-eight feet. You can't miss it. It's the one with the coconut trees sprouting in corned beef cans on the deck, surrounded by a multitude of rust circles where previous ones kicked the bucket!"

"You can see that there are actually weeds growing through the deck," added Peter.

"Oh, I think I know the one you mean," said Alan, nodding. "It's the one with the blue dodger."

"Yeah," said Bob, warming to the tale. "And it's got a collection of dead batteries and lengths of rusty chain draped over different things on the deck. And odd lengths of rope that are *so* worn out they resemble feather dusters. Halyards that have rotted off are left hanging halfway up the mast. It's just unbelievable!" He said with a chuckle, "The blocks are so corroded you could soak them in a five-gallon bucket of WD-40 for five years and they still wouldn't move!" He laughed and took a drink of his coffee before renewing his assault. "There is so much growth on the bottom of the boat that it would keep a family of vegetarians in food for six months!"

Alan and Peter roared with laughter. "You're kidding!" said Alan in disbelief.

"No!" Bob continued with enthusiasm, "The barnacles on the bottom are so thick that to get them off would be like an archaeological dig! It would treat a mere scraper with contempt. You'd need an underwater jackhammer to get 'em off!" They all laughed at the image. Alan started to ask another question, but Bob hadn't finished. "The propeller is so fouled that it resembles something like a beach ball! And that blue dodger you're talking about has perished in the sun, with all the stitching hanging out. The whole thing is held together with silicone and duct tape!"

They laughed again and took several minutes to settle down to the original story. Finally Alan asked, "So what happened to the boat?"

"It was just before you got here," said Peter. "The bloke was supposed to be delivering this tiny little boat to a mate of his in New Zealand. It was a twenty-two footer—twenty-five at the most—fiberglass, with a rough wooden doghouse. A piece of shit really, but probably with lots of insurance! Not worth much more than a piece of driftwood."

"Peter and I were looking at each other like, 'This looks like a bloody setup,'" said Bob. "We figured we're not going to see this joker again. He's obviously not going to make it in this pile of shit."

"I'd be nervous about sailing it in Pago Harbor, let alone taking it into the open ocean!" Peter emphasized.

"It wasn't worth two fucking bob, so he'd obviously made a deal with the owner. He was supposedly going to deliver it to New Zealand—*deliver* being the operative word—but in actual fact, the deal would have been to deliver it straight to the bottom of the ocean to Davey Jones's locker and split the insurance money!"

"He was a fat little bastard. He hardly fit in the cockpit," said Peter. "If he had to turn the boat in a hurry, the tiller would get lost in his gut!"

"If you can imagine a light on his head, he would have made a good marker buoy!" said Bob. "He looked like he had a built-in life ring under his T-shirt. If he had to abandon ship, floatation would not be a problem."

"So what happened to the boat?" pursued Alan.

"Well," said Bob, "the fading hippy said good-bye with a certain exuberance, like 'At last there's a major change in the course of my life. I'm finally getting rid of this loser.'"

"He took off one day, and was only about half a day out," said Peter. "He made sure the water depth was phenomenal—something like five thousand feet—and then opened the sea cocks so he was sure to lose the boat."

"He said the sea was rough and he nearly got turned over," said Bob, "but the skipper of the freighter that picked him up told the harbormaster that it was as flat as a plate of piss. He'd obviously studied up on the ships' arrivals and departures and placed himself in the path of one of these.

Timing was critical. He had to time it to get there before the next freighter arrived; otherwise, he would have to float around for another three days and he might not make it. This was the most dangerous part of the whole thing! He probably just stepped into the life raft and then let off the distress flares." He took a sip of coffee to whet his whistle before continuing.

"The freighter skipper says that one of the flares nearly hit a bloke on the bridge in the face! I imagine he set off a broadside of red flares and miraculously they saw him. The skipper said it was pretty difficult to miss *this* fireworks display! The deadbeat loser told the captain that he'd hit something and was taking on water. He didn't even get his feet wet! They brought him back to the old washed-out hippy lady, and her exuberance changed when she realized that Jonah had returned." He pronounced these last three words slowly and dramatically. "She was decidedly down in the mouth when they saved him. She probably thought, 'Why couldn't you leave him out there and bring the boat back?' Since then, they've kind of just faded into the woodwork."

Chapter 29

The Haulout

The *Ron* rode gently at anchor in the morning breeze, a hot tropical wind that ruffled the surface of the water without providing much relief. The crew was sitting under the sun awning in the cockpit having a coffee and running through the list for the haulout that was booked for that day. During the trip from Vava'u, the boat had taken on progressively more water, and Bob wanted to make the most of their time up on the hard to have a good look at the hull and fix any problems before embarking on the 2,500-mile trip to Honolulu.

"That list's as long as a roll of shithouse paper," said Peter. "We'll be up on the hard for a month."

"Better that than a short trip to the bottom halfway there," Bob joked, and they all laughed.

"What the hell have you got on there, Bob?" asked Alan.

"Well, for starters, we're going to have to look at the stem and check the seams. And while we're at it, we'll antifoul the bottom."

"So that's why we've got two miles of caulking cotton," Alan observed. "I thought you were going to tie that to a mooring buoy so we could find our way back from the marine railway."

The wind was increasing and funneled down the harbor, a good indicator of a coming shower. The *Ron* rocked slightly as the wind pushed it back, stretching out the anchor chain. Above the sound of the wind in the rigging, they heard the distant calls of Asian voices. Turning astern and looking toward the sound, they could make out several crewmen on the nearest Korean long-liner waving from the foredeck. Peter studied the activity on the boat. "What's all that palaver?"

"I can't see what they're on about," said Alan, squinting.

"There, in the water!" Bob pointed to a spot about a hundred feet away. A head was just visible among the choppy waves. An arm lashed the air and then disappeared. Peter instinctively bounced to his feet, took two steps to the rail, and plunged into the murky water. With powerful strokes, he reached the man and grabbed him by the hair just as he dropped below the surface again. As Peter hauled him up, the man grabbed weakly at him. Filthy water poured from his mouth, and his frantic eyes darted around. With a twist of his arm, Peter flipped the man over onto his back and began to tow him back toward the *Ron*.

Bob looked down at the dinghy to see the aft section deflated and floating limply in the water, the outboard barely visible below the surface. He called out, "The Avon's rooted, Peter! You're going to have to swim!"

Alan pulled off his T-shirt and stood by with a boat hook on the aft deck, ready to assist. As Peter drew alongside, Bob and Alan reached down and grabbed the man by his arms and pulled him aboard. He slumped limply to the deck, coughing and sputtering. Peter climbed aboard, rivulets of dark, shimmering water running down him.

Bob regarded Peter, who blinked at him with red eyes and spat over the side. "Welcome back aboard, cesspit Pete!" he said.

Peter looked down at his filthy T-shirt. "Don't strike a bloody match near me, mate, or I'll burst into flames!" he said.

The man groaned, lifted his head, and threw up onto the neat teak deck.

"We'll have to add that to the list, I guess," commented Alan, leaning down to give the unfortunate sailor a sip of freshwater.

From across the harbor, a decrepit wooden launch made its way toward the *Ron*. Within a few minutes, six hard-eyed Korean sailors pulled up and gestured to their missing crewman, who had now raised himself into a sitting position, his head hanging down despondently. With the exchange of a few words, the victim edged over to the boarding gate and was roughly assisted into the launch. Without a word, the launch pulled away and turned toward the sailors' ship.

"Poor bastard," said Alan. "I've seen these Korean boats come into Vancouver. They've only got two choices for national service—the army or the fishing fleet."

"This one apparently didn't like either one," said Bob. "Now, let's get the decks cleaned up and get going before Peter curdles the milk."

———

The *Ron* chugged slowly toward the marine railway, where a huge platform was being prepared to haul vessels needing repair out of the water. The platform ran down a concrete slope on a set of rails until it was submerged, and then the ships were loaded alone or, in the case of smaller ships, together with other vessels, and hauled up by a chain using a massive winch. After an hour or so of jockeying around, the Samoan workers managed to position the *Ron* on the platform along with several others, including an American yacht, a couple of small local fishing boats, and a fifty-foot wooden, junk-rigged vessel.

The workers swam around them in the filthy water, wearing only *lava lavas* and diving masks, apparently oblivious to the toxic soup. They dived under each hull to place various-sized wooden support blocks in a complex system intended to hold the ships upright once the platform was hauled out of the water. The crew helped lash the *Ron* to the vertical steel frame of the platform and then watched nervously as an Asian long-liner pulled in behind them. The crew paid close attention for the next hour while this load was secured. Finally the platform was winched up the slope inch by inch until the last one in line was clear of the water.

With the *Ron* up on the hard, the boatyard crew leaned a steel ladder against its side, and the crew climbed down to the dripping platform. Peter clutched his shower kit and a towel. "Well, let's get to work," announced Bob, glancing over at Alan with a wink.

Asian long-liner awaiting repair at the marine railway

Alan, Bob, and Don place fenders as the *Ron* is secured on the marine railway

Alan places a fender as some of the boatyard crew swim below

Boatyard worker nicknamed Slim takes a rest

Long-liner pulls in to the marine railway behind the *Ron*

Foreman checks that the *Ron* is secure

"After I have a shower," reminded Peter.

"You don't smell so bad now," replied Bob. "I'm kind of getting used to you now that you've dried out a bit."

"Pig's ass! I'm going to clean all of this shit off me before these railway jokers take a liking to me." Peter strode off to find a shower, but was surprised to hear from the yard boss that there wasn't one. "Where do these blokes clean up then?" he asked.

"Chain wash," was all he said.

Peter looked around, perplexed. "Chain wash?" he repeated. He saw the chain that ran from the platform up to the winch shed. The huge links of the chain were about two feet long and a foot wide. The weight of the platform and its load pulled the chain so tight that it was suspended a foot above the concrete ramp. Over the chain where it entered the shed, he detected a water pipe and showerhead. Understanding the boss's meaning, he looked around until he found a spigot and turned it on. Sure enough, the shower sprayed onto the chain, cleaning it to some degree of the salt and debris of the harbor as it passed underneath. Straddling the chain, Peter was able to find a public, but not too uncomfortable, seat and scrub himself clean of the morning's coating. A shout from the platform interrupted his wash.

"Hey Pete, you're creating an oil slick back here!" Bob chided.

Peter finished up and rejoined the crew at the boat. "How d'ya like that, mate?" he beamed, pulling up the front of his clean T-shirt and sniffing it for effect. "Fresh as a flower!"

"Well, you shouldn't have bothered with the country club, Pete," laughed Alan. "Here comes a Samoan shower."

"Shower, my ass," said Bob, casting a glance upward. "It's going to piss down."

Right on cue, the sky opened up and the downpour began. Peter rushed forward to join the crew under the hull for protection. The deluge soon collected on the decks and poured out the scuppers, cascading down the hull and washing the collection of seaweed, oily harbor water, and other collected rubbish down upon them. They quickly moved to avoid the deluge.

"It's like Niagara Falls!" Peter exclaimed.

"Welcome back!" laughed Bob, and gestured to Peter's T-shirt, which was now as filthy as the rest of them.

The tropical rain ended almost as quickly as it had started. Bob and Alan surveyed the hull while Peter went in search of the loo.

"It's going to need a lot of work," noted Bob. "There's more involved than I thought. The garboard needs work, there's a scarf joint in the stem that's opened up, and a bunch of the caulking has disappeared. Some parts of the hull aren't as good as that junk over there." He gestured to the fishing boat. "That must be the great-great-grandfather of those old rust buckets at the end of the harbor. It's got to be sixty years old and based on a design by the great marine architect Confucius three thousand years ago. It probably sailed here all the way from China."

Activity had begun around all of the boats on the railway. Blocked up on the port side of the *Ron* was the American yacht, crewed by an ex-navy man, his wife, and their fifteen-year-old son, Joey, who wore a hearing aid in each ear. The family was headed to New Zealand, where they felt that they would survive the inevitable nuclear holocaust. They, too, were inspecting their boat, and the father was indicating to his son the extent of the work that they would have to do to clean and paint their hull.

Astern, the rusty ninety-foot long-liner was undergoing a more direct assessment. Three of the crew and an obviously more senior officer were making a circuit around the hull. At intervals, the officer would point to a spot, and one of the crew would wind up with a sledgehammer and kabong the hull. If the sledge rebounded cleanly, they moved on to the next spot; but if the hammer hit with a thud, they would take their second precision instrument, a pickax, and conduct another scientific test. The pickax sometimes only chipped off great chunks of rusty metal, but occasionally it disappeared clean through the rusty steel plates. At these weak points, the crew worked the pickax out in an increasing circle until they hit solid metal. These places were marked for future work.

Bob and Alan had already completed their survey when Peter returned. He jerked his thumb over his shoulder and said, "The yard boss just told me they lock us in at six o'clock every night. That's their idea of security."

"That's all right," responded Bob. "Let's sit and have a beer until they're gone, and then we'll sort out a plan."

As darkness was setting in, the *Ron*'s crew sidled along the eight-foot-high chain link fence topped with barbed wire that protected the marine railway until they found a spot that was conveniently hidden from view on the street side by a large, leafy bush. "This should do," said Bob, indicating a likely spot.

Alan pressed his hand against the fence to test the tension of the mesh. "This'll be fine. There's enough slack," he said. He selected a wire strand and, using a pair of bolt cutters, made a neat cut at the bottom to separate it from the wire that ran along the bottom of the mesh, and then followed the zigzag pattern of the strand to the top and cut it there too. Next, with Bob and Peter on either side pulling the mesh toward him, he twisted the loosened wire around and around until it corkscrewed halfway out of the fence, leaving an almost invisible slot at the bottom. The protruding wire was hidden from view by the bush. Alan said, "I've had miles of this stuff installed back home. It's a piece of cake! I'll put it back together before we go."

Satisfied with their private entrance, they stashed the cutters in the grass, squeezed through the narrow slot, and disappeared down the road to find something to eat.

Chapter 30

Sharkbite Charlie and the Bowling Alley

The Bowling Alley Bar and Disco at the head of the harbor was a convenient choice. The crew stopped as they entered to watch the players. It was an awesome sight. The full-sized balls were dwarfed in the huge hands of the big Samoans. They wound up and flung the balls with such force that, if all the players threw the balls at the same time, it would have the same effect as a full cannon broadside of a man-of-war. Due to their size, the players were unable to bend down to effect the normal release of the ball. Instead, they hurled the balls so that they landed halfway down the lane and with one bounce struck the unsuspecting pins.

They ran into Charles van der Water as they passed. Everyone called him Charles to his face, but in private, he was known as "Sharkbite Charlie." Charlie had been traveling on a yacht two years before when he had an unfortunate accident. He was snorkeling just off the remote island of Suwarrow in the Cook Islands and spearfishing to get some fresh meat. He'd speared a big fish but hadn't killed it, and the fish swam into the coral. Charlie had to go to the surface for air before he could go after it.

A blacktip shark, sensing the struggle, swam in as Charlie returned to retrieve his catch. Just as he reached for the spear impaling the quivering fish, the shark arched his back, signaling an attack, and moved in with a quick thrust of its tail. Seeing the shark, Charlie grabbed the spear and thrust it at the shark to fend it off. A shark's eyesight is notoriously bad, so it depends more on its other senses. The shark glanced off the fish-bearing spear and grabbed Charlie's hand instead. The shark shook it with a tearing motion before sensing that this prey was too big and released it to swim off. In shock and in excruciating pain, Charlie swam to the surface with blood pouring from the wound.

The skipper did what he could for him before setting off with all sails flying and motor running for American Samoa. Charlie almost bled to death during the three-day trip. When they arrived, he was rushed to the Lyndon B. Johnson Tropical Medical Center, where they performed emergency surgery. They saved his hand and tried to rejoin the three severed tendons but failed, leaving his hand permanently contorted into a claw shape.

Charlie had taken a job at the bowling alley during his recuperation. Among his other duties, he took charge of drilling the bowling balls, which were, of necessity, custom-made.

"How's it going, Charles? Any good-looking girls here tonight?" asked Bob.

"One that I recognize," he said with the trace of a smile. "What mischief are you guys up to?"

"Aw, we've finally put the *Ron* up on the marine railway, and we've come around for a meal and a couple of quiet drinks."

"Quiet? That'll be the day!"

"Are you nearly done?" asked Peter.

"I'm off in about an hour."

"Why don't you come upstairs for a drink after?"

"Yeah, okay. If you're buying."

———

The upstairs of the bowling alley was fitted out as a bar, disco, and restaurant and was one of the prime nightspots in Pago Pago. The crew settled in at the bar. It was early, so there were only a few of the local patrons and nobody was dancing on the tiny dance floor. The recorded music played in the background anyway. As the barman served up a round of beer, Alan noticed the bottle of scotch whiskey on the shelf behind the bar. "It's been awhile since I had a glass of scotch," he said to the barman. "I'll have one when you come around again."

The generous shot of scotch went down very smoothly, as did the second. By the time the bar began to fill up, Alan was in a joyous mood, so when a slim young lady approached and asked if the seat next to him was free, he was only too happy for the company. Bob was sitting on his left and looked across with a sly smile. Alan and the young lady fell into a lively conversation, and as he ordered another scotch for himself and a drink for the lady, he glanced at Bob and raised his eyebrows to indicate that he was enjoying himself. The level stare and slight shake of the head that he received in return puzzled him. Undaunted, Alan picked up on their conversation. "Yes, Peter and I rode up on the cable car to the top of Rainmaker Mountain and made the hike down. Have you been up there?"

"Yes," said his companion, "but when I was walking down, I fell and cut my leg. Do you want to see my scar?" Without waiting for a response, she hiked up her long dress to expose a slender leg. Alan blinked and then squinted in the low light. While he was unable to really make out the wound, he took this as a friendly gesture. He glanced back over to Bob and Peter and gave them a wink. He was mystified and a little troubled by their lack of encouragement. In his fog, he returned to the young lady. "Would you like to dance?" she asked.

Alan took a moment to consider this. He was uncertain now of his luck and wondered what Bob and Peter knew that he didn't. "Perhaps Bob would like to have a dance first," he suggested, leaning back and looking over to Bob.

"No way, Jose," Bob responded firmly.

Alan looked up at the barman for a clue, but he just wiped a glass studiously with a cloth and stared, noncommittally, into the distance. After a short pause, Alan tried again. "Well, maybe Peter would."

"Not me, mate!" said Peter and took a drink of his beer.

This sudden turn to gentlemanly behavior raised the alarm. Alan stared carefully at the young lady through the scotch mist created by the alcohol and observed the flower in the middle of her hair. Slowly he began to see the nature of his crewmates' refusal. He was staggered by his mistake. He pushed the glass of whiskey on the bar away from him and turned back to the *fa'afafine*. "Maybe you can find a young lady to dance with you instead, mate," he said, remembering Bob's advice and trying to hide his indignation. The *fa'afafine* slipped off the seat and strolled away. Alan turned to Bob and Peter, who were now in stitches with laughter. "Some mates you are!" he snorted.

"Don't worry," said Bob, laughing. "We wouldn't have let you go on much longer!"

"Yeah," Peter joined in, "only until you proposed to him!"

It was long past midnight when the crew came careening back down the road, seeking the entry through the fence that they had created. They called to one another over the thundering racket of the diesel engines of the power plant across the street. "It's in here," insisted Bob, thrashing aside the bushes.

"No, it's not," argued Peter. "I'm sure it was after the lamppost."

"It's nearer the corner," said Alan, staggering slightly and feeling along the fence.

For some time they scoured back and forth before finally finding their secret entrance. They pulled the opening apart and slid through. "Make sure you lock the gate behind you, Pete," Bob admonished. "We wouldn't want Alan getting out and roaming around without us. You never know what he'd get up to!"

Chapter 31

The Haulout Continues

It was early morning when Alan limped into the main saloon, wincing and holding his head. Bob was lying on his back on one of the settees, his forearm over his eyes and one leg dangling off the cushion so that his foot rested at an awkward angle on the cabin sole.

"What's that awful smell?" Alan asked.

"The wind must have shifted," Bob groaned. "That's the sweet smell of the tuna factories just up the harbor. It's enough to gag a maggot!"

Alan gasped at the stench and glanced up to the main hatch above him. "And I guess if we opened the hatch, it would only get worse. But it must be forty degrees or more in here already."

"At least," chimed in Peter, coming into the saloon from the galley with three cups of black coffee. "How's the head?"

"Rotten. With that bloody power plant hammering away all night, I feel like I've been tortured by a bass drum player." He took the coffee and collapsed onto one of the other settees. "What time did the railway crew pick up this morning?"

"Must have been six o'clock," said Bob. "The worst thing is that they're such a cheery lot you can't really hate them."

"I'll just take a few minutes to try," said Alan wryly.

Bob sat up slowly and carefully swung his other leg around to join the first one and positioned them both to provide the much-needed support. He leaned forward, picked up the coffee, and took a sip. "Let's get out of here and get some grub over on the other side of the harbor before my skull breaks."

The crew sat at a table in Soli's Restaurant and Bar overlooking the harbor and hoed into their breakfast with gusto. Peter turned to Alan and asked, "Who was that bloke you were talking to at dinner last night?"

Alan reached for the salt and sprinkled a little on his eggs before answering. "He's an American guy. Pretty interesting. Runs the 'Black Ship'—the slop bucket that takes the offal from the StarKist and Van Camp tuna canneries and dumps it out at sea twice a day. He says they used to just pump it into the harbor."

"Yes, the improvement is obvious," said Bob sarcastically. "If Charlie the Tuna knew what went on in that factory, he probably wouldn't want to be there."

"By the smell of it, you're right," said Peter.

"Do you know they can turn out two hundred tons of fish a day from each plant?" said Alan. "They do all the gutting and cleaning by hand here. They only make minimum wages, but lots of the workers come here from Tonga to get US dollars and send them home."

Bob refilled his coffee and considered, "Wonder what he gets paid for running the shit wagon?"

"The company gets a thousand dollars a day, but I don't know what he gets himself."

"Not bad wages for an undertaker," said Peter. "I bet there's a bloody great feeding frenzy out there when he dumps the shit."

"He says that the sharks would put the Amazon piranhas to shame! Tigers, hammerheads—the works."

"Remind me to mark in the ship's log not to go under and scrub the hull in Samoa," remarked Bob.

266

The "Black Ship" passing the Rainmaker Hotel to dump offal at sea

The crew managed to regain their strength quickly and were soon back at the boatyard and on to the work of cleaning the hull. They dressed only in shorts and flip-flops, sweating heavily in the oppressive humidity, and became mottled all over with seaweed, flakes of red paint, and bits of seashells. From time to time, they turned the hose over their heads in a futile attempt to cool off. They were well into it when Don wandered into the marine railway.

"How's it going, fellas?" said Don.

"Not bad, Don," replied Bob, straightening up and stepping aside to stand in the shade of the boat. "Did you get all the gear that you needed?"

"Most of it. You never know what you're going to find in this place. I've got a few days to spare before I fly back. Do you guys need a hand?"

"If you've got nothing better to do. You've done plenty of caulking. We've got about seven miles to do here. Alan and Peter are about to learn the fine art of reefing out the old cotton, so anytime's a good time."

By late afternoon, the caulking crew had set up a good system. Peter and Alan made up the advance guard. Peter used the bent tang of an old chisel as a reefing iron to break through the hardened linseed oil putty and fish out the old caulking cotton. Once he had a piece that was long enough to grab onto, he pulled it out of the groove between the planks until he got to a weak section and it broke, and then he started again. Behind him, Alan cleaned the remaining debris from the groove with a similarly modified chisel to leave it clean for the new caulking.

Don followed, deftly feeding the new string of caulking cotton with two fingers and the thumb of his left hand to one of a variety of caulking irons of different thicknesses that he held between the other two fingers and his palm. With the long-headed, T-shaped caulking mallet in his right hand, he used one of those caulking irons to tap the cotton into the groove

Don Coleman caulking the hull of the *Ron*

Caulking finished and ready for bottom paint

about every four inches, leaving a loop of cotton between. At the end of each plank, he returned to the loops and tapped them home. Finally, he went over the whole length again with a setting iron to finish it off. Each step of the setting iron along the joint usually took three hits. The first two fell with a dull thump as the caulking cotton was driven deep into the groove, and the third resulted in a solid, woody thud as the cotton reached resistance. In Don's expert hands, the mallet sang as he fell into a regular rhythm: thump, thump, *thud;* thump, thump, *thud.*

Working from the waterline down to the turn of the bilge was straightforward, but as he started to work underneath the hull, he had to perform great contortions to position himself properly to work the mallet. Peter and Alan had finished removing all of the loose caulking and putty and came back to where Don was working. They watched the master at work for a while to learn the technique.

"You make that look easy," said Peter.

Don straightened up and looked over at the two. "It is with a little practice," he said with a straight face. "Why don't you guys give it a try while I go look at the stem with Bob?"

Peter took the mallet and setting iron while Alan picked up the paint and started to prepare the newly caulked grooves for the new linseed oil putty. After half an hour, Peter crept out from under the hull and stretched. He winced as he worked out the kinks in his neck and back, and then turned to Alan. "That's real hard yakka!" he said.

"'Yakka?'" said Alan with a puzzled look. "What's that mean?"

"Something you know very little about Alan—hard work! Here you are, mate—it's all yours. Get stuck into it!"

"Sure, I'll give it a try," said Alan and took over for a turn while Peter went up to the bow to check on the progress at the stem.

But instead of inspecting the stem, Bob was looking up at the sky. "There's an old Samoan saying that when a cloud sits on Rainmaker Mountain, it'll rain in ten minutes."

"Are they that accurate?" inquired Peter.

As the heavy drops began to dance off the platform, Bob replied, "I guess not! Here we go into the rinse cycle again!"

The crew took shelter as usual under the hull, careful now to stay away from the runoff from the scuppers. The rain didn't last for long, though, and after half an hour, the steam was rising in the hot sun and they returned to their work.

After a spell of caulking, Alan relinquished the tools to Don and went forward to check out the state of the bow. "How's it look, Bob?" he asked.

"The stem's split at one of the scarf joints." To illustrate, he jammed his finger into the space between two of the three pieces that fit together to form the curve of the bow. "Looks like the headstay's been pulled too tight. The bolts might be broken. We'd never be able to spring the planks and replace the stem in the time that we've got before they dump us back in the water. The best we can do is clean it up and jam some caulking into it to make it watertight. I'll get Don to help me with that when I slack off the headstay to check the gammon iron. Then we'll screw a thick copper plate over the joint. That'll take care of it 'til it gets to a real boatyard."

He gestured further along the hull. "I think we've got some keel bolts loose too," he continued. "We'll lift the cabin sole," he said, reciting new additions to the list, "and I'll have you two get down in the bilge and tighten 'em up. For Christ sake, don't snap any of 'em or geez, what a job we'll have trying to drive 'em out through the bottom. While we're in there, we'll take out those big bronze bungs down by the keel and flush out the bilges. That'll give us a chance to clean out that boxful of wooden matches that's floating around in there so they don't jam the bilge pump again."

The work carried on like this for several days. Bob would inspect different parts of the boat and keep finding more to fix. The crew worked on, from first light to dark, in the sweltering heat and amid the constant din of the power plant and stench of the canneries. Every day the work was interrupted by the cry, "Rinse cycle on the way!" During the downpour, the temperature would drop by a few degrees, only to rocket back up when the sun emerged and the air was filled with steam.

It was in one of the idle moments that these downpours provided that Bob patted his belly and commented, "I think I'm losing weight. It must be the heat."

"Losing weight?" said Alan incredulously. "With the amount of beer you've been putting away, I kinda doubt it."

"They said don't drink the water," Bob joked.

"Yes, but when they said drink from a bottle, they didn't mean the green ones."

Bob snorted. "Well, at least I'm healthy."

Behind the *Ron,* the repairs were underway on the long-liner. The *Ron's* crew kept a careful eye on their progress since the end of that work would likely signal the whole repair fleet's return to Pago Pago Harbor. Bob stopped to check the caulking crew's progress.

"How's it going, fellas?"

"We're keeping ahead of the watch factory," smiled Don, nodding toward the long-liner. Behind them the Korean crew were applying themselves with enthusiasm. At each of the previously determined weak points, they would weld on a roughly cut steel plate that would cover the rusty bit. They would begin by tack-welding the plate at the top, and then take their multipurpose sledgehammer and bash at it until it kind of conformed to the shape of the hull. At that point, they would finish welding around it and slap some paint on it before moving on to the next spot.

In contrast, the tradesman working on the junk just across the platform from them appeared to be doing all of his work with a carving knife. He spent hours a day working on a piece of wood, at intervals checking his progress against the propeller shaft. "What's he doing?" asked Peter. "He's been whittling away on that same piece of wood for days."

"By the look of it, he's making a new propeller shaft bearing from a piece of lignum vitae," said Bob.

"Lignum what?"

"Lignum vitae—a very hard tropical wood used for bearings, cleats, block sheaves, and other nautical shit like that."

"Does it work?"

"It'll probably outlive you. And that won't be hard if you don't get back to work on that caulking."

"It looks like I'll have a short reprieve, skipper," said Peter, laughing and looking skyward. "We're in for another rinse cycle!"

Next to the *Ron*, Joey and his dad, also named Bob, were redoing the bottom paint on their boat. This is normally a routine, mundane chore, but they provided some light entertainment for the *Ron*'s crew. "Dad" would work on one side and Joey on the other. Every few minutes Dad would walk around and look at what his son had done. "You're putting the paint on too thick, Joey," he would chastise in an exasperated tone. Joey would spread the paint out some more and continue with his work. A few minutes later, his dad was back. "You're putting the paint on too thin, Joey," he would say, and Joey would apply some more paint and carry on. A few minutes later, the same thing would happen. The *Ron*'s crew looked at each other as this performance was repeated but knew enough not to criticize the skipper about his own yacht. Eventually, Joey quietly put down his paintbrush and turned down the volume on both of his hearing aids. This appeared to alleviate, at least for him, the constant nagging.

Since it was not a very long job, Joey and his dad soon finished their work and, along with mother Frieda, began hanging around to watch the work on the *Ron* and chat with the crew. They were nice people and generously offered their help. The *Ron*'s crew had to admit that the finished job on their own hull was first class, so once the caulking was complete, Bob succeeded in putting their experience to work as part of the painting crew. This sped up the work tremendously and allowed them to stay ahead of the watch factory. He teamed Joey up with Peter and Don on one side. Joey worked happily away with them and exchanged sailing tales as they worked. On the other side, Bob and Alan had their hands full keeping Dad focused on his work since he constantly wanted to check on Joey to make sure that he was doing a good job. To help, they placed some old barrels strategically at the bow and stern to obstruct him from taking surreptitious looks at the progress on the other side. When they were done, Bob inspected the work and couldn't help taking the opportunity to comment. "Pretty good job, fellas," he said, and then added with a grin, "even if it's a bit thin in places on our side."

The following day, Bob announced to the crew, "It looks like the watch factory's going out of business. They'll probably put us in at the next high tide. Let's do a final check before we get wet, so we don't end our trip in the middle of the harbor."

Four hours later, the diesel winch started up with a roar, and soon the railway platform was rattling slowly down the tracks. It stopped when the long-liner was afloat. "We'll have to sit here for a minute until the rust bucket gets its engine started," said Bob.

Peter looked doubtfully at the fishing boat. "And what if it doesn't?"

"Then we'll have to tow it out with the Avon and the outboard," Bob joked. "That's if it'd stay inflated long enough!"

They didn't need to put the dinghy to the test, as it turned out, and two hours later, the *Ron* was returned to its anchorage. They were getting closer to their departure.

Chapter 32

A Suspicious Sinking

Later that week the crew was trudging through town as a rusty Asian long-liner, the *Kwang Myong 65*, chugged by, heading out of the harbor. She was about ninety feet in length and was typical of the aging Asian fishing fleet. She had a high wheelhouse and bow, with a low waist from which the small crew set the miles of mainline with the fishing lines suspended below it, along with the hundreds of bamboo poles and floats above that supported the mainline and marked its location. This one, however, sat noticeably down in the stern, with about a twenty-degree list to port. In fact, it looked most unseaworthy. Fortunately for the crew of the *Kwang Myong 65*, it was one of those unusually calm days in the tropics where the trade winds had disappeared, to be replaced by low, ragged clouds that trapped an oppressive humidity below them. The *Ron*'s crew watched the long-liner push past, its image barely reflected in the flat, oily-looking water, until it was lost from their view. Soon after, they went their separate ways to take care of various tasks, arranging to meet at the Rainmaker Hotel near the entrance to the harbor for lunch.

Like in any port town, news of a calamity travels quickly, even if it isn't all true, so when Peter bumped into Alan heading down to the hotel, they had already heard a variety of stories about the long-liner having gone up on the reef. Regardless of the circumstances, the outcome was not a great surprise. There are numerous cases in the South Pacific of similarly abject commercial vessels conveniently running onto reefs and all of the crew miraculously being saved by lifeboats, by a nearby emergency service, or even by walking ashore. The rusty hulks that are left behind mark the entrance to many harbors. Rumors suggest that these events are often cases of financial rather than nautical distress.

They met Bob at the hotel as planned. He was working on a Steinlager beer—not an unfamiliar image—while he sat at a table in the restaurant that looked over the harbor entrance and the reef some two miles away. "That shit box has gone up on the reef," he observed as they walked in.

Peter and Alan sat down. "Yeah, we heard about it," said Alan, peering up the harbor. "Is it still afloat?"

"Take a look. Sitting up on the east side," Bob said, pointing.

"I heard that it sprung a leak," said Peter, following his gaze.

"Like an insurance leak," said Bob. "Anyway, let's order some lunch and watch the circus."

Lunch had just arrived when the harbor tug came by, pushing a huge bow wave as it hurriedly made its way out to the fishing boat. They watched from this vantage point as the tug approached, slowed, nudged up to the distressed vessel, and took the boat's crew aboard. When all were safe, the tug's crew fixed a line to the stern of the boat to try to pull it off the reef. "She looks like she's pretty hard aground," said Peter. "Just look how high the bow is."

"And aren't we on a falling tide?" asked Bob.

"Yeah, high tide was about an hour ago," said Alan.

It took some work, but eventually the fishing boat was pulled free of the reef to float unevenly in the still water. "Look how low she's sitting!" Alan remarked. "Looks pretty bad."

"She might have holed when she hit," Bob speculated.

The armchair salvagers continued to offer their opinions as they ate their lunch, and by the time they had finished eating, the tug had tied a line to the bow and taken her in tow. As the tug came abreast of the hotel, they could see that the fishing boat's condition had worsened. "She's starting to sit even lower in the water," said Bob. "The bloody stern's submerged now."

View of Pago Pago Harbor entrance and reefs from the cable car atop Rainmaker Mountain

A still and humid day in Pago Pago Harbor

"Look at that!" Peter exclaimed, and pointed to the beach. Bobbing in the water and floating toward shore like a tiny armada were hundreds of round glass fishing floats. The village children were wading into the water to retrieve them, laughing and playing with them as they did.

"They've come loose from the hold, I expect," said Bob.

"Here comes the cavalry!" said Alan, as a police car drove off the road and onto the beach, lights flashing and siren blaring. It came to a stop, and two heavyset policemen in dark blue uniforms got out, waiting on the sand until the pint-sized perpetrators began to emerge from the water with their prizes. They tried frantically to stop the children, but in spite of their superior size and authority, they were outclassed in terms of agility, and the scene became more like a segment from the Keystone Cops. Empty-handed, the two officers finally gave up their pursuit.

"We'd better get down to the boat and see where they dump that shit box," said Bob, getting up.

They paid their bill and turned to leave. "Thanks! We'll be back for the evening performance!" Peter said to the hostess as they left.

The crew hurried as fast as they could through the steamy afternoon heat of Pago Pago to get back to the *Ron* to make sure it was safe. As they passed the post office, they heard the familiar tone of the Honda motorbike and turned to see Gary putt-putting along the road, grinning from ear to ear. Leonard was on the back, almost obscured by a clutch of large glass floats that he struggled to control, looking like something out of Barnum and Bailey. Gary slowed only enough to crow to them. "You wouldn't read about it!" he said in his New Zealand jargon. "Each one of these bastards is worth fifty dollars back home!"

"That Gary, he loves something for nothing!" laughed Bob. "Look at 'im. He's as happy as a pig in shit!"

They could see the progress of the tug in the harbor as they walked. It had safely passed the *Ron* now, and the stern of the fishing boat sank lower and lower as the tug fought to get its tow to the marine railway. It

Sunken long-liner Kwang Myong 65

was a losing battle. By now more than half of the boat was underwater, and it began to threaten to submerge the stern of the tug. The tug kept on as long as it could, but just short of the railway, the skipper must have decided that he couldn't slow to make the turn to head into the ramp without the boat sinking completely. Instead, he gunned the engine to make one last push toward shallow water at the end of the harbor, and at the last second, cut the long-liner free, the stern of the tug visibly bobbing up clear of the surface as it did. Within thirty seconds, the fishing boat had all but vanished, with only fifteen feet of its rusty bow protruding above the dark water, leaving behind a trail of oil and debris.

Chapter 33

A Mission of Mercy

A week or so later, Alan and Peter were refinishing the brightwork on the *Ron* when they saw a skiff motoring toward them. As it came closer, they recognized Mike and Shawn, two commercial divers they had met who were working on the construction of a new marine railway. Alan put down his sandpaper and walked astern to catch the painter as they came alongside.

"How're ya doin', guys?" Alan called to them over the sound of the engine.

"Great, Al," said Mike as he fended off to prevent the rough edge of the skiff from scuffing the hull.

Alan tied the line to the stern cleat, and Shawn shut off the engine. "Come aboard. It's about time for a union break. Coffee?"

"Sure," said Mike as he grabbed the boarding ladder and climbed up to the deck.

"Yeah, thanks," added Shawn, following.

"G'day, fellas!" called Peter from the bosun's chair halfway up the mast. Mike and Shawn looked up, shielding their eyes from the sun.

"Hi, Pete!" called Shawn.

Mike waved. "Nice to see you doing some work for a change! Where's Bob?"

"He's gone in to town to make some calls," replied Peter, "leaving us to do all the work!"

The two visitors ducked under the sun awning and sat down in the cockpit. "Beautiful yacht," observed Shawn, looking down into the main saloon.

Alan returned with the coffee and passed up two mugs. "I'll give you guys the tour before you go," he said, and then climbed up the companionway ladder with two more mugs.

Peter had lowered himself to the deck and joined them in the cockpit. "What're you guys up to today?" he asked.

Mike took a sip of his coffee before replying. "We got the contract to go down and take a look at that sunken fishing boat. It looks pretty shady. We had a quick look, but we could only find superficial damage to the hull."

"But surprise, surprise," Shawn interjected, "some of the sea cocks were open! The insurance adjuster from Hong Kong was here a couple of days ago. He's kinda suspicious, so he's asked us to check the boat out and write a report."

"He had the ship's manifest," continued Mike. "It was provisioned for three months. Part of the deal is that we can have the Steinlager beer that's on board if we can get it off. We've already got the diving platform alongside. Our Samoan helper, Paul, is getting the equipment set up. We thought maybe you and Peter would give us a hand to haul it up. There's no money involved, but whatever beer we recover, we'll split 50–50."

"Sounds like a worthwhile cause!" suggested Peter.

"Yeah," agreed Alan. "And I think Bob would see the wisdom of it!" he said with a grin.

"Well, we've got all of the gear ready to go. Can you come over this morning?"

"Don't see why not," said Alan, looking over at Peter.

"No time like the present," agreed Peter with a nod.

"That's great," said Mike. "You guys finish up what you're doing, and we'll get going when you're ready."

"Suits me," said Alan. "I'll leave Bob a note."

When Bob returned in the dinghy a couple of hours later, he was puzzled to find the boat empty. On the chart table, he found a note. It read: "On a mission of mercy. Back for happy hour."

Alan and Peter were suited up on the diving platform, with masks, fins, weights, buoyancy compensators, and tanks nearby, ready to jump into the water in case of an emergency. Mike, Shawn, and Joe, their helper, were down below, retrieving the crates of beer and putting them into a big cargo net. Alan and Peter hauled up the last load onto the deck and stacked them along with the others into two neat piles. They could tell from the bubbles that the divers were ascending along the line that guided them through the soupy mix of water, silt, and debris that surrounded the wreck.

As the divers broke the surface, Alan and Peter quickly grabbed their gear so that they could climb up the short ladder onto the platform before peeling off their own wet suits.

"Nice work, fellas!" said Alan in greeting.

"And none too soon," announced Peter. "I was just about to pop the cap on some of the cargo to replace some valuable fluids!"

"How'd it go?" asked Alan, offering Mike a big bottle of water.

"About as expected," he replied, peeling off the top of his wet suit and taking the water bottle. "We got all the information the insurance company was looking for." He took a long drink before passing the bottle around.

"And nineteen crates of Steinlager in the bargain. That's 228 bottles," said Alan. "Not a bad job!"

"That should keep our thirst at bay for a couple of weeks," added Peter. "That's over 450 pints of beer by my calculation!"

"All in a day's work around here," said Shawn with a chuckle.

"What's next?" asked Peter.

"Let's get this gear stowed," said Mike. "Joe," he called to their young helper, "how about getting the motor started, and I'll get us untied."

They pulled away from the wreck, the skiff pulling the diving platform and leaving a sickly green-brown wake.

———

Bob was standing on deck as they approached. As they got closer, he could see the crates of bottles stacked on the deck. "I thought you guys were going off to save some damsel in distress!"

"Even better!" called Peter.

Alan threw a line to Bob, and they maneuvered the platform alongside.

"You've got to earn your share, Bob," said Peter. "We've done all the hard yakka; now get your big fucking paws around these as we pass them up!"

It didn't take long before their nine and a half dozen quart-sized bottles were stacked on the afterdeck of the *Ron*.

"Okay, we're gonna get the platform put away and this beer unloaded," said Mike when they'd finished.

"Come on back when you're done, and we'll knock the top off a few," invited Peter.

"Naw, gotta get this beer home, or it'll disappear," replied Mike. "Thanks for your help. See you guys later."

Alan cast off the mooring line, and the skiff pulled gently away.

"He's right," said Bob. "We're going to have to stow these below; otherwise, they'll disappear in the dark of night."

"Where do you want them?" asked Alan.

"In the bilges with the rest, I guess," said Bob, surveying the pile. "I reckon we can get at least thirty bottles forward of the water tanks and twenty or more aft." He stopped and made a mental calculation. "Then we'll just have to drink the rest."

"Let me take a look," suggested Alan. "You never know."

Chapter 34

Flying the Flag

"I t's 7 a.m. in Pago Pago. It's thirty-seven degrees and one hundred percent humidity. This is radio WVUV FM in American Samoa. Stay tuned for the local and international news, followed by Casey Kasem's Top 40."

Cheery Polynesian instrumental music played in the background as the radio announcer continued with the broadcast. It looked like another stinker of a day in Pago Pago Harbor. In the main saloon, the crew was sipping their coffee as Bob went through his morning ritual of checking the seemingly unending list of work. The skylights overhead were open to encourage what little breeze there might be to enter and provide some relief. Bob looked up from his deliberations and stated conclusively, "We're going to have to make up a new gammon iron. I found some cracks in the old one, and we don't want to lose the bowsprit. We'll have to go around to the marine railway to get it done."

"When are you planning to go?" asked Alan nonchalantly.

"I've got to make a drawing and get some measurements together—probably about eleven, I guess. Why?" asked Bob suspiciously.

"Because I've kinda got a date for lunch."

"What?" asked Peter with surprise.

"With who?" asked Bob, raising his eyebrows.

"An American woman I met in town."

"So that's the reason you've been going to the post office every day and coming back empty-handed!" said Bob as it suddenly dawned on him.

"Well, somebody's got to keep the Samoan economy afloat while you go and have fun," Peter jibed. "Don't give a thought to us, mate. Go and enjoy yourself. We'll be right!"

"We know what you'll be doing!" said Bob.

"She's not like that," Alan protested. "We just met. She seems like a really nice girl."

"Then ask her if she's got a couple of really nice girlfriends," suggested Bob.

"Yeah, a man's not a camel, you know!" Peter chimed in.

It was after eleven when Bob stood in the cockpit with his drawing, pencil, and tape measure, ready to go. Peter came up the companionway. "Right-oh, let's get moving," said Bob. "Where's the bosun?"

"Still in the head preening himself for his big date."

"What? He's been in there for a bloody hour! Get yer ass up here, bosun!" he called down the companionway. "Let's get this show on the road!" A few moments later, Alan emerged, scrubbed, trimmed, and dressed in his cleanest gear. "Come on, bucko," insisted Bob. "You don't want to keep the lady waiting."

They all climbed down into the dinghy, which was in surprisingly good health, and motored downwind to avoid an early soaking by the spray from the bow. They ended up coming ashore below Soli's Restaurant and Bar, a quarter of a mile or so down the harbor from the rock mole. They carried the dinghy over the sharp oyster shells that lined the shore and tied it to one of the pilings that supported the deck of the bar.

"We'll be a couple of hours getting this gammon iron done," said Bob. "We'll meet back here. See if you can drag your ass back before midnight, bosun." Alan assured them that he would and walked off toward town.

"We're going around to see Big Charlie," Bob said, turning to Peter. "We'll need to take him some beer."

"Shit, we should have grabbed some of that Steinlager from on board," said Peter.

"Too late now. We're not going back out for it," said Bob.

"Okay, then, let's go over to the store and pick him up a six-pack," Peter suggested.

"A six-pack? He has that for morning tea!" Bob exclaimed with an animated look of surprise. "And we don't want to insult him. We'd better get him a dozen big Steinlager."

"You mean the quart size?"

"Of course."

With the Steinlager in hand, they stood waiting for the local bus. Bob explained to Peter whom they were going to meet. "Big Charlie is *the man* at the railway. Nothing happens without his say-so."

"Why do they call him Big Charlie?"

"Just wait 'til you see this dude. He's about six-foot-fourteen and weighs four hundred and fifty pounds. You know how some people tear telephone books in half? Well, this dude tears anvils in half!"

"Sounds like he deserves plenty of respect," said Peter.

"Yeah," Bob replied. "He's so big he doesn't fit into any normal clothes on the island. The only thing that fits him is a *lava lava* the size of a three-man tent!"

Big Charlie lived up to his billing. He stood up as he saw them walk into the machine shed. He was bigger than a sumo wrestler, towering over the workers, and as big around as a bull. His enormous feet hung out over the sides of his flip-flops like slabs of meat that are too big for their plates, and his neck seemed to be missing, his huge head instead sitting squarely on his massive shoulders. He wore only a *lava lava* around his waist that barely contained his bulging belly, but his arms and legs appeared to be solid muscle. When he started to walk toward them, the floorboards sagged with complaint. He gave a small smile as he approached. "*Malo*, Captain Bob," he said in a deep, clear voice and extended his hand.

Bob shook it or, rather, responded to the shake. "*Malo*. How are ya, Charlie? This is a mate of mine, Peter, from Australia."

"G'day, Charlie," Peter said, extending his hand politely. Charlie shook Peter's hand, the hand itself and part of his lower arm enveloped by the giant mitt. Peter winced inwardly at the grip.

"I brought you some lunch," said Bob, smiling as he picked up the crate and passed it to Charlie.

"*Fa'afetai*. What are you up to, Bob?"

"I need to make a new gammon iron."

"No problem. I'll get a couple of guys to set up the forge. You've got the measurements?"

"It's all right here." Bob held up the drawing, and then together he and Charlie selected the metal that they needed and Charlie put his men to work. Bob and Peter shared some of Charlie's "lunch" as they oversaw the operation.

⋯⋯⋯⋯

Several hours later, Bob and Peter stepped off the bus outside Soli's Restaurant and Bar carrying the completed gammon iron. They walked down to the beach to find the dinghy gone. Peter pointed out to the *Ron*. "There it is," he said. "Alan's beat us back. That's a surprise."

Bob held his hand up to shade his eyes from the sun. "What are those fucking flags in the rigging?" he said with surprise.

"Don't know. Can you see what they are?" asked Peter.

"Wait a minute, wait a minute, wait a minute," Bob muttered. "I can just make them out. They're signal codes. B—'I am taking in or discharging explosives' … X—'stop carrying out your intentions and watch for my signals' … Letter R—that's 'Romeo.'"

290

They both burst out laughing. "That clever bastard!" Peter exclaimed. "I saw him reading the signal book. At least he's put it to good use!"

"Look at us!" said Bob. "We're dripping in sweat just standing still. I can only imagine that they're working up a hell of a sweat down below!"

"Come on, it's stinking hot out here," said Peter. "Let's get inside for a couple of cold ones and put 'em on Alan's bar bill."

They walked into the luxury of the air-conditioning of Soli's and ordered two cold Budweisers at the bar. One of the unique features of the establishment was the row of one-armed bandits that sat along one wall. Strangely, these were the only gambling machines on the island; they made one wonder what special arrangements were in place to allow these machines to operate. Perched on a stool in front of one of these machines was Andy, an American man in his midsixties with thinning white hair. He was scruffily dressed and grasped a drink in one hand that he sipped at intervals between plugging quarters into the machine and pulling the handle with the other. He had a rough, weather-beaten face and looked a lot like the late actor Richard Boone. In contrast, seated alongside him at the next machine was his wife, Marie, petite and immaculately groomed. She clutched her trademark, Seagram's Seven and 7UP.

Andy acknowledged them with a gruff "howdy" as Bob and Peter walked by to take a table by the window overlooking the harbor. This vantage point gave them a good view of the *Ron* as well as the other yachts and all of the maritime comings and goings at this end of the harbor.

Peter looked over at Andy. "That Andy and his missus are in here all the time. What do they bloody do for money?"

"He's one of the few people I know who spend their whole life trying to avoid doing an honest day's work and is successful at it," Bob replied. "Apart from having the biggest porno collection in the world, he buys and sells those Asian rust buckets."

"You wouldn't think there's much money in those."

"They get about five to ten thousand apiece. But this island runs on graft and corruption, so he gets all the government contracts for abandoned boats that can't pay their harbor fees. He's got contacts in Korea, and he's got a Samoan guy in government that helps him fix up the deals."

"But who does he sell the boats to?"

"Most of the boats are presold before he's even bought them. He told me last month that he sold five of them to a Chinese guy. They left the harbor with the best one of the bunch towing the other four. When I told him I didn't think they'd make it, he turned to me and said, 'I don't give a shit. I've got my money in the bank.'"

"Unbelievable. Sounds like a real wheeler-dealer."

"He's a funny bastard. He got a new truck last week. He'd waited for *months* for this fucking thing to come from the U.S. They unloaded it on the dock—brand-new. He went to pick it up, pissed to the gills, and only drove it as far as here. He tried to park it and says it got stuck in gear. Well, I don't know how fast he was going, but he ran right over one of those rusty little local cars and smashed into that brick wall. It was a write-off, and it only had twelve miles on it!"

"Hey! There goes Alan!" Peter interrupted, pointing to the *Ron*.

The flags had been taken down, and the dinghy with two people aboard was motoring up the harbor.

"Where's he going?" Bob asked, puzzled.

"Probably to the LBJ Hospital to get rehydrated. I think they're probably both down a couple of pints."

"Serves 'em right."

"Well, I hope the outboard doesn't stop because he won't have the strength to pull the string to restart it!"

"He's going to be awhile before he gets back here. What're we going to do?" asked Bob rhetorically.

"We don't have much choice," Peter replied, sitting back in his chair. "We're just going to have to sit here and have a couple more beers."

"Maybe we should try something more expensive," suggested Bob. "After all, we're not paying for it."

Peter smiled and nodded. "That sounds fair."

Chapter 35

Diving on the Tuna Seiners

It was late one afternoon when Alan and Peter walked again through the cluster of vessels at the marine railway. As they neared an American yacht, the young skipper straightened up from his work scraping the bottom of the hull. "How's it goin', fellas?" he called to them.

"Pretty good, mate," replied Peter.

"Yeah, good, Frank," said Alan. "Have you seen Mike and Shawn today?"

"Yeah, they're working off the skiff down at the concrete pilings," he said, pointing the way with his scraper.

They walked in the direction he had indicated down to the edge of the water. The ten-by-twenty-foot timber diving platform was anchored about ten feet from them in the shallow water. Shawn was sitting on a wooden crate, hunched over with his back toward them. Beside him a gasoline engine rattled away with a steady rhythm, turning a compressor and feeding air down the long rubber hose that snaked over the side to Mike, who was apparently working down below.

Alan called out, "Hey, Shawn!" But even from this close, he couldn't be heard over the racket of the engine.

"He hasn't moved. Must be asleep," laughed Peter.

Suddenly Shawn leaped to his feet and jerked up on the fishing rod that they could now see him holding with both hands. The tip of the rod doubled over, quivering, as Shawn strained to reel in his catch.

"It must be something big!" exclaimed Peter.

"Maybe he's hooked his brother!" said Alan with a laugh.

Proving him wrong, at the other end of the platform, Mike's head broke the surface and he started to climb up the ladder. As he did, Shawn succeeded in hauling a very unhappy three-foot-long baby hammerhead shark clear of the water. He swung it onto the platform, narrowly missing his startled brother, who froze as the shark thrashed and gnashed violently between them. Shawn appeared unsure of his next move, but he was relieved of the need to decide when the shark broke free of the hook, writhing vigorously, and bounced its way across the platform, over the edge, and back into the murky water. Shawn put down the fishing rod and turned around to shut off the engine. He saw Peter and Alan and waved. Mike finished climbing onto the skiff. He pulled off his helmet, but before he could say anything to Shawn, he also saw the two.

"Hi, guys!" called Mike.

"Hi, Mike. I don't suppose you saw that hammerhead's mother down there?" asked Alan.

"You're kidding! I can hardly see my hand in front of my face, but I'm sure she was close by." He stripped off his wet suit to avoid baking in the heat. "Where's Bob?" he asked.

"He's gone to visit a friend," Peter replied, "so we've got some time to ourselves."

"We thought we'd come over to see how things are going," said Alan.

"Well, if you've got nothing to do, would you be interested in giving Shawn and me a hand cleaning a couple of those big American tuna seiners?"

"What's involved?" asked Alan.

"We've done a visual underwater inspection. The hulls are pretty good, but the props and rudders are fairly fouled and the anodes are shot on both of them."

Anodes are used to reduce corrosion on all kinds of boats. Different metals together in seawater create an electric current like a battery, called electrolysis, and result in corrosion of metal parts. The anodes are made of zinc, which corrodes more easily than other metals, and reduce the damage to the boat by sacrificing themselves before the important parts of the boat are affected. These anodes gradually disappear and need to be replaced from time to time.

"So it's mainly cleaning them and zapping on some new anodes with the electric welder," he said casually. "It's worth a hundred bucks US a day for each of you, and, of course, as much Steinlager as you need to wash the salt out of your throats at the end of the day."

"When do we start?" asked Peter keenly, looking over to Alan.

"I'm in," said Alan.

"What about eleven tomorrow morning? Shawn and I'll bring the skiff across to the wharf, get the diving platform set up, and then come over to your boat and pick you up."

"Sounds real good," said Peter.

"Okay, guys. We'll see you tomorrow then."

Alan and Peter stood on the diving platform in the midday sun, their diving gear at their feet. From their vantage point alongside the first tuna seiner, they could appreciate the immensity of the vessel. The ship's gunwale towered at least thirty feet above them, and like others in the fleet, it stretched over two hundred feet from bow to stern. Mike had told them that each one cost over twelve million US dollars to build and could go to sea for up to three months at a time. Like the vessels Alan had seen the day he arrived, every one of the boats in the fleet carried a Hughes 500 helicopter strapped onto a landing pad that they used to scout for the tuna.

"This is going to be a big job," said Alan as he inched closer to the edge of the platform, trying to get into the narrow band of shade produced by the flare of the hull.

American tuna seiner *Montana* in Pago Pago Harbor

"I can't wait to get into the water and cool off," said Peter, joining him. "With this heat, let's hope it takes all day. And at a hundred US a day, I don't care if it takes all week!"

Mike and Shawn had gone to shore in the workboat to pick up the zinc anodes and now arrived back and began unloading half a dozen of them onto the platform. Alan and Peter walked across the platform to give them a hand, and Alan leaned over into the boat to pick one up. They were silver-colored ingots, about a foot and a half long, eight inches wide and four inches thick. The surface was rough, but with a shiny finish that made them look like they were still molten. A flat steel bar was embedded just below the surface and protruded about eight inches from each end. He grabbed one, lifting it by one of its metal tails. "Boy, these are heavy!" he remarked.

"Yeah, they weigh close to forty pounds each," said Mike as he heaved one onto the platform. "And they cost twenty-five dollars apiece, so don't drop any or you'll be twenty-five bucks short in your pay!"

"They're sure enormous compared to the ones on the *Ron*," said Peter. "The one on the *Ron's* prop shaft isn't much bigger than a bar of soap!" He carefully lifted the last one aboard. "Let's get geared up and into the water, Al, before we both get roasted. Although," he said, glancing down, "I must say the water doesn't look all that appealing. Just look at the film of diesel on the surface."

They began pulling on their wet suits as Mike, already geared up, slipped into the water with the electric welding torch. He called back, "I'll go down and get organized. Peter, you grab the first anode and meet me down near the keel. The visibility is only about fifteen feet, so just follow my bubbles."

Peter dropped over the edge of the platform into the water. He added a little extra air to his buoyancy vest and called to Shawn, "Hand me one of those anodes, mate."

Shawn picked up the anode in both hands and dropped down into a crouching position at the edge of the platform. "Now, there's one thing that you've got to be careful about," Shawn cautioned him.

"What's that?"

"When Mike starts welding, make goddamned sure you've got those metal tails in good contact with the bare metal of the hull," he said with a mischievous grin. "Otherwise you'll get your ass fried!"

"Oh," Peter said hesitantly.

"Don't worry. It probably won't kill ya," Shawn added, and without waiting, thrust the anode into Peter's still outstretched hand.

Peter quickly put his regulator in his mouth. With the sudden extra weight overcoming the now insufficient buoyancy, Peter sunk like a rock, vigorously kicking and simultaneously adding air to his vest, regaining his buoyancy just as he came level with Mike at a depth of twenty-five feet. He cradled the valuable anode against his chest and swam toward Mike nonchalantly, as if this was the way he had intended to make his entrance. Moments later, Peter saw Alan arrive at the keel.

Mike had by now attached the ground clamp to the keel and scraped away the paint to the bare metal. Peter held the anode in both hands, pushing it against the keel while at the same time kicking with his flippers to try to maintain a solid contact as Shawn had instructed. With the anode in place, Mike touched the electrode to the metal tail with a flash of light.

From the first instant, Peter could feel a tingling in his fingers. The involuntary contractions of the muscles tightened his grip on the anode, but resulted in a slight decrease in the pressure he was able to bring to bear against the keel. He clenched his teeth and kicked harder, breathing heavily with the exertion and sucking hard on his air supply, blowing an almost constant stream of bubbles from his regulator. The tingling quickly developed into tiny spasms, so that his grip was loosened, weakening the contact between the metal strap and the keel and causing more of the current to course through not just his hands now, but into his arms and shoulders. One of the steel straps finally lost contact, and his head jerked back in a final convulsion as he was forced to release the anode. It dropped immediately into the gloom below, but Peter didn't see it. Suddenly forty pounds lighter, he shot upward toward the surface, out of Alan and Mike's sight. His initial trajectory was interrupted by his contact with the steel hull, but the additional buoyancy forced him up higher, bouncing him along the curved hull. He blew out through his regulator, simultaneously purging air from his vest to prevent him from bursting to the surface and ending up with an air embolism. A few seconds later, he emerged gently next to the platform.

"Done already?" Shawn snickered.

Peter had a rush of anger, frustration, and above all else, the thought that he didn't want to lose twenty-five dollars from the day's pay. He cast Shawn a determined glance, put the regulator back in his mouth, ducked his head, and with a swish of his fins disappeared once again below the surface. Alan was halfway to the surface as Peter appeared and swam straight past him and into the murk below the keel. He kept going down and down, waiting for the bottom to come into view. He was surprised that it was so deep and that the visibility actually increased as he went deeper. When he finally saw the contrast of the lost anode against the muddy bottom, he looked at his depth gauge and found he was at fifty feet. He grabbed the anode and instinctively looked around while adding air to his vest.

Peter had to kick hard to reach the level of the keel again, and when he emerged through the swirling haze, he saw Mike and Alan hovering together, waiting for him. As soon as they saw what he was carrying, Mike shook his head in apparent disbelief, and a stream of bubbles spewed from Alan's regulator as he laughed out loud. They saw that Peter had found a second anode! Peter swam straight past them and continued upward. Breaking the surface once again beside the platform, Peter held the two anodes up for Shawn to see. He spat out his regulator and shouted triumphantly, "I got the bastard, and another one for good measure! Quick, grab one!" Shawn bent down and hauled one of them onto the platform. Reaching for his regulator, Peter called, "It looks like I'm not the only person that's dropped one. And I expect another twenty-five bucks in my pay packet as well!" Shawn grinned, and Peter vanished below the surface.

Back down at the keel, Peter signaled to Alan, who nodded and took one tail of the anode. They adjusted their buoyancy and together placed the anode into position. Looking relieved, Mike leaned forward to commence welding. This time both Peter and Alan pushed as hard as they could to ensure that a good contact was maintained with the hull. To be sure, Alan reached one arm under the keel, gripping the other side to get a better purchase. As Mike started welding, they both began to feel a slight tingle in their fingers, prompting them to put in an even greater effort.

The next two minutes seemed like an eternity. Their muscles began to burn as the electrocutioner completed one side and then finally finished the other before they were able to rest their aching limbs. Mike signaled to them to go to the surface and bring down another anode.

Floating at the surface, Alan turned to Peter and said with a grin, "I think we've just about got this figured out now!"

"Yeah, it only took us an hour and a half to do a five-minute job, and I don't know about you but I'm stuffed already! I think—hey, what's happened to your hand? Look at the blood pissing out of it!" Peter said in surprise.

"Shit, I've sliced the bloody thing open!" exclaimed Alan, staring at his palm. "It must have been those damned barnacles on the keel!"

"Let me have a look!" called Shawn as he bent down on the edge of the diving platform. Alan swam over and held up his hand for Shawn to look at. Shawn studied it for a few seconds. "I don't think it's as bad as it looks." He found some antibiotic cream in the first-aid kit and smeared it on. "Here, put on my neoprene diving gloves. The pressure should stop the bleeding, and we'll clean it up properly at the end of the day."

"How do they feel?" asked Peter as Alan finished pulling on the gloves.

"That does the trick. Hand us down another anode, Shawn. We'd better get our asses moving, or Mike'll think we've quit already!"

By late that afternoon they had finished welding the last of the anodes. They loaded their gear into the workboat and climbed in. Mike fired up the outboard. "I don't know about you, but I'm knackered!" said Peter.

"Me too," said Alan. "My arms and hands are shot!"

"Nothing a hot shower and a couple of cold beers won't fix!" shouted Mike above the roar of the motor.

———

The next morning when Alan and Peter stepped onto the diving platform, Shawn was standing over a strange-looking device. At first glance it looked like a commercial floor polisher crossed with an octopus. It had two brushes about eighteen inches in diameter mounted side by side on a metal frame. At the rear of the frame, a pair of hoses extended from each side, leading to two coils of black hose. Peter walked across to Shawn. "What is this mechanical monstrosity?" he asked.

"It's for scrubbing the hull. Mike's gonna give 'em a quick once-over."

"Is it easy to use?" asked Alan, joining them.

"Well, it probably won't kill ya," he began. Alan and Peter exchanged glances. "But if you give it too much juice," Shawn continued, "it'll take off with ya."

"Let's get geared up and get it in the water," said Mike. "You guys can start on the first boat with a scraper and wire brush. Al, you take the rudder, and Pete, you do the propeller."

From a distance of about twenty feet, Peter could see the outline of the rudder and propeller. As he swam closer, he could make out the details. It was a four-bladed propeller with a diameter of about twelve feet, supported on about an eight-inch-diameter driveshaft. It had come to a stop with one pair of the opposing blades almost vertical. It was badly fouled with a variety of marine growth, including barnacles and coral. He headed for the prop, and Alan, swimming nearby, headed for the rudder.

Hanging onto one of the horizontal blades of the prop with one hand, Peter realized the enormity of the job and thought to himself that he should have had that extra piece of toast for breakfast. He started in with the scraper and was soon surrounded by a cloud of particles suspended in the water around him. This reduced the visibility to about a foot, so that he could just make out his hand in front of his face. In this visual isolation, Peter's imagination began to go to work. *What*, he thought, *would prevent the ship's engineer from starting up the engine and turning him into mincemeat?* He imagined a school of hammerhead sharks in a feeding frenzy, chomping on his remains. He quickly looked around him in a futile attempt to guard against such an imagined attack.

A short distance away, Alan hung onto the edge of the rudder. It was huge compared to the *Ron's,* rectangular in shape and some eighteen feet high by eight feet wide. He scraped away at the accumulation of growth as he was enveloped in his own cloud of muck. He thought about how many meals this would make and chuckled to himself. Alan worked methodically, starting at the bottom on the starboard side and cleaning a swath about three feet wide from the forward edge to the trailing edge and then moving around to the port side and cleaning toward the front. He was about halfway through his first tank of air when he got up to the level of the lower blade of the propeller.

Peter was just starting work on the second blade of the prop, still surrounded in a cloud of debris, when a black fin flashed in front of his eyes. Instinctively he lashed out with the scraper to fend it off, striking it a solid blow. Then, pushing himself off from the prop with all his might, he swam hard for clearer water, his head swiveling frantically, searching for the shark.

Simultaneously, Alan felt what could only be a shark attacking his flipper. He jerked his leg away and cast a quick glance blindly toward it, and then began swimming as hard as he could. He didn't know where he was going yet, but far away from here seemed like a good start! Alan tried to focus on the direction of the bubbles boiling from his regulator inches in front of his face, vainly seeking a clue to whether he was going up, down, or level, just as he emerged into clearer water.

Up ahead, Peter froze as a huge hulk shot out of the murk toward him, knowing from the shape that it could only be a hammerhead. He raised the only weapon at hand—the scraper—in a farcical gesture to defend himself. Alan collided with him, and the two instantly recoiled before each recognized the other. Peter grabbed Alan's arm and held the open palm of his other hand over his head like a fin to indicate a shark.

Alan nodded vigorously and pointed to his fin, seeing it clearly for the first time, and frowned to see that it was intact.

Peter flashed his open palm in front of his mask and made a slashing motion with the scraper.

Then they both stopped for a moment and looked at one another as the realization sunk in that they had attacked one another. They hung there together for a few seconds and then they saw Mike about fifteen feet away, following their bubbles toward them. He looked at them suspiciously and made an "O" shape with his thumb and forefinger, asking "are you okay?" They nodded nonchalantly, signaling "okay" to each other and then to Mike. Peter indicated that they were going up for air, and they slowly ascended toward the skiff.

It took five tanks of air for each of them to complete both boats, all without any further "shark" incidents. By four o'clock, they were relaxing on the platform with a couple of Steinlagers.

"You guys handled that pretty well for first-timers!" said Mike.

Alan looked over at Peter, and they both burst out laughing. "Yeah, it was a piece of cake except for the phantom shark!" said Peter.

"What's this about a phantom shark?" asked Shawn.

"Ah, don't worry about it," replied Alan. "It was just a figment of our imaginations. What about a couple more beers?"

Chapter 36

———◆—×—◆———

Rust Bucket Rodeo

The *Ron*'s crew was taking refuge down below from a torrential rain, whiling away the time reading and intermittently mopping up drips from the skylights that were now exposed to the elements after the removal of the sun awnings in preparation for their departure. The rain lasted about an hour, and as the intensity decreased, it was supplemented by a series of wind squalls. Due to the narrowing of the harbor and the surrounding mountains, these winds were accelerated into intense but short-lived gusts of up to thirty or forty knots. The crew had moved the yacht farther down the harbor to tie up to a huge mooring buoy designed to secure offshore vessels, so they were less concerned by these regular events than when they had been at anchor. However, without the attenuating effect of the heavy anchor chain, the wind that now whistled through the rigging made the *Ron* jerk at its short tether like a mad bull, lurching back and forth at its mooring. They were shifted by each lurch but tried to ignore the imposition. Above the noise of these events, they suddenly heard the distant sounds of shouting. "What the hell's that?" asked Peter. He climbed up the companionway and stuck his head out into the rain for a look.

"What is it?" asked Bob.

"Can't see." Peter climbed into the cockpit for a better view. Bob and Alan climbed out behind him, shielding their eyes from the driving rain.

"It looks like Bob and Joey over on the shore," said Alan, pointing.

"They're yelling," said Peter.

"Holy shit! Those two rust buckets have let go!" cried Bob.

They looked a mile up the harbor to where the two abandoned, ninety-foot long-liners had been tied up together to a mooring buoy like their own. They were lying broadside to the gusts and blowing slowly down the harbor like a rusty steel avalanche.

"Looks like the cable has parted," said Alan.

"They'll miss us, but they'll clean up Bob and Joey's boat and probably the others too!" added Peter, looking down the harbor to where three yachts were anchored.

"How's the dinghy?" asked Bob, looking quickly over the side. To his amazement, the Avon was both inflated and upright. "One of the rust buckets has an anchor hanging off the bow," he said. "Maybe we can knock it loose!"

They jumped into the dinghy, fired up the outboard, and headed off into the short, filthy chop of the harbor. With Bob at the outboard, Peter and Alan crouched low on either side of the bow in a hopeless attempt to avoid the blowing spray. Bob held his hand in front of his face so he could see where he was going. "It looks like there's what's left of a ladder hanging down on one of them. Maybe we can use that to get aboard," Bob called. He maneuvered alongside to match the speed of the drifting boats. Peter stood up on the pontoon and jumped onto the lowest rung of the ladder. The wooden step disintegrated and Peter dropped promptly into the harbor. He emerged instantly and grabbed onto the side of the dinghy, spitting and swearing. "Quit fooling around, Pete. This is serious shit!" called Bob.

"Up yours!" came Peter's retort.

Alan grabbed the cables that formed the sides of the ladder and hoisted himself up to one of the remaining steps higher up, cautiously testing the rungs and climbing slowly up the side, favoring the parts of the rungs closest to the cables. Seeing it was safe, Bob scrambled up behind him, calling over his shoulder to Peter as he clambered into the dinghy, "It's all yours, Pete!"

Alan jumped onto the deck with Bob close behind. They ran forward along the rusty deck through an obstacle course of old cable, rotten boards, and chunks of old line. From the bow Bob peered down the harbor in the direction of the anchored yachts. They were closing slowly but steadily on them. "Hope this works! We don't have much time!"

The rusty anchor chain ran out of the chain locker below their feet through a spillpipe and over the chainwheel of an old winch before passing fifteen feet across the deck and feeding down a hawsepipe to the anchor. Looking at the winch, Bob said, "There's no stopper on the chain. That's good. All we have to do is free this brake, and the weight of the anchor should do the rest."

Alan looked at the wheel at the back of the winch near the spillpipe. It was about eighteen inches in diameter and was attached to a long threaded shaft. He could see that turning the wheel would loosen a thick steel band that wrapped around the horizontal drum of the winch and allow it to turn. "It looks like it's rusted solid," he said. He tested his theory by grabbing the brake wheel and trying to turn it, without success. Bob joined him, but despite their combined effort, it wouldn't budge.

"There was some old pipe back there," said Bob. "I'll be right back."

"How's it going?" shouted Peter from the dinghy below.

Alan looked down over the side. "Just great. The winch is jammed with rust. Any bright ideas?"

"WD-40!"

Bob returned with a rusty, six-foot piece of pipe. He jammed it through the spokes of the wheel and caught the end under the body of the winch for leverage. "Stand clear!" he cautioned and leaned on the pipe. It had no effect.

"You'll have to do better than that," said Alan. Bob repositioned the pipe so the free end was higher, and together they hung on the end of it with their full weight. The pipe flexed, but the wheel did not turn. They tried again, this time bouncing on the end of the pipe to try to break the wheel free. "I think it moved!" said Alan.

With the fourth try, the wheel began to turn, and they descended slowly until the end of the pipe was level with the deck. Bob extracted the pipe and jammed it in up higher and leaned on it again. The wheel moved more easily this time, and the first link of the chain scraped over the rim of the spillpipe in a tentative attempt to escape the rusting hulk. With one more turn of the wheel, the chain slowly started to move under the weight of the anchor, the links clanking by, one by one, like the loud ticking of a clock, each link fitting precisely into the like shape of the slowly turning chainwheel of the winch.

With a sudden squeal, the winch brake came free, and the chain's tune escalated in seconds into a machine gun-like stutter as the chain pulled up from the chain locker with increasing speed and disappeared over the side. Before they could tighten the brake wheel again, the chain accelerated and began to gallop, the chain leading to the hawsepipe oscillating up and down in a wave, causing an occasional link to skip off the winch that had restrained it, the chain lurching violently before chasing away even faster. The chain was tearing out of the locker with a deafening clatter as it described a writhing arc leading from the chainwheel to the hawsepipe, sending a shower of rust into the air that rained down upon them. Alan and Bob stood back and looked at one another as the chain made its hasty escape.

"Hope the end's tied onto something!" called Alan.

"Hope it didn't land on Peter!" Bob called back, and they both turned to look over the bow. Peter was keeping pace with them some twenty feet away.

"And what do you do for your next trick?" Peter shouted up at them.

"That's the only one we had!" Alan called back.

With that, the chain came to a jarring halt, descending in a final insult against the winch, and the deck jerked sideways under their feet. They staggered, grabbing for the rail for support, and then quickly regained their balance, their ears ringing from the din in the sudden silence.

"I think it's stopped," said Alan, leaning back against the railing.

"Stay back in case it lets go again," cautioned Bob.

The boats started to slow and turn as their combined weight began to straighten out the anchor chain. There was a lurch as the anchor grabbed and then let go, another lurch, and then it appeared that it had dug into the mud. Alan looked astern. "She's about a hundred and fifty feet from the mooring buoy!" he called to Peter. "I think she's got it!"

"And none too soon!" said Bob.

Alan relaxed a little and looked him up and down. Rust flakes clung to Bob's wet clothes and skin so densely that with the help of the rain, the stains resulting from each flake had begun to coalesce, forming an almost uniform redness. Only the whites of his eyes and his teeth revealed their original color. "You're a mess!" said Alan.

"So are you."

"Peter's the only clean one among us," said Alan with a chuckle.

"Yes, but at least we don't smell like an oily rag!" Bob observed.

———

The *Ron*'s crew was cleaning up on the aft deck when Bob and Joey came alongside in their dinghy to thank them.

"That was close! If I was mayor of Pago Pago, I'd give you guys the keys to the city!" declared Dad. "In this case, I hope this will do." He deposited two dozen cans of beer and two bottles of rum on the deck.

"Thanks!" said Bob. "But remember: don't try that yourself. We're The Professionals!"

Chapter 37

---◈◆◈◆◈---

Final Preparations

Peter and Alan sat on the foredeck, surrounded by billows of sail, each of them working with a leather sewing palm and needle. They had spent all morning tearing out the chafed sections of three rows of stitching that secured one of the seams. Now they worked to restitch the seams using an age-old method. Each of them held a needle that was threaded onto opposite ends of a long loop of sail thread. Working from opposite sides of the sail, as one passed his needle through the existing hole, the other took it from the opposite side and pulled it tight. Then he pushed his own needle through the same hole in the other direction, and the other pulled it tight. Every ten to fifteen stitches, they would pull the thread through a block of beeswax to lubricate it so that it would run smoothly through the heavy material. They repeated this process until the loop diminished to an unworkable length, and then they tied it off. They would then tie up a new loop and start again, overlapping the last five or six stitches to lock the previous thread into place. The end result was a precise, tight, even seam that would rival or exceed the best machine sewing.

"How's that look to you, Al?"

"Looks okay to me so far."

"Well, we'd better make sure we get these seams even and tight. You know how particular Bob is."

"Do I ever!"

The first one of these they had done had not lived up to Bob's expectations. He had expressed his dissatisfaction by tearing the whole thing out with his knife and then showed them himself how it was done. Their subsequent efforts had been much better.

Suddenly Peter looked up and over Alan's shoulder with alarm. "Tie ho!" he called out before jumping up and darting past him, aft toward the companionway.

Alan paused and called after him, "What the hell does that mean, 'tie ho'? I swear you two just make this stuff up!" He laughed and shook his head as he put down his needle and began to turn around to see what had caused Peter's rapid departure. "Why can't you just speak English? I mean, plain, simple English," he reasoned.

"It means 'stop'!" Peter replied with a laugh as he slid closed the companionway hatch.

"Stop? What for?" Alan asked as he looked up to see the squall descend upon him.

"Here comes another rinse cycle!" Peter laughed again from the security of the companionway. And the sky opened up.

The rain finally abated and the steaming decks dried enough so that Alan and Peter could continue work on the sails. Bob, meanwhile, had been below for several hours working on some mysterious project. From time to time, they had observed him with a selection of narrow wooden lathes with curious marks on them. He spent his time on his knees, hidden in a cabinet under the chart table up to the waist, occasionally emitting oaths that usually preceded his emergence from the crevice for a union break. This time it involved replenishing his precious body fluids with one or two bottles of Steinlager. Eventually he came up the companionway with his magic sticks.

"I'm going ashore to have a bracket welded up," he declared. He looked over the side at the dinghy. It was a pathetic sight. Half-deflated, its wrinkled pontoons undulated with the passing waves. He shook his head. "We need the dinghy doctor to do some emergency surgery!" he called.

Alan groaned. "What's wrong with it now?"

"It's lost a lot of blood—needs a tourniquet and a transfusion right away."

"Okay," said Alan, and he pushed the sail aside. "I'll get out my dinghy first-aid kit and have a look." He took a few steps and dropped down the forward hatch to his forepeak lair, where the tools were kept.

———

With the dinghy patched again and pumped up as hard as possible, Bob putt-putted away to see Big Charlie at the marine railway to get the bracket made up. Alan returned to the sail repair with Peter. "After this, we'll have other trades to fall back on," said Alan.

"Yeah, I'm going to start a seamstress shop back in Sydney!" Peter joked.

"Maybe I'll do some dinghy repair consulting on the side. I can see it now, 'Yes, sir! Give it two patches and call me in the morning!'"

Bob returned later that morning, having exchanged his magic sticks for some bits of metal tack welded together. He checked on the crew and seemed to mentally measure how much of the seam they had done, and then he disappeared below to the cabinet and a lot of bashing, banging, and colorful language ensued. After an hour of this, he reappeared on deck.

"I'm off to the welder again, fellas," he called as he stepped into the cockpit. He grimaced as he looked down at the dinghy. One side retained most of its air, but the other was deflated and incapacitated, looking like it had suffered a stroke. "That's it!" he shouted indignantly. "We're going to fix this thing once and for all!"

After Alan had staunched the flow of air and recharged it, Bob once again took off for shore, this time heading in the direction of the tuna seiners. After an hour, Bob returned with an air of triumph. "This'll fix el diablo!" he declared, holding aloft two mysterious cans. "The skipper of one of those seiners says they have this in their repair kits for their survival rafts. Says it sticks like shit to a blanket."

They pulled the dinghy on deck and cleaned it off to perform the final act of redemption. "Take the lid off that tin and put some of the glue in a jar," Bob instructed. "We have to add a shot of this accelerator, and then we've got about ten minutes before it goes off. This stuff's dynamite, so be careful not to get your hands stuck together or you'll look like an altar boy for the rest of your days." They placed an enormous patch over all of the other patches and sat back to let it cure.

"I'll get some lunch together while that glue does its stuff," said Alan. He passed up a couple of bottles of beer and disappeared into the galley. He was soon back with a plate of sandwiches and three bowls of muddy brown liquid. Bob looked quizzically at the bowls.

"I didn't think we had any soup left," he said. "What's this?"

Alan smiled proudly. "Neither did I," he said, "but I found these cans in the bilge with the corned beef. They had something about 'beans' written on them. I couldn't read the whole thing, but I opened them up and they seemed to be all right."

"Beans?" said Bob, looking up with a puzzled gaze. "You mean refried beans? What did you do to it?"

"Well, the beans were all stuck together when I put them in the saucepan, so I added a can of water to it. Worked like a charm, don't you think?" he said, beaming at his achievement.

"Added water? To refried beans?"

"Yeah, is it still too thick?"

"Refried bean soup?" Bob asked incredulously.

"Yeah, is it okay?"

"Refried bean soup?" Bob repeated.

"You don't like it?" Alan asked, concerned.

"I love refried beans," said Bob, "but not with water! Don't you have any Mexicans up there in Canada?" Without waiting for an answer, he turned to Peter. "Enter this in the log, mate," Bob announced officially.

"Today the bosun created a new Canadian cuisine—refried bean soup." They all laughed at the characterization.

"It's original and tasty," Alan lampooned. "I should send this in to Campbell's. They'd probably give me a royalty on every tin!"

"Yeah," chimed in Peter. "If you got one cent a tin, you'd make at *least* a dollar fifty a year!"

"And that's worldwide sales," added Bob with a laugh.

Along with Alan's other bosun duties came the ship's carpentry. Fortunately he had some skills in this area, but the tasks were made difficult by a lack of tools and materials. Being a resourceful sort, though, he looked for opportunities to make the best of a bad situation. One of the ongoing problems aboard ship was the deterioration of the dinghy bellows. Bob suggested that it must have been the same model year as the dinghy and was expiring at about the same rate. Alan thought this entirely possible, as he had patched and repaired the gusset, valve, and hose of the bellows with equal frequency as he had revived the dinghy itself. In spite of his ministrations, the contraption still wheezed and gulped with a lopsided motion whenever forced into use. To make it even more difficult, the spring that was meant to return it to its wedge shape after you stood on it had taken its leave, and the only way to use it now was to grasp the two oval-shaped sides, one in each hand, and push and pull on them in an accordion-like fashion while trying not to pinch your fingers in the process. The situation had become even more desperate now, though, as the plywood that formed the sides of the bellows had started to delaminate and peel apart, threatening the contraption with complete disintegration.

On one of their trips back from the market, Alan came across a shipping pallet lying alongside the path near the commercial docks. Taking his knife from his belt, he sliced a long sliver from the edge of one plank and looked at it thoughtfully.

"What have you got there, bosun?" asked Bob.

"Mahogany, I think," he replied, scraping the surface of the plank to expose the grain. "Not good mahogany, but not too many knots. I think it'll do for what I need."

"And what's that?" Peter asked curiously.

"It'll be a surprise!" Alan replied. He looked around to see if there was anyone who would lay claim to his treasure. Seeing no one, he said, "Give me a hand, and we'll get this back to the boat."

They managed to balance the pallet on their knees in the dinghy on the trip back to the *Ron,* and Alan immediately set to work dismantling it into its constituent planks. He chose the best ones and disappeared into the forepeak to reconstruct the dinghy bellows. The dull, rusty, tenon saw and chisels made it tough work, but he brutalized the mahogany roughly into the shape required. After several sweaty sessions at the workbench—and as many sessions recuperating with a beer in the relative coolness of the cockpit—he had fashioned an acceptable replacement.

"Not bad, bosun," complimented Bob, "even if it does look a bit crude."

"It's a poor craftsman that blames his tools," said Alan, "but those rusty old things make it pretty damned hard to make a decent job of it."

"Don't worry," Bob comforted. "I'll buy you a shiny new set of tools at Kilgo's as soon as we get up to Honolulu."

"That's great," Alan replied, "because there's nothing available here. Just as long as I don't need to fix anything in a hurry in the meantime."

For the next week, the crew continued to work through the list, making marked progress even in the tropical heat. The work topside exposed them to the intense heat of the sun, while the work below subjected them to the sweltering stillness. At one point, Alan extracted himself from under the chart table, dripping with sweat.

"That's the last bolt, Bob," he gasped.

"You've got that pump mounted good and solid?"

"Yep. That old oak's as hard as a pharaoh's heart, but it's done."

"And the belt and pulley are lined up?"

"Perfectly. It'll run like a top."

"Good. I hope we don't have to use this thing, but I have a funny feeling about it."

"That's just the corned mutton you ate last night."

"Yeah, that was great. One plate of corned mutton a day, and you'll never get scurvy."

"That's limes. Anyway, one plate of corned mutton a day, and I wouldn't live long enough to get scurvy."

"Careful, bosun. Refusing rations is an offense punishable by a double ration of corned mutton!"

Alan ignored the threat.

"I'll see how Peter's doing with stowing the sails," Bob continued. "I've just about finished the provisioning list. We'll get going on the water and grub tomorrow."

While Bob scouted out the shops and arranged for their supplies, Peter and Alan filled the water tanks. This chore alone consumed two days. Depending on el diablo, they shuttled back and forth from the boat to the shore, transporting four five-gallon plastic jerricans full of water at a time. On every other trip, they stopped to pump up the dinghy, which had miraculously developed at least one more leak.

The following day Bob took off on his shopping trip and turned up at the rock mole in an old, rusted-out Toyota taxi with their first load of provisions. He hailed the *Ron,* and the crew came ashore and began loading the provisions into the dinghy. Bob took off for another load.

"Did you see how much refried beans Bob's bought?" Peter asked. "He's got enough to feed half the Mexican army!"

"And the corned mutton!" Alan exclaimed. "I think I'm going to chance the punishment."

"Maybe some of this will fall over the side on the way out to the *Ron.*"

"Waste of time. He'd just go buy some more."

They had almost finished stowing the first load when Bob arrived back in the taxi with the next one. "I hope there's no more refried beans in that lot, Bob," Peter needled.

"And no more corned mutton," said Alan.

"It could be worse," Bob retorted.

"How?" asked Peter in surprise.

"In the old days, they used to carry casks of salt horse."

"And this is better?" Alan countered.

It took two more taxi loads to complete the provisioning of the preserved foods. There was no more mutton. The next task was to stock up on the additional liquids for the trip. This required some careful selection, and the object of their desires was the government liquor store. The crew trooped into the store, consulted their list, and started to load up one of the shopping carts. It was double the size of the carts at a local grocery store.

"Have a go at this!" called Peter. Bob and Alan joined him to inspect the wares. "The gin is cheaper than the 7UP!"

"'You're losing money drinking water,' to quote Gary," said Alan.

"Yeah, 'you wouldn't read about it!'" Peter joined in, "but do you think the prices are right?"

"Well, I'm not going to tell them that they're not," Bob replied practically. "Last time I was here, there was one bloke who emptied one of his water tanks and filled it with rum! It'd be hard for customs at the next port of call to find that."

"Unless they wanted a drink of water," said Peter.

"How much do you think we need?" asked Alan.

"Well, we'll need the regular rations, and some for the life raft if we have to abandon ship," said Bob.

"That's supposed to be water," Alan suggested.

"Well," Bob considered, "we'll take enough to face the ocean with confidence."

It took several more loads in the dinghy to finish the liquid provisions. Alan took charge of stowing the precious cargo in the bilges, making optimal use of the available space.

As soon as the provisioning was underway, Bob had begun making regular trips to the weather station near the airport for the latest satellite weather pictures. It was run by the National Oceanic and Atmospheric Administration, abbreviated NOAA but pronounced *noah* for short. It was getting toward the beginning of the cyclone season, and they wanted to be careful to avoid any obvious problems. To complicate things, Peter had developed a throat infection through contact with someone on one of their forays ashore, and he had deteriorated over the last few days. He was now restricted to his bunk.

"I'm heading round to the weather station," said Bob, "and on the way, I'll drop Peter off at the LBJ Hospital to get checked out. He's got a fever as well now."

"I'll come too," Alan offered. "I need to stock up the first-aid kit anyway. I can get a lot of the stuff at the hospital."

They were waiting by the rock mole for a local *aiga* bus to come by when Gary and Leonard zoomed past on the motorcycle, apparently going spearfishing. Gary gave a wave as they passed, the earflaps of his leather aviator's hat flapping in the breeze and an extinguished cigarette glued to his lower lip that no amount of wind could dislodge. On the back sat Leonard, knees sticking out like a schooner going downwind wing-on-wing, holding on to the fishing spears and grinning like the Cheshire cat.

"That's a sight you don't see very often," commented Alan.

"Thank Christ for that," wheezed Peter, showing that he hadn't lost his sense of humor.

They didn't have to wait long before the bus arrived and they were on their way. Alan and Peter got off the bus at the LBJ Tropical Medical Hospital, and Bob carried on to the NOAA office.

After leaving Peter at the outpatient ward to see a doctor, Alan went in search of the necessary supplies. His first stop was the hospital's pharmacy. He had a list of items that would excite the interest of most customs officers, but things that are an absolute necessity for yachts at sea. He spoke to the woman behind the counter, a large, pleasant-looking Samoan woman neatly dressed in a flowered *lava lava*.

"Hi," Alan opened amiably. "I'm the first-aid officer on our yacht, and I need to restock our first-aid kit for our trip to Hawaii." He held up a piece of paper and smiled. "I have a small list."

"Let's take a look," she replied warmly. He passed the paper across to her, and she unfolded it to its full length. She studied it for a moment, and then her eyes widened and she looked back at Alan. "What are you preparing for, Pearl Harbor?"

"We've got a long voyage ahead of us, and I need to be prepared." He smiled engagingly.

"Well, I can give you the iodine, ether, syringes, bandages, splints, adhesive tape, and some of these other things, but most of these drugs you'll need a prescription for. And I wouldn't know where to find the scalpels, surgical saw, needles, and surgical sutures." She looked at Alan again, this time suspiciously.

"Fine," Alan said cheerfully. "Let's put together what you have. But I really need the pharmaceuticals. You have to be prepared for anything at sea."

She considered for a moment, and then said, "Do you have any identification?"

"Certainly. Here are the yacht's papers, my passport, and the crew list."

She looked them over, not appearing to know exactly what she was looking for, but since it all looked very official, she handed the documents back and nodded. "Okay, I'll give you all the drugs, but I'm going to have to call the surgeon on duty about the other things. That's up to him."

She began assembling the goods. Before long, an American doctor arrived and introduced himself. "I understand that you're looking for some surgical equipment." He looked Alan up and down. "Are you qualified to use them?"

"I'm the yacht's first-aid officer. We've got a long voyage ahead of us," Alan repeated, "and I need to be prepared." He smiled again.

"Such as ..." the doctor prompted.

"There are lots of hazards at sea on a wooden yacht. Splinters need to be removed, fingers get squashed, heads get bashed by the boom, someone slips with a knife. There's a lot that can happen."

"Well, you can forget the surgical saw. There are only two in the whole hospital, and I'm not sure that I'd want to let you loose with one anyway. But I can find most of these other things for you."

Disappointed by missing out on a new saw but buoyed by the success of his shopping trip, Alan was in a happy frame of mind when he retrieved the newly medicated and revived Peter. He flagged down a bus for the trip back around the island to the *Ron*, a rather large package of medicinal goods tucked under his arm.

"The weather looks clear," Bob reported when they returned.

"That's too bad," said Alan, "because the mate has a five-day course of antibiotics to take and he's supposed to rest."

"Well, there's no point in leaving with him flat in his bunk," said Bob. He contemplated for a moment. "Maybe if I have him gargle with rum every half hour, he'll be cured faster."

"In this case—and it would be an isolated case, I'm sure—I'd suggest going with the conventional treatment," Alan counseled, and then turned back to the weather. "What's the long-range forecast?"

"Looks all right for now. We'll fuel up in a couple of days so we're ready. But we'll wait 'til we're set to go before we put on a load of fresh fruit and vegetables from the market. How'd you make out with the bandages?"

"Not bad," Alan replied. "I got most of what I needed. I couldn't get the saw, though."

"Saw?" Bob queried.

"Yeah, the surgical saw."

"The what?"

"Surgical saw," Alan repeated.

"What are you planning to amputate?"

"We've got a long voyage ahead of us," Alan repeated yet again, but this time with a twinkle in his eye, "and I need to be prepared."

Bob laughed, now understanding Alan's ploy. "Well, it was a clever idea, bosun," he said, "but it looks like you're going to have to wait until we get to Kilgo's after all. And if it comes to amputation, I suppose you can use that rusty old hacksaw in the foc'sle. Just make sure you soak it in lots of alcohol first!"

"As long as I'm the one doing the sawing!" said Alan.

For the next few days, Peter recuperated, waited on by Alan and Bob. Alan administered the medicine and soup—not of the refried bean variety—and Bob insisted on administering the rum. Three days later, Bob resumed his ritual trip to the weather office. He returned with heaps of paper and an overabundance of information, including winds, currents, water temperatures, wave heights, weather balloon results, and phases of the moon. The two lonely men who staffed the station were always grateful for the company of someone interested in their craft. Bob sifted through it all to check the conditions for the trip.

"It looks pretty good out there," he reported. "As long as the mate's up for it, we'll shove off in two days' time."

Chapter 38

---◆◇◆◇◆---

The Aborted Trip

The last weather report showed a clear run to Honolulu, with only a small depression in the vicinity of Palmyra Atoll. Bob took the dinghy to shore to clear customs, and at ten o'clock in the morning in a light rain under a heavy sky, the crew sweated up the mainsail and the *Ron* finally made way out of the harbor. As they motored along, Bob stood at the stern pulpit and cast a hibiscus blossom into the yacht's wake.

"What's that about, Bob?" asked Alan.

"Just paying my respects to the princess of the sea," he replied.

"Will that bring us luck?"

"It won't do us any harm," he said solemnly. He stared after it for a few seconds, and then he brightened and pulled a dirty white rag from his pocket. He waved ceremoniously to the scene disappearing behind them. "Good-bye, rust buckets; good-bye, StarKist," called Bob.

"Good-bye, Rosie!" said Alan and Peter in unison.

"Any more of that Rosie shit, and somebody'll be swinging from the yardarm!" Bob responded with fake indignation. Alan and Peter laughed at this good-natured humor.

"What's that funny smell?" asked Peter with a straight face.

"That's fresh air!" said Alan on cue.

321

Ron of Argyll leaving Pago Pago Harbor en route to Honolulu

Bob rolled his eyes. "Abbott and Costello. This is going to be a long trip."

"Yeah, and we don't work for corned mutton!" Alan feigned protest.

"To hell with corned mutton," said Peter. "Once we're clear of the island, we'll set up our fishing line and catch some fresh tuna!"

"We'll set a course to give us as much easting as we can get," said Bob, getting back to business. "It's definitely going to be in our favor when we get the wind shift across the equator to the northeast trades. We don't want to get stuck on the backside of Hawaii and have to beat our way back up for three days."

The conditions for their departure were ideal. The trade winds held at a steady ten to fifteen knots, with regular, steady seas, and the *Ron* made up to six knots as they cruised easily along under main, jib, and staysail. They checked the bilge at each change of watch and cleared up any water with three or four strokes on the handle of the big, double-diaphragm bilge pump.

"The caulking seems to be holding," said Bob. "The dribble of water is probably just seeping in at the stem."

"The last time I took a gander at it, it looked all right," said Peter.

"We did a really skookum job," Alan confirmed.

Bob looked at him quizzically. "We did what?" he asked.

Alan looked from one to the other of them for a sign of recognition. "A really skookum job," Alan repeated.

"What the hell does that mean—*skookum*?" asked Peter.

"Really solid, really strong," explained Alan.

"Is that a Canadianism?" asked Peter.

"I think you're just making that up!" said Bob with a laugh as he headed up to the cockpit for the first night watch.

It was a perfect night for sailing. The rain had stopped and the skies had cleared to a degree, revealing some of the millions of stars spread out above him. With the steady wind and easy seas, Bob settled comfortably in the cockpit and tucked the tiller under his arm. Down below, Peter and

Alan were setting up the charts for the voyage. Suddenly from the cockpit, they heard, "What the hell—you slimy son of a bitch!" and the sudden commotion of a struggle. Before they could make it to the companionway, the noise abruptly stopped. Without warning, a large blue flying fish landed at their feet, followed by a stream of oaths. "Cut the guts out of that bastard and toss him in the pan!"

"You all right up there?" asked Alan, peering up the companionway steps into the dark.

"Yeah. It only slapped me in the face, but it surprised the shit out of me."

Before long, the aroma of frying flying fish wafted through the yacht, and the voyage resumed in peace.

———

In these favorable conditions, the watches were set at three hours on and six hours off. This allowed the crew sufficient rest and time to attend to shipboard duties. As is often the case on an oceangoing yacht, unless there are sail changes or other situations to attend to on deck, the off-watch crew got as much rest as possible.

Peter was on the helm the next night, well into his watch and enjoying the serenity of the ocean. He was happy to be back at sea aboard this old friend and was reminiscing about the adventures he had experienced since leaving Sydney, when he noticed a gradual slowing of the boat. Puzzled, he looked around as the mass of sail strained ahead, pulling the yacht noticeably down at the bow. Sensing that the wind had not changed, he took a flashlight and looked astern. Streaming out behind the boat as far as he could see was what appeared to be a length of fishing net. Peter roused Bob and Alan from belowdeck.

"What's the problem, mate?" Bob called up.

"We're hung up on a chunk of net!" Peter called with an urgency in his voice. "We've got to get some of this sail down!"

They dropped the jib and staysail, and then eased the main to take the drive out of it. The boat bucked in the seas, held almost stationary by the drag of the net on the keel.

"Get a boat hook and pull this shit off!" called Bob. "We've got to get free of the net, and for Christ's sake, keep it out of the rudder!"

Peter grabbed a boat hook, and Bob illuminated the net with the flashlight. Peter wrapped one arm around the mizzen shroud and, with the boat hook in the other hand, managed to hook onto the net. He heaved a part of the net to within reach of Bob and Alan, who leaned over the rail and slashed at it with their knives as the net rose and fell with the motion of the seas.

"I can't hold it up for long!" Peter grunted, and finally had to lower the net down. He rested for a few minutes and then hooked onto it again. This time Bob and Alan each grabbed onto the net with one hand to help support it and were able to cut it with better effect. They were making slow but steady progress when there was a sudden lurch and a piece of the net caught on the rudder, swinging the tiller violently across the cockpit and then sweeping it back and forth with each rise and fall. They stood clear, huddled together at the stern.

"We've got to get this thing clear before it rips the rudder out of the boat!" Bob declared.

They turned back to their work and fought for over an hour against the net as the boat wallowed in the swells. They took turns pulling the net up with the boat hook while the other two grabbed it and cut it away, their fingers and hands becoming badly cut from the barnacle- and coral-encrusted mesh. Occasionally a wave would hit them side-on and wash over the deck. Alan spat to clear the seawater from his mouth. "What I wouldn't give for the rinse cycle right now!" he said.

"And some corned mutton!" added Bob.

They labored on, struggling to release the yacht from the death grip of the rogue net. Gradually the weight of the net decreased until it finally parted and dropped off, leaving the yacht to swim free. The three of them sank to the deck. "It's almost light," Bob observed. "Let's heave her to and have something to eat. I think we've earned it."

"I'm rat shit! And look at my bloody hands!" exclaimed Peter, holding them up in front of him. "They're cut to ribbons!"

"You're no Robinson Crusoe," said Alan, inspecting them. He looked down at his own. "Mine are pretty bad too. How're yours, Bob?"

"McDonald's hamburger patties!"

"Let me get something on them. I've got just what the doctor ordered," said Alan. He disappeared below and returned with an enormous, dark-colored apothecary bottle. "This'll fix what ails you guys."

Bob and Peter dutifully held their hands out over the side as instructed, like Oliver Twist begging for more. "Is this going to hurt, doctor?" asked Bob as Alan held the bottle over the outstretched palms. He poured the iodine over the cuts, and the pain appeared in Bob's eyes.

"No," he replied. "And don't get any of that on the deck—I just washed it," he said with a faint smile.

Bob bit his lip, and Alan turned to Peter, who looked up apprehensively. "Get on with it, Alan. I don't believe a word you say!" he said resignedly.

At this point, Bob couldn't contain himself any longer, and he erupted with, "Holy shit!"

Almost in unison, Peter cried out too. "Aaaagh!"

He joined Bob in an Irish jig about the deck, flapping their hands in a vain attempt to reduce the stinging. Wincing, Bob and Peter turned to Alan, and a cruel smile spread across Bob's face. "Now it's your turn!" said Bob, and unceremoniously doused Alan's wounds with the iodine.

In spite of a brave effort, Alan let go a "Yowowowowow!" like an Austrian yodel and shook his hands. "Whose idea was this anyway?"

"Yours!" was their pained reply.

The crew raised the jib and staysail as quickly as their lacerated hands and aching limbs would allow them, every contact with their hands a new revelation in pain. The wind filled the sails, and the boat made way again. Bob took the helm to resume course, while Peter went below to make up some hot food. They sat together in the cockpit for their meal.

"You know, we saw some drift nets on the way down from Vancouver," said Alan. He told them of the experience aboard *Second Chance*.

"We'll have to wean them off fish and introduce them to the delights of corned mutton!" said Bob. "Work on that while I get some sleep."

On the afternoon of the fifth day, the sky changed. Bob looked aloft and saw the approach of a bank of heavy, low cloud from the southeast. He called below to the crew, "The party's over, fellas! It looks like the shit's gonna hit the fan in about twelve hours. I would guess it's only local, but let's get everything battened down just in case."

By midnight, the wind had increased to gale force, and the *Ron* roared along under double-reefed main and staysail. After each watch, the crew took a turn on the pump. The water had increased during the night, and it now took about a hundred throws of the pump to dry the bilge.

"This is starting to look familiar," said Peter as he finished his turn on the pump.

"Yeah, I've seen this movie before too," said Alan, coming into the main saloon from the galley with a mug of coffee. "I wonder where it's coming in."

Before Peter could answer, Bob's angry voice caught their attention. It sounded as though he was having an argument with someone.

"What now?" asked Alan, putting down the mug, and both of them bolted for the companionway. As they scrambled up the steps, they heard Bob more clearly. "Go to hell, you mother—"

Peter stuck his head out of the companionway to see Bob at the tiller, waving his free hand about his head in obvious frustration. Alan clambered up beside Peter, the two of them cautious not to venture too far without their safety lines.

"What the hell's going on?" Alan asked Peter.

"Don't know. He's gone mad!"

Just then a dark shape darted across the stern of the boat, only inches from Bob's head. Bob swung out at it, but the shape turned neatly as it passed, avoiding this defensive maneuver.

"What the hell was that?" called Peter.

"It's a bloody big bird!" came Bob's reply as he cast about for the next attack. "He just started dive-bombing me!"

"Maybe he's a friend of that flying fish you met the other night," Peter offered, "and he's pissed off that you ate him!" The bird suddenly appeared from the other side, turning expertly in the gusty winds to graze Bob's sou'wester and dipping its wing to miss the running backstay. "It looks like an albatross," said Peter.

"Well, if it *is* an albatross, I sure don't want to kill it and end up like the crew in *The Rime of the Ancient Mariner*," said Bob cautiously. "A leaky boat is bad enough without a curse as well!"

"It's hard to tell in the dark, but I don't think it's that big," said Alan. "It could be a tropic bird or a frigate bird."

"It's a bloody loony bird, I reckon!" laughed Peter. "You might end up with breakfast out of this, Bob!"

The bird swept by again.

"You sure seem to be an attraction to the local wildlife," said Alan from the safety of the doghouse. "Try to discourage him, Bob, 'cause I'm on watch next."

"I'll keep an eye on him for a while," Peter said to Alan. "You'd better get some sleep."

"Sounds good to me. Mind your friend doesn't shit on the decks, Bob!" he called, and disappeared below.

Peter jumped up into the leeward doghouse berth and kept a watch on things. Every few minutes, the bird would dart out of the blackness and zoom past Bob at the helm, passing within inches but never touching him. Satisfied that the bird was not intent on skewering the helmsman, Peter decided to turn in as well.

Over the next twenty-four hours, the frigate bird—for that was what they were able to determine it to be in the daylight—kept up its harassment, while the weather conditions continued to deteriorate, with increasing wind and seas. The leaking also got worse, so that at the end of each watch, the water would be about a foot and a half deep in the bilge, only a few inches below the cabin sole. The crew coming off watch would crouch over the larger of the two manual bilge pumps, leaning into the long handle with his sore, red-stained hands and counting each painful stroke until the bilge was dry. It was taking up to half an hour of hot, nauseating work, and the fatigue was beginning to show. The count on the pump was up to four hundred. During his turn on the pump, the handle broke off in Alan's hands.

"Take a look at this, Peter."

"That's not a good sign."

"No, and Bob'll take it off my wages."

"Well, just tell him the guts just fell out of it. Good thing we've got a backup."

"Yeah, but it's only a single-action pump. It'll take twice as long."

"Before you know it, we'll be getting up to pump an hour before going to bed."

This turned out to be not far from the truth—the effort to clear the bilge was taking over an hour and nearly a thousand strokes.

———

Only the soles of Bob's feet were visible as he searched in the forepeak for the source of the leak. He extracted himself and returned to the main saloon. "Well, it's not coming in much there. I think the problem's under the water tanks amidships. It could be a sprung garboard. We'll have to pump it dry again, so I can see."

Alan nodded resignedly. "I'll try not to break the pump this time."

"Don't worry about it. We'll get the engine-driven pump going."

Alan raised his eyes and intoned dramatically, "Oh, princess of the sea, please let the engine start and save my weary body."

Up in the cockpit, Peter hunched over in his foul-weather gear, bracing himself with his legs across the narrow cockpit, his arms outstretched and his swollen hands gripping the tiller. Heavy rain sluiced down on him. He lifted his head as he heard the engine start, and he saw a large, black rubber hose flop onto the deck and immediately begin to expel a gusher of water out through the scuppers.

"What a beautiful sound!" he shouted over the noise of the engine. He ducked as the frigate bird hurtled past, apparently unperturbed by the noise.

Alan's grinning face appeared in the companionway. "We may be out of a job, mate!"

"Yeah, none too soon. Any luck finding the leak?"

"Not yet. And it's getting worse. We're only three miles from land the way it stands."

"Three miles from land?"

"Yep, straight down, that is."

Bob came up the companionway steps, and Alan moved to one side so that they could stand side by side. "Well, fellas," Bob announced, "we can't depend on the engine to keep us afloat. We're still 1,800 miles from Honolulu. If we keep punching this old girl into these short, steep seas, we'll tear her apart. We're going to have to turn her around."

Bob and Alan retreated to the main saloon and turned out in their foul-weather gear to tack the boat. The wind had begun to drop somewhat, and the driving rain had almost stopped. Bob had knocked the pump out of gear so that they could use the engine to assist them with their turn. Now they eased her through the eye of the wind.

"Take it easy bringing that boom across. We don't want to slam her around," Bob cautioned.

When they had completed the tack and set the sails for their new course, Bob shifted the engine back into neutral. "Go down and flick that pump into gear, Peter," he called out. "We'll dry out the bilge and see how much she's going to make now."

"She's sure riding better on this point of sail," said Alan. "I'm glad it stopped raining too, but it's too bad this isn't the direction to Honolulu."

They could soon see that the inflow of water was noticeably reduced. "With the pressure off her, the water's really gone down," remarked Bob. "We'll see how often we need to run the pump. With the wind the way it is, let's leave the reefs in the main. We'll soon see what she's going to do."

They sat dejectedly in the cockpit, making themselves as comfortable as they could. "Hey, where's that annoying bloody bird gone?" said Alan, looking about.

"Yeah, it looks like he's disappeared!" said Peter, who then hunched his shoulders and peered around defensively in case he'd spoken too soon.

"Maybe he doesn't like the smell of diesel," Bob speculated.

"Well, whatever it is, I'm glad he's buggered off," said Alan. "Anyway, I could sure use some grub."

"You're going to have to tie ho on the grub," said Bob. "Go down and grab that bottle of black rum from the cabin, and we'll splice the main brace."

"More than once," said Peter. "We've bloody well earned it in the last few days. In fact, I'd like a double splice!"

After an hour of celebration, Alan yawned. "Well, my main brace is well and truly spliced, and I'm starving!"

"Okay," said Bob. "I'll go below and whip up some gourmet delight."

"Not that corned mutton again," said Alan.

"No, I promise it will be something entirely different," said Bob. "Let me surprise you!"

Before long, Bob came up the companionway carrying two large bowls of steaming food. Alan reached for his bowl expectantly. He looked at it and his head jerked up. "What's this? You said you were going to surprise me!"

"It's Palm corned *beef*," Bob said emphatically, "fresh from the can, and *undiluted* refried beans," he added, defying gastronomic criticism. "Surprise!"

Six days of nursing the boat along brought the *Ron* back to Pago Pago Harbor. "Hello, rust buckets. Hello, StarKist," called Bob dramatically as they passed the reef. "We're back."

The *Ron* motored down the harbor, and they tied up to one of the buoys at the far end. Peter and Alan finished pumping up the dinghy and fitted the outboard.

"This won't take long, fellas," said Bob. "Clean up the main saloon a bit so I can bring the customs bloke aboard."

The chief customs officer was surprised to see Bob back again. "How come you're back so soon?" he asked.

"A lot of trouble with the boat," Bob replied. "I suppose you guys want to come down and have a look at us."

The chief looked around the office and selected the most junior customs officer. "He'll go with you," he said. He gestured toward a young, but fully-formed, rhinoceros of a lad and dismissed him with a wave of his hand. Junior followed Bob out of the door, struggling to keep his two hundred-pound bulk up with him.

"Where is your boat?" he asked.

"Off Soli's Restaurant," answered Bob.

"At 'e end of harbor?"

"Yeah."

They strode on in silence. After a few minutes, Junior asked, "You got dinghy?"

"Yeah."

Silence.

"You got outboard?"

Bob thought about this for a second. "Yeah, but not work. We have to rowed," said Bob, imitating the local jargon.

They walked along in the hot sun, and Junior began to perspire. Bob saw this and walked a little faster.

"How big your dinghy?"

"Only small," replied Bob, spreading his hands two feet apart.

Silence.

"*How* big your dinghy?" Junior inquired again, as if he had not understood.

"Only small." Bob's palms were now only eighteen inches apart. "And we have to rowed," he emphasized.

After a few more steps, Junior stopped. He thumbed through the papers on his clipboard and said, "You knowed my boss in there. If he ask if I inspect the boat, you say 'yes,' okay?"

Bob looked down at the lad, who was in obvious distress, and shrugged. "Okay," he said, as if he were doing Junior a favor.

Relieved, Junior passed the clipboard to Bob to sign the papers, and then he ambled off at a more leisurely pace.

Bob carried on, smiling to himself with the satisfaction that he had avoided this bureaucratic chore and taking time to enjoy the little zephyr that swept by. At the same time, he noticed the tiny white flowers that pushed through the scrub along the side of the road. He approached Soli's Restaurant, musing about their salvation and the happiness of life—until he saw el diablo. It was flat.

Chapter 39

---※◆◆◆◆◆◆◆◆◆◆◆◆◆◆◆---

Tiki

It took the crew a day in the calm of the harbor to confirm the source of the leaks. While the leaking between the planks was indeed the main source of the water, as Andrew had suspected in Vava'u, the problem wasn't the caulking. They discovered that a lot of the caulking cotton they had so painstakingly hammered in had been spit out from between the planks into the bilge from the pressure of the water. This indicated that the problem was more serious. Bob's consultation with an American marine surveyor confirmed his suspicion that the oak ribs had been weakened by age and deterioration, allowing the bronze fasteners to move and the planks to open up under the vastly increased downward pressure of the mast when sailing hard on the wind.

It took them another two weeks to patch up the problem to the point where they were confident that she would stay afloat without constant supervision, but the *Ron* would never make the trip to Hawaii in this condition. Satisfied with this temporary repair and with arrangements in place for someone to look after the boat, the crew decided that it was about time to make the trip up to Honolulu—by airplane this time—for some rest and recuperation. Besides, Bob had run out of time and needed to get back up there to meet another commitment. They took advantage of an introductory offer of a ninety-nine-dollar return airfare by a previously unknown airline with a single Boeing 707 and took off for civilization.

Like any sailors, they were anxious to get their mail. Before leaving port on their aborted trip, they had written family and friends to tell them to send any future mail to Honolulu and left instructions with the post office in Pago Pago to forward any mail that arrived after their departure to Honolulu as well. It was now six weeks since they'd left port, and they were looking forward to finding some letters waiting for them when they got to Hawaii. So one morning they were packing their gear in the cabin of the *Ron,* and later that day they were stepping out of a taxi at the front door of the Waikiki Yacht Club.

"Here you go, mate," said Peter, handing the driver a ten-dollar bill. "Keep the change. And get someone to take a look at that left front wheel. She drags a bit when you turn to the left." He slammed the back door and looked at the pile of seabags that Bob and Alan had unloaded onto the sidewalk. "What're we going to do with these?"

"The office manager is a friend of mine," said Bob. "He'll let us stick them in the back room while we have a beer. Give us a hand getting them inside."

He rang the intercom beside the door, and the crackly sound of a man's voice replied with a relaxed, "Aloha!"

"Aloha, mate!" Bob responded in an emphasized Kiwi accent. "Pop the door open, would ya, George, and pour us three cold beers!"

"What the hell—are you kidding me, man?" came the startled reply, and the latch clicked open.

Bob frowned and looked back at Peter and Alan with a puzzled look. "What's got into George?" he asked out loud, pulling on the open door. They both shook their heads. "Well, let's get this gear inside and see what's going on in the joint."

They propped the bags inside the door and wandered through the lounge. The bar area stretched almost half the length of the narrow building and opened all along one side to the boat slips a few steps away. It was just after four in the afternoon, and a few regulars were scattered around the small, round tables in idle conversation. Some of them stopped talking as the three walked in. George was gawking through the office window, his mouth open and a blank look on his face. On seeing the three sailors, he opened the office door and walked slowly into the bar, staring.

The bartender was a longtime fixture at the club, and he beamed a big smile as they approached. "Good to see you, Bob!" he called. "Hi, guys!" he waved to Peter and Alan. George still had not spoken.

"How's it going, Clyde?" said Bob. "Line us up three beers, would you? And what's up with George?" he asked, gesturing with his thumb toward the ashen-faced man. "You don't look too good, George," he said, bending down and staring seriously into the wide eyes.

George hesitated a moment longer and leaned on the edge of the bar for support before finally blurting out, "You're dead!"

"I promise not to take offense at that if this beer is on the house!" Peter quipped, and took a long drink.

Alan raised his glass. "And for an extra beer, we'll walk through a wall for you," he offered, "but hauntings cost a full meal."

"What's this 'dead' shit?" asked Bob, looking around at the patrons, who by now were whispering among themselves and pointing toward the crew.

Before anyone could answer, a tall, lanky American guy strolled in from the direction of the docks. "Bob!" he called. It was Lon, a friend of Bob's and a resident of the floating Ala Wai community. "I thought that was you!"

"Hi, Lon," replied Bob. "You remember Alan."

"Sure. Hi, Al."

"Good to see you again, Lon."

"And this is our mate, Peter, from Oz," said Bob.

"G'day, Lon," said Peter.

"Nice to meet ya, Pete. So where's the boat, Bob?"

"Back in Pago Harbor," replied Bob. "We had a little problem keeping the ocean on the right side of the wood. What's up around here? Everyone acts like they're surprised to see us."

"That's 'cuz everyone thinks you're at the bottom of the ocean!" said Lon with a laugh. "We heard you'd left Samoa, and when you didn't arrive, we all figured you'd gone down in the hurricane!"

"Hey there, Bob!"

Bob looked around to see another friend arriving. He shook Bob's hand warmly. He was an older man, and even with his slight stoop, you could see that he was well over six feet tall. "Hi, Slim," Bob replied with a broad smile.

"It's good to see you!" said Slim. "We thought you'd bought it out there! Let me buy you guys a drink."

"We shouldn't. We're dead, you know," Bob replied archly. "But since we've got Saint Peter here with us," he put his arm around Peter's shoulder, "maybe we can make an exception." The small group laughed.

"And this must be the Dark Prince for good measure," said Slim, shaking Alan's hand. Alan responded with a mischievous grin.

"Closer than you'd think!" said Peter. "He's got a devilish way about him!"

"This is Alan from Canada and Peter from Oz," said Bob. "This is Slim. He knows all about the dark side. His boat's called *Red Witch*."

"Good to meet you, Slim," said Alan. "So what happened here during the hurricane?"

⸺

Stories were told from both sides, and as more people arrived at the end of the workday, the stories were retold and more details revealed about the day the hurricane hit. The Honolulu *Star-Bulletin* and the Honolulu *Advertiser* together told the most complete story of the event. They reported that it was a late-season storm and the first hurricane to hit the islands in more than a quarter of a century. Hurricane Iwa came ashore on November 23, 1982, traveling at a speed of forty miles an hour, with winds gusting up to 120 miles an hour. It created a storm surge along the coast of Kauai of six to eight feet, which caused the evacuation of over 5,800 people from shoreline areas and flattened homes several hundred feet inland. One sailor aboard a destroyer leaving Pearl Harbor ahead of the storm was killed, and several others were injured by the heavy seas, while a number of small vessels in harbors along the coast were either sunk or grounded.

The surge washed sand along the streets of Waikiki, and the passing squall line associated with the hurricane was likely responsible for spawning a string of tornadoes. A number of small aircraft were damaged, including a DC-3 that was propelled across the runways at Honolulu International Airport. Passengers in the terminal were injured by fragments of a plate glass window that imploded under the pressure of the gusts. Power was out for over a week in many areas, and long-distance telephone communication was cut off entirely when both satellite and undersea cable links were severed. The total damage to property and public utilities was estimated at about $200 million.

The crew milled about the bar, celebrating life and sharing the camaraderie common to mariners everywhere. Amid the hubbub, Alan turned to the bartender and said, "'Iwa' is an odd name for a hurricane. They're usually given men's or women's names, like Hurricane Sally or something like that. What's that mean anyway?"

Bob was nearby and listened for the reply. The response only served to further the mystery of their charmed preservation. "That's easy," the bartender replied. "*Iwa* is the Hawaiian word for the frigate bird."

Bob was silent for a moment, and then set his glass down on the bar. He seemed to contemplate something before walking purposefully out onto the terrace that looked over the yacht basin.

Peter saw him go and strolled over to Alan. "Where's Bob going?"

"Damned if I know." He told Peter about the name of the hurricane.

"Bloody hell!" Peter exclaimed. "Maybe there's something to Bob's supernatural shit after all!"

The bartender overheard them and interjected, "Bob knows he has something to do."

They watched him walk over to a Hawaiian ti tree. He carefully picked a long, slender leaf and smoothed it between his fingers and thumb, accentuating its boatlike v-shape. Then he walked to the breakwater and down onto the sand. Bob stood there in silence for a moment and then bent down, placed the leaf on the rippled surface of the water, and pushed it gently out to sea.

"Tiki will be happy now," said the bartender with a smile.

In ancient Hawai'i, the ti plant was thought to have great spiritual power. By making this tribute to Kanaloa, the Hawaiian sea god and one of the four major Tiki gods, Bob was recognizing the protection provided to him and his shipmates. Bob rejoined them and picked up his glass, making only a slight nod to the bartender. "It's been quite a trip!" he said.

They were silent for a while as they sipped their beer and the significance of the events sunk in. Finally Bob broke the silence. "Let's have another beer," he said. He looked around at the growing crowd. "Better make it two."

About the Authors

"Hollywood" Bob Rossiter has a history of life on the sea. He started out studying mechanical engineering and displayed a talent for designing and building racing cars, a passion that led to his becoming the co-owner and editor of the first New Zealand hot rod magazine. But like many other Kiwis, he found his true vocation on the ocean. From his home in New Zealand, Bob made his way as a fisherman, sailor, and ferryboat captain. He spent time around the islands of Polynesia, both as a fishing guide and as a sailor, and lived in Marina del Rey, California, working as a shipwright on the yachts of the Hollywood set, leading to his meeting distinguished actor Hal Holbrook and their voyage across the Pacific to New Zealand.

Bob spent the subsequent years living with his American wife aboard their ferro-cement sloop *Greystone* in Ala Wai Marina in Honolulu. From this base of operations, he worked as a delivery skipper, transporting yachts between Hawaii and California and from Hawaii to Vancouver, Alaska, and Japan. He also worked as a marine services consultant and wooden yacht maintenance expert, better known in the Honolulu yachting community as the proprietor of Varnish World. While in Hawaii, Bob expanded his interests by studying acting and had parts in television commercials filmed there.

Bob retired from full-time marine work in 1995 and moved ashore with his wife to the US mainland. They now make their home in the Arkansas countryside and take expeditions together on their Honda Goldwing motorcycle. Bob still does some consulting work, and they are making plans to retire for good to their property in New Zealand.

Peter Jinks left his home in the south of England at seventeen to immigrate to Australia. By the time he met Bob and Alan, he had spent almost half his life on the road, working as needed to fund his adventures. When he ran out of money, he started a window-cleaning business in Denmark, worked as a freelance photographer in South America, Russia, and Japan, had a fur coat business in Afghanistan, worked as a crocodile hunter in Costa Rica, started a marriage agency with a business partner in Sydney that was written up in *Time* magazine, and went from selling end-of-line shoes for cash in the local Sydney flea market to a partnership in two top-grossing city shoe stores. Along the way, Peter was featured for a time as the Foster's Man in Foster's Lager television commercials and has done other acting parts.

Peter has circled the globe over fifteen times and has stamps in his passports from over one hundred countries to prove it. He has traveled by air, train, motorcycle, passenger ship, hitchhiking, mule, four-wheel drive, and sailing ship.

Married in 1989, Peter and his wife have traveled together to Israel, Egypt, Africa, Asia, Europe, Canada, and the United States. They have two daughters and have lived with them in the Cook Islands and Bolivia. An entrepreneur and still an ardent traveler, Peter and his family live at Bondi Beach in Sydney, where he owns a real estate consultancy, specializing as a buyer's agent for top-end residential properties.

Alan Boreham emigrated from England to Canada with his family when he was two. He grew up on Vancouver Island off the west coast, spending a lot of time on the water with his father and friends. After completing a degree in civil engineering in Vancouver, he began his travels with a trip back to the United Kingdom and on to Western Europe, which only whetted his appetite for more. After three years of work, he left for the offshore sailing voyages described in *Beer in the Bilges*. Following that, Alan traveled by sailing yachts west from American Samoa to Tonga, Fiji, Vanuatu, and the Santa Cruz Islands.

He returned to Vancouver in 1983 to resume his career in the field of fisheries and the environment. At the same time, Alan became a director of Cooper Boating, Canada's largest sailing school and yacht-charter company, where he ran programs to teach adults to sail. He also volunteered with the Canadian Yachting Association and trained sailing instructors, giving him the opportunity to travel to France to teach in an international sailing schools exchange program.

His further travels have taken him across Canada and the United States, back to England and France, and to Denmark and the Channel Islands, as well as to Peru, Bolivia, Beijing, Australia, New Zealand, French Polynesia, and the Cook Islands. Alan's trips have included travel aboard power or sailing yachts in the Atlantic Ocean, the North and South Pacific Oceans, the Indian Ocean, and the Coral Sea.

Alan has now retired from a career that included working extensively on fisheries programs for Aboriginal people in Canada, participating as Canada's national correspondent for the Canada-U.S.A. Pacific Salmon Treaty, and managing a program to improve the sustainability of Canada's fisheries. He lives in Vancouver and works as a travel writer, focusing on unusual and historically significant destinations.

The three coauthors are currently collaborating on further works of fiction and nonfiction.

Glossary

aiga	Samoan word meaning family or community; pronounced *eyengah* with a nasal "n"
backwind	to have the wind on the lee, or back, side of a sail
barbie	Aussie slang meaning barbeque
bearing away	to move the bow of a sailboat away from the direction of the wind
beating	sailing as close to the wind as possible
belaying pin	a wooden or metal pin fitted into a rail of a sailboat around which a rope is made fast
bilge	the lowest space inside a ship, between the sides of the hull and the keel
block	a nautical term for several kinds of pulleys, which are comprised of one or more sheaves (pulley wheels) encased between two cheeks (sides)
boom	a spar used to hold the foot of a fore-and-aft sail
boom gallows	a fixed frame used to stow the end of a boom
breast line	a mooring line that runs perpendicularly from a ship to a dock
brightwork	varnished woodwork or polished metal
broad reach	a point of sail in which the vessel is heading off the wind, but not directly downwind
bure	Fijian word for house
caulking	the cotton or oakum driven in between a ship's planking

chainwheel	the wheel of a winch that is shaped around its perimeter to fit a chain as the wheel turns
cleat	a metal or wood fitting with arms on which to belay a rope, especially sheets or halyards
close-hauled	having the sails trimmed as flat as possible in order to sail a vessel as close to the wind as it will go
cockpit	a well or space, sunken below deck level and often with seats, where the helmsman steers the vessel and the crew operates
courtesy flag	the sail of a foreign country flown by a visiting vessel as a sign of courtesy when visiting that country
crutch	a movable form of boom gallows used to stow the end of a boom
cutter-rigged sloop	a single-masted, fore-and-aft rigged vessel having two foresails, namely a jib and a staysail
dead reckoning	an abbreviation of deduced reckoning; a calculation of a vessel's position by knowing its distance and direction from a known position
doghouse	a raised portion of the ship's deck that is used to provide more headroom below, to protect the companionway, or as a sleeping space near the cockpit
easting	the easterly component of a ship's course; especially important in the trade winds, where eastward progress is made difficult due to the direction of the prevailing winds
eye of the wind	the direction the wind is blowing from
fa'afafine	Samoan word for a biological male, who is either raised as a female to help with household duties when there are no women, or not enough women, in a family, or a male who chooses to act like a female in manner and dress; considered as a third gender in Samoan culture; literally "ladylike" in Samoan; also *fakaleiti* in Tonga and *mahu* in Hawaiian; not to be confused with the western concept of homosexual or gay

fa'afetai	Samoan word for thank you
fale	Samoan and Tongan word for house, pronounced *fahlay*
forepeak	the area below deck in the bow of a vessel; usually separated from the rest of the ship by a bulkhead
gaff	the spar that is used to extend the upper edge of a four-cornered sail from a mast
gaff-rigged	a sailboat that is rigged with one or more four-cornered fore-and-aft sails
garboard	the plank of a hull closest to the keel
genoa	a large jib that overlaps the mast
gimbaled	able to tip freely in all directions
GPS	abbreviation for global positioning system
gybe	to move the stern of the sailboat through the eye of the wind; also known as to jibe
ham radio	amateur shortwave radio
hanks	a set of hoops, rings, or fasteners at the luff of a fore-and-aft sail to attach it to the forestay
hard on the wind	sailing close to the wind
hard yakka	Aussie or Kiwi slang meaning hard work
hauling the sails	to shift or alter the position of a sail
hawsepipe	a pipe or opening in the bow of a vessel through which an anchor rode would normally pass
head	marine toilet; also, the top corner of a triangular sail
heave to	to stop a vessel by lashing the helm in a position that opposes the action of the sails
helm's alee	the warning from the helmsman that he is about to tack (or come about)
hove to	the past tense of heave-to
'io	Tonga word meaning yes
iron horse	an iron rail fixed to the foredeck along which the sheet tackle for the staysail boom is allowed to travel, making it a self-tending sail

347

jib	foresail
ketch	a two-masted vessel with the mizzen stepped forward of the rudder post
knackered	Aussie or Kiwi slang meaning physically exhausted
knot	a nautical measure of speed measured in nautical miles per hour, which is approximately 15% faster than a statute, or land, mile per hour
lava lava	a wraparound skirt of Polynesia, commonly worn by both men and women
lazarette	a storage space near a vessel's stern
lazy sheet	the rope (sheet) used to control a foresail that is not currently under tension
lee cloth	a wooden, mesh, or fabric barrier that is drawn up alongside a bunk to prevent a person from rolling out when the ship heels
lee shore	a shoreline that is to leeward of a vessel, presenting a danger of shipwreck if the vessel is unable to maneuver away from it
leeward	the direction or side opposite from which the wind is coming
luff	to steer closer to the wind; also, the leading edge of a fore-and-aft sail
mainsail	the principal sail on a vessel; on a sloop, the sail set from the mast
mainsheet	the rope that controls the position of the foot of a mainsail
malo	Samoan word for hello
mizzen	the aft mast on a ketch or yawl
nautical mile	a measure of distance derived from the circumference of the earth; a distance approximately 15% greater than a statute, or land, mile
northing	the northerly component of a ship's course
number two sail	the second largest jib

off the wind	a point of sail where the vessel is sailing in a direction ranging from 90 degrees to 180 degrees relative to the direction of the wind
on the wind	a point of sail where the vessel is sailing in a direction ranging from approximately 45 degrees to 90 degrees relative to the direction of the wind
Pago Pago	capital of American Samoa; pronounced *pango pango* with a nasal "n"
palagi	Polynesian word for stranger or foreigner; often used when referring to Caucasians; pronounced *palangi* with a nasal "n"
pandanus	the leaf of a tropical plant that is used to make woven products such as mats
peak	the outermost end of a gaff; also, to raise a gaff or yard more nearly vertical
peak halyard	the line used to lift the after, or peak, end of a gaff or yard
pissed	drunk
pissed to the gills	very drunk
port	left side
port light	a glass window in the hull of a ship that cannot be opened
port tack	sailing with the principal sail (usually the mainsail) set to the starboard side
pulpit	a metal railing, usually at the bow of a vessel (bow pulpit), but also at the stern of a vessel, if fitted (stern pulpit)
ratlines	small lines tied horizontally across the shrouds, with equal spacing between them, to serve as steps
reach	a point of sail between beating and running
ready about	a command given by the helmsman for the crew to get ready to tack (or come about)
reef (a sail)	to reduce the area of sail

ribs	the curved wooden frames that make up the structure of the hull of a ship
rooted	Aussie or Kiwi slang meaning worn-out or exhausted; also, something that is broken or unusable; stuffed
running	sailing dead downwind
running backstay	a backstay on a mast that can be tensioned or released
sextant	a nautical navigation instrument used to measure the angle of the sun in relation to the horizon
sheet	a rope or ropes attached to the lower, aft corner of a sail (clew) and used to control its position
sheila	Aussie or Kiwi slang meaning a girl or woman
ship's log	a ship's official record
skeg	the aft part of a vessel's keel that supports the rudder on a full-keeled sailboat, or a separate fin or blade that extends down from the hull behind the keel to support the propeller shaft in a fin-keeled sailboat
sloop	a single-masted, fore-and-aft rigged vessel
sole	the floor of a ship's cockpit or cabin
spillpipe	a pipe leading to the anchor locker which the anchor chain runs through
spreader	horizontal arms attached to the mast that change the angle of the shrouds
spring line	a mooring line that runs at an angle from a ship to a dock
starboard	right side
starboard tack	sailing with the principal sail (usually the mainsail) set to the port side
staysail	the inner foresail on a cutter rig
stopper	a plug to fill an opening; also, a device that stops or checks movement
stuffed	Aussie or Kiwi slang meaning worn-out or exhausted; something that is broken or unusable; rooted

sulu	a wraparound skirt of Melanesia; similar to *lava lava* in Polynesia
tack	to move the bow of the sailboat through the eye of the wind; also, the relative position of a vessel with respect to the directions of the wind, such as a *port tack* or a *starboard tack;* also, the corner of a sail at the bottom of the luff
tau lava	alternate Tongan word for a wraparound skirt of Polynesia; *lava lava*
throat	the innermost, concave end of a gaff, where it fits to the mast
throat halyard	the line used to lift the forward, or throat, end of a gaff or yard
tofa	Tongan word for good-bye
toque	a bowl-shaped knitted hat, originally made of wool, without a peak, which is worn to keep warm; it is pulled on over the head and sometimes covers the ears; sometimes referred to as a ski hat
tucker	Aussie or Kiwi slang meaning food
upwind	refers to a sailing direction that is less than 90 degrees from the eye of the wind
VHF radio	abbreviation for very high frequency radio
westing	the westerly component of a ship's course
winch	a windlass used for raising a sail, control of its sheets, or the raising or lowering of anchor rode
windward	the direction or side that the wind is coming from
yachties	owners or crew of sailboats

CPSIA information can be obtained at www.ICGtesting.com
Printed in the USA
LVOW042126070912

297959LV00002B/7/P

9 781475 928808